COSTUME

COST

PERFORMING

Photographs by Pravina Shukla
and Henry Glassie

PRAVINA
SHUKLA

UME

DENTITIES THROUGH DRESS

INDIANA UNIVERSITY PRESS
Bloomington and Indianapolis

This book is a publication of

Indiana University Press
Office of Scholarly Publishing
Herman B Wells Library 350
1320 East 10th Street
Bloomington, Indiana 47405 USA

iupress.indiana.edu

♾ The paper used in this publication meets
the minimum requirements of the American
National Standard for Information Sciences—
Permanence of Paper for Printed Library
Materials, ANSI Z39.48–1992.

Manufactured in China

Cataloging information is available
from the Library of Congress.

ISBN 978-0-253-01577-8 (paperback)
ISBN 978-0-253-01581-5 (ebook)

1 2 3 4 5 20 19 18 17 16 15

For Henry, with love

CONTENTS

ACKNOWLEDGMENTS

MY AIM IN WRITING THIS BOOK WAS TO UNDERSTAND HOW COSTUME enables individuals to perform identities that are not expressed through daily dress. As a folklorist, I conducted case studies using ethnographic methods to show how costume functions to express identity in contexts full of intention and meaning. During this project, which began in 2007, I have accumulated debts to many individuals who have taught me about the significance of costume.

My first debt is to the people who furthered my intellectual pursuit by providing me with hours of recorded interviews and allowing me to observe, photograph, and understand costumes in use, both abroad and here in the United States. Two people in particular gave me much support and encouragement at the project's beginning—Ellen Adair and Kersti Jobs-Björklöf. Both Ellen and Kersti spent many hours talking to me about the nuanced ways in which costume functions: Ellen on how costumes communicate on the professional theater stage and Kersti on how folk costumes express identity and heritage in contemporary Sweden. Ellen and Kersti not only shared their expertise with me; they also led me to other people to interview.

Though I grew up in São Paulo, Brazil, the carnival costumes of Bahia were a new topic for me. I was excited to learn about Salvador's *blocos Afro* and *afoxés*. In Olodum I thank João Jorge Santos Rodrigues, Tita Lopes, and Alberto Pita. In Ilê Aiyê I thank Antônio Carlos dos Santos "Vovô." I am especially grateful to my friends in Filhos de Gandhy: Professor Agnaldo Silva, Ildo Sousa, and Francisco Santos. For over fifteen years of friendship in Salvador, I thank Fátima Miranda. I am also grateful to my colleagues Henry Drewal and Eduardo Brondízio, and especially to Steve Selka who read an early draft of the Brazil chapter.

I thank Kersti Jobs-Björklöf and Kerstin Sinha for reading a draft of the Sweden chapter carefully, for suggesting many useful changes, and for translating original texts into English for me. In Sweden I thank Kersti and Sune Björklöf for providing me a place to stay in Dalarna; Sune unfortunately passed away before this book went to press. In Leksand I am also grateful to Britta and Sven Roos; to Ulla Björklöf, her mother Karin Gärdsback, and her two aunts, Britta Matsson and Anna Halvares; to Ingrid Samuelsson at the Leksand Handcraft shop; to Katarina Karlsson Nordqvist at the Sätergläntan College of Handcrafts; to Eva Erkers in Floda. In Stockholm I acknowledge the help of Mats Widbom, Barbro Klein, Lizette Gráden, and Ulrich Lange.

My gratitude extends to many people in the United States who were generous with their time, helping me see the link between costume and history in the three chapters on reenactment. I thank Sarah Lash, P. J. Schultz, Jarett Diamond, Carolyn Jenkinson, and Aimee Formo of the Society for Creativity Anachronism. Among Civil War reenactors I thank the following living historians: Wayne Brunson, Mark LaPointe, Jay Vogel, Frank Orlando, Mike Sipes, Jim Opdenaker, Niles Clark, and Dwight Hensley. At Colonial Williamsburg I thank the scholars and interpreters who shared information with me: Brenda Rosseau, Linda Baumgarten, Janea Whitacre, Sarah Woodyard, Mark Schneider, James Ingram, and Terry Thon. I am especially indebted to Mark Hutter, talented tailor, scholar, colleague, and friend.

Many busy theater professionals took time to meet with me, providing me with great insight into their artistic endeavors. I thank the following playwrights, directors, costume designers, and actors for their thoughtful knowledge about theatrical costume: Rafael Jaen, Lewis Wheeler, Eric Gilde, Molly Trainer, Spiro Veloudos, Vincent Woods, and Charles Morey. I single out, once again, Ellen Adair, for her tremendous help and for reading a draft of the theater and concluding chapters.

My gratitude extends to my teachers and mentors at Berkeley and UCLA. I remember the late Alan Dundes and continue to be grateful to Michael Owen Jones, Doran Ross, David Mayo, Fran Krystock, Owen Moore, Donald Cosentino, and Robert Georges. I am sustained in intellectual camaraderie by fellow folklorists John Burrison, Ray Cashman, Lorraine Walsh Cashman, Michael Foster, Diane Goldstein, Jason Jackson, Tim Lloyd, John McDowell, Tom Mould, Jerry Pocius, and Terry Zug. For help with this book, I also thank John Cash, Harry Glassie, Gregory Hansen, and Rich Walter. My interest in the serious study of dress has been fueled by my colleagues in the Costume Society of America, especially Cristina Bates, Anne Bissonnette, Robin Campbell, Cynthia Cooper, Sally Helvenston Gray, Mark Hutter, Susan Neill, and Sarah Woodyard. I am grateful to Linda Welters for reading a draft of this book, and for providing me with many useful comments and suggestions. The idea for this book arose during an early conversation with Joanne Eicher, and I thank Joanne for all she has done to champion the study of dress.

For financial support of my fieldwork in Brazil and across the United States, I acknowledge the following sources: UCLA Fowler Museum of Cultural History Robert C. Altman Memorial Award, UCLA Fowler Museum of Cultural History Arnold Rubin Memorial Award, Los Angeles Bead Society, Indiana University College Arts and Humanities Institute, and Indiana University Center for Latin American and Caribbean Studies.

I am, of course, indebted to the able staff at the Indiana University Press for their help throughout the long process of publication, especially to Janet Rabinowitch, Rebecca Tolen, Bernadette Zoss, Dan Pyle, and to Jill R. Hughes for her copyediting. I especially thank Darja Malcolm-Clarke for her help, and Jennifer L. Witzke for her beautiful design.

I end my list of debt by acknowledging my family, the people I have loved the longest; I owe them my complete devotion. My mother, Neeru Shukla, to whom I dedicated my first book, continues to be a source of strength for me. My sisters, Divya and Bobby, have supported every endeavor I have embarked on, and being with them in California continues to be a highlight in my life. With happiness I celebrate the growth of our small family unit, welcoming its new members: Paul, Arjun, Layla, Chris, and little Mina, the newest member of our family.

My greatest debt is to my husband, Henry Glassie, to whom I dedicate this book. A fellow folklorist, Henry inspires me in our shared effort to understand the world through its artistic excellence. Henry accompanied me on every one of this book's fieldtrips, taking many of the photographs published here, and he read the manuscript carefully. Henry's book *The Potter's Art*—an examination of cultural phenomena through distinct ethnographic case studies—provided a model for my book. For his unconditional support and affection—and for filling my days with joy—I dedicate this book to Henry with all of my love.

COSTUME

INTRODUCTION
Special Clothing for Extraordinary Contexts

T IS THE THIRD OF JULY, AND TENS OF THOUSANDS OF PEOPLE ARE gathered on a farm just outside of Gettysburg, Pennsylvania. A young couple walks by, wearing matching T-shirts: his says "Civil War Nut's Husband"; hers reads "Civil War Nut's Wife." A man in baggy khaki shorts has a T-shirt that reads "Fort Bragg FIRE Emergency Services"; his companion sports a baseball cap that says "U.S. Army." A little boy is dressed as a Union soldier, in blue pants and shirt, a kepi on his head, with a yellow cavalry sash tied at his waist, proudly carrying a toy infantryman's rifle. On Sutler's Row, at the photography studio, a young man poses in a wool Union uniform, indistinguishable from a real one except that it is open in back and fastened with long ties. At the Activities Tent a camera crew awaits, every man clad in shorts, sunglasses, bandanas on their heads, with large laminated "Press" badges dangling from their vests. Outside the tent stands an elegant bearded man in an impeccably tailored, pale gray uniform. He has come from upstate New York to address the crowd in the role of General Robert E. Lee. All of these people express their identities by what they wear.[1]

DRESS AS MATERIAL CULTURE

We all dress to accommodate social and environmental factors and to reflect our personal aesthetics and identities. Sending meaningful messages through dress is one way people engage in a daily artful endeavor, participating in what folklorists call "creativity in everyday life" or "artistic communication in small groups."[2] Clothing is a palpable, immediate, and intimate form of material culture, which is defined by folklorist Henry Glassie as "culture made material." The study of material culture, he writes, is "the study of creativity in context."[3]

This book is a study of individuals and society, of creativity and social communication. I study dress in its immediate context of the human actors who

Posing for a portrait at the reenactment of the Battle of Gettysburg. Gettysburg, Pennsylvania, 2010.

construct, inhabit, behold, and judge garments and their accessories. I join my colleagues—dress scholars, historians, and curators—by contributing to our common intellectual endeavor a folkloristic approach to the study of dress, treating costume as artistic communication, as a marker of identity, as an outlet for personality, and as a vehicle for social and cultural expression.

My orientation has been shaped by folkloristic studies of material culture that have developed in exchange with performance theory, a paradigm that emphasizes the individual in the social moment of creativity.[4] We understand the act of creation by attending at once to individuals and their circumstances, paying attention to standards, to acts of desire, and to the forces of consumption and social response. Scholars of material culture, working in diverse media—architecture, ceramics and textiles, metal, and wood—have provided models that enable consideration of form and function, creation and consumption, and the historical and social forces that bring beauty, meaning, and the power of communication to the things people make.[5] Key to communication is the expression of personal identity through the material objects we make, shape, and use.

That daily dress reflects personal identity is an obvious point; what we wear is affected by our body, age, gender, socioeconomic class, personality, our taste and style. Dress is who we are. Costume, on the other hand, is often described as the clothing of who we are not. The dictionary defines "costume" as the clothing of another place or another time, or as clothing fit for performance: the garments worn by people in faraway China, the clothing of the Victorian era in the United States, or the flamboyant dress of participants in the Mardi Gras parade of New Orleans. Generally, costume is thought to be the clothing of others, the people we are pretending to be. In this book I show that costume—like dress—is the clothing of who we are but that it signals a different self, one other than that expressed through daily dress.

DRESS AND COSTUME

There are discernible differences between what we call "dress" and what we mean by "costume," differences in form, materials, and construction, as well as in intended meanings and contexts of wear. Mary Ellen Roach-Higgins and Joanne B. Eicher have famously defined dress as "modifications of the body and/or supplements to the body."[6] Costume, according to these two authors, delineates the modifications and supplementations "that indicate the 'out-of-everyday' social role or activity."[7] Writing in Valerie Steele's *The Berg Companion to Fashion*, Eicher argues that costume is used by individuals to express a "performance identity" while dress is used to establish "identity in everyday life."[8] Scholars of dress agree that, ultimately, the chief difference between costume and dress lies in the ability of garments to differently project identity.[9] Costume is usually set apart from dress in its rarity, cost, and elaborate materials, trims, and embellishments, and in its pronounced silhouette or exaggerated proportions. It is not meant to be ordinary, but, rather, evocative, urging the daily further along an artistic trajectory that leads to heightened communication and often culminates in a spectacle for public consumption. Costume designer Pamela Keech, when asked to describe the difference between costume and clothing, answered, "I think it's the motivation. A person who gets up in the morning and gets dressed without giving it much thought is putting on *clothing*. But a person who gets dressed for the effect it will create is putting on *costume*."[10]

Some people who carefully compose their daily ensembles become icons; in effect, they wear a costume every day. Frida Kahlo, Iris Apfel, and Daphne Guinness are examples of individuals who consistently construct a self-conscious presentation of self through dress.[11] Some celebrities have developed such an emblematic style that one can impersonate them by wearing similar clothing. In Harmony Korine's movie *Mr. Lonely*, characters live their lives as Marilyn Monroe, Michael Jackson, Madonna, Abraham Lincoln, Queen Elizabeth II, and Charlie Chaplin. None of the people look like the celebrities they enact, but they dress like them, and that's enough to effect personification. Characters in the film assert that they impersonate the famous "to become who we want to be." One character says, "We have become who we wish we were."[12] The act of dressing up in costume—whether for the fictional characters in a film or for ordinary people everywhere—can become a means of achieving a self-conscious definition of the self.

The intended meaning, or effect, of garments depends on the specific context of wear. Similar garments can project different messages in different contexts. A sari worn by a woman in India is daily dress; the same garment worn by flight attendants on Air India is a uniform; worn for Halloween in the United States it becomes a costume. Sometimes the different demands on the garment affect their construction: they might look the same, though they are not. A policeman's uniform made by a regional theater company will have reinforced seams for the script's rough fight scenes, and it may have hidden Velcro fasteners that allow for quick costume changes between acts. A common garment can become a costume through the behavior of its wearer: the actor who wears a policeman's uniform onstage might not act like an officer reporting to work in uniform. A nurse's uniform worn at the hospital allows the wearer access to patients and presumes specialized medical knowledge. A nurse's costume worn during a college party will be quite different; it will probably be shorter and sexier: the pastel scrub top and pants of the hospital nurse will be replaced with a skimpy, tight white dress worn with fishnet stockings and high heels. The costumed nurse might be drunk, but the hospital's nurse must remain sober and alert. If a medical emergency arises at the costume party, no one would presume that the young woman with the nurse's cap and stethoscope would be of any use.

Costume—as opposed to uniform—is defined by the wearer's intentions and behaviors, and it is evaluated by the audience on the basis of garment construction, fabrics, ensemble, and accessories, as well as by its fitness for the occasion. Wearing a cute little French maid uniform to the office on October 31 is acceptable, perhaps even creative, daring, or sexy. Wearing the same outfit to work on a random day—say, April 9 or July 7—would be considered outlandish and abnormal, possibly even a sign of mental instability.[13]

There is an implicit alternative persona that the costume permits its wearer to assume. In addressing the dichotomy of dress and costume, both Valerie Steele and Joanne B. Eicher, leading dress scholars, raise the issue of the wearer's identity as a defining feature of costume. In her foreword to *Dress for Thrills*, a catalog of antique Halloween costumes, Steele says that to dress up "is to escape from the constraints of ordinary life and adopt a new identity."[14] Eicher, writing in *The Berg Companion to Fashion*, Steele's encyclopedia of dress, defines costume as "hiding or temporarily cancelling an individual's everyday identity," and goes on to say that "in contrast to costume, dress establishes individual identity within a cultural context."[15]

In this book I explore the connections between identity and costume, showing how costume functions to help individuals elect, embrace, and display special identities that are not expressed through daily dress. We all have multiple identities, and some of these are expressed only by means of a costume. Through particular case studies and deep ethnographic data, I show how costume always functions to express identity. Many of the examples of costume discussed in this book are described by their wearers as transformative, changing both the wearers and the beholders somehow, capable of taking them to mythical places, emotional depths, and on magical journeys. In costume, people are engaged in some sort of performance, inhabiting one of the stages or dreams of their lives. They choose their clothing to fit the aim of their performance, its audience, and their own intention of meaningful communication. Messages are sent and received between individuals within a mutually understood cultural context, and for this communication to occur it is necessary to have a social unit comprised of collaborators, beholders, and enablers. Identity is both ascribed and elected within this group. The individual is always viewed in relation to a community or society, so we must approach costume by acknowledging the people surrounding the garment, those who make the transmission of elected identity possible.

For the majority of Americans the most familiar experience of costuming occurs during Halloween. For children it is an annual excuse to dress up and go door to door for candy. For adults Halloween is a socially acceptable occasion for costuming, a time to dress up for work and parties. A brief look at Halloween foreshadows the concepts and themes I raise throughout the book, helping us recognize the nuanced ways in which multiple identities can be communicated simultaneously through costume use.

SPIRITED INDIVIDUALITY: HALLOWEEN

Halloween as celebrated in the United States has been greatly influenced by the Celtic festival of Samhain. There are echoes of the Irish folk traditions of mumming, wrenboys, and strawboys in the customs of house visitation and rhyming in disguise, playing pranks on neighbors, and demanding treats.[16] What was for many years a children's costumed activity of begging for candy—trick-or-treat—has now become a significant adult costumed social event. In 2010, of the 65 percent of Americans who celebrated Halloween, 33 percent dressed up in costume. In 2009 it was estimated that $1.75 billion was spent on costumes, with 47 million adults and 58 million children dressing up for Halloween.[17] Almost as many adults as children now dress up on October 31, and this trend is reflected in the number of costumes designed for adults. Many businesses encourage their employees to dress in costume for work on Halloween.[18] In 2007 the Ticketmaster corporate headquarters in Los Angeles set up a photo wall with fake spiderwebs and a "Morgue" sign, against which the staff posed for pictures, displaying a wide variety of costumes, including the traditional (witch, mummy); popular culture (Velma from *Scooby Doo,* Napoleon from *Napoleon Dynamite*); celebrities (Amy Winehouse); cute (Minnie Mouse, fairy); ethnic (kimono); and literary (Hester Prynne from *The Scarlet Letter*). These costumes reflect the general patterns, yet being worn for work there was an understandable lack of provocative attire. A popular costume website, buycostumes.com, has almost four thousand different adult choices in such thematic categories as "Classic," "Historical," "Horror/Gothic," "Humorous," "Food and Beverage," and also by body type, "Plus Size Costumes." The two largest subcategories of adult costumes are "Sexy" (1,085 options) and "TV and Movie Character" (1,084 options).

I documented and photographed Halloween costumes in Bloomington, Indiana, in 2007 and again in 2009–2012, observing the children's costumes worn

Tom Daddono as Oompa Loompa from *Charlie and the Chocolate Factory*. Halloween, Bloomington, Indiana, 2012.

for an afternoon of trick-or-treating in suburban neighborhoods and in the shopping mall, and adult costumes at evening college parties.[19] Clear patterns emerged: most costumes are readymade, with a few put together or handcrafted. Little boys were often dressed as superheroes (Spiderman, Superman, Iron Man) and little girls as Disney princesses (Belle, Snow White, Cinderella). These are licensed costumes, all alike, and sanctioned by the Disney or Marvel Comics corporations.[20] In 2007 I photographed a girl dressed as Princess Fiona from the cartoon movie *Shrek*. She wore a homemade version of the costume—flowing purple and green dress, necklaces, tiara. Since she was not wearing the officially licensed ensemble, she grumpily explained to me, in exasperation, who she was supposed to be. While her costume impressionistically resembled the cartoon princess in palette and tone, it was not the version that others around her recognized. For many years creativity and artistry were expressed through the making of costumes, usually by a mother or grandmother, though sometimes by the

Shannon Larson as Pris Stratton from *Blade Runner.* Halloween, Bloomington, Indiana, 2012.

wearers themselves. Commercial costumes became widely available starting in the 1930s,[21] and today the creativity of the wearer is mainly expressed by the choice of a readymade, commercial ensemble that suggests a character or signals a theme.

Among the costumes for the college-aged, I observed that young women often wore commercial "sexy" ensembles with a low-cut top, a miniskirt with a puffy crinoline, striped socks, and high-heeled Mary Jane buckle shoes. Male students were dressed as goofy and funny characters, as women, as babies, or as skit characters from *Saturday Night Live.* The women's aim was to be alluring, while the men wanted to be humorous—in the same way that when they pose for photos at other times, females generally try to look sexy, males funny. On Halloween sexy women and funny men prominently featured their faces; they were not masked, not anonymous, not exactly in disguise. The aim was to reveal a facet of their identity through their choice of costume and associated behavior. Sometimes creativity and wit are the driving forces. In 2010, for example, I photographed three friends—each wearing a pair of mouse ears, sunglasses, and holding a walking stick. As the Three Blind Mice, they were clever, original, and their costumes linked them to one another.

In 2008 I photographed the thirty-fifth annual Greenwich Village Halloween Parade in New York City. This much-documented pageant features visual and performance artists and their professional, expensive, and elaborate costumes, which have been illustrated by anthropologist Jack Kugelmass in his book *Masked Culture: The Greenwich Village Halloween Parade*. The commercial costumes bought by college students from websites were rare among the revelers. In this celebrated event, which includes more than two million participants and spectators, a few interesting tendencies for the public communication of identity were apparent, and these foreshadow some of the findings in this book. Sociability was an obvious goal, and there were many groups of friends dressed in coordinated "ensemble" costumes, thus reinforcing their bonds to one another. (Many commercial costumes are marketed as pairs or ensembles, targeting couples, trick-or-treating friends, or siblings to wear matching or complementary attire.) One group of a dozen friends, both male and female, all dressed alike as the fitness fanatic Richard Simmons: each wore a big curly wig, pink-and-white-striped running shorts, and a baggy pink tank top, carrying different messages: "Candy Kills," "Don't Do Doritos," and "Dance Your Pants Off." Four Japanese friends

Spidermen. Halloween, Bloomington, Indiana, 2007.

"Sewage W. Bush." Greenwich Village Halloween Parade, New York, 2008.

went as Teletubbies, and two older men performed a drag song-and-dance show, each in a blue satin dress, satin gloves, feathers, corsage, wig, costume jewelry, and makeup.

Costumes grant their wearers a chance to be social and an opportunity to make public statements. Many of the costumed participants in Greenwich Village seized this moment to communicate to the world, knowing that the national and international media would be present,[22] and the time was ripe during the Halloween of 2008, since the presidential election was only a week away. A man in a George W. Bush face mask wore a toilet seat around his neck and held a sign: "Sewage W. Bush / ready-to-flush . . . / eight years of liarrhea." An attractive young woman mocked Sarah Palin by wearing her dark hair pulled back, red lipstick and glasses, and a sexy sequined dress with a sash that read "Miss Vice President."[23] A man wearing a suit and tie with the initials "CEO" pinned on his lapel had a gold lamé parachute over his head, from which dangled paper currency.

These people, like many we will meet in this book, used costume to carry political and social messages. One man, Christopher Puzzele, wore a giant condom over his head with the sign "I do *not* want kids.com," while handing out flyers advertising his online dating service for those who do not wish to procreate. As a person who rejects the prospect of parenthood, Puzzele feels he is discriminated against in popular dating sites and wanted to call attention to his position by his outrageous costume (he told me in a follow-up email that hundreds of people took his picture and his flyer that night).

For some people, dressing up for Halloween is a way to get a bagful of candy. For others it is a chance to look desirable and alluring or funny and wacky at a college party. Or it can be an opportunity for artistry and communication, fulfilling creative desires while constructing a platform for social and political critique. And for others, perhaps for most, it is a chance for psychological release, a way to bring personality to the fore in projections of identity beyond what is possible through daily dress. These many functions are not separated categorically in action; in fact, they often fuse in the simultaneity of costumed performance.

With a seemingly endless number of costumes to choose from, the one a person selects will inevitably reflect several aspects of his or her identity. On Halloween of 2007, for instance, I photographed and interviewed an undergraduate student, Joseph Howard Burnette II, who was dressed as Chad Gray, the lead singer of the heavy metal band Mudvayne.[24] Joseph wore denim overalls, a white "wife beater" tank top, chains around his neck, and a spray of fake blood all over his face and body. He attached braided strings to his beard to make it look like the lead singer's long goatee, and he dyed his hair light blue on the sides to simulate a shaved head, and colored it red on top to look like Gray's red Mohawk.

Joseph has been dressing up as Chad Gray for the last three Halloweens, he told me, but varying his impersonation every year. Part of the artistic pleasure for Joseph is to improvise on the general aesthetic of Chad Gray. The lead singer, he said, "does something different with how he looks" for every concert, so in 2007 Joseph came up with the idea of dried blood on his face, achieved by smearing liquid latex over red lipstick marks. It was not something that Chad Gray had ever done, but it was an opportunity for Joseph to express his originality: "Due to the fact that he's ever changing his image, I thought it would be interesting to change it myself, see what I could come up with, with what he has started."

The costume provides an outlet for personal creativity, and it enables the wearer to connect to a social group, as the New York parade demonstrated. By dressing like the singer, Joseph visually connects himself to other Mudvayne fans who recognize the impersonation and communicates his commitment to the band and their music. He told me that it is uncommon for people to dress up as Chad Gray, though he has seen a few at the concerts, but "it takes a big fan to be willing to masquerade to that level." For insiders, Joseph conveys a mutual passion for the band. For outsiders, he introduces them to Mudvayne, since many people don't know of the band or of the lead singer, and they will ask him about them, as I did when I first met Joseph on Halloween day.

Costumes invite others to join in: they can become vehicles to instruct people about the values, aesthetics, and culture that a particular costume embodies. During the last three Halloweens when Joseph went as Chad Gray, that was one of his aims: "You know, every time somebody asked me who I was, it was my opportunity to advertise, more or less. Which is why I wore the costume. You know, I try to be a walking, talking advertisement for Mudvayne."

The Halloween costume carries personal creativity, social identity, and it can afford the wearer a chance to educate the beholder, whether the education is aesthetic or political. The main function of costume, including Halloween costume, is to express the personal identity of the wearer. Folklorist John McDowell's study of Halloween costumes among undergraduates at Indiana University in 1982 supports this conclusion, as do the analytic papers on Halloween costume from my own students at the same university twenty years later.[25] Hundreds of undergraduate Midwestern students confirmed that, far from donning a separate identity, they were communicating a deep sense of themselves. Joseph Burnette identifies so deeply with Mudvayne—their lyrics, their style, their music—that dressing as their leader is a way to externalize a meaningful internal sentiment: "They embody everything that I love, more or less. Or a huge portion of what I love. So by masquerading as the lead singer, I'm capturing that this is me. They just kind of embody me." The costume also functions psychologically, for it gives Joseph a moment of flamboyant notice: "I like being known. I hate just being that kid in the corner. I like being the center of attention. I would be lying if I said anything else." Joseph, like many people around the world, feels trapped in a single version of himself. He rightly observes that men have fewer aesthetic options when it comes to dress than women, and he gets tired of seeing "the same image in the mirror every day." By wearing a Halloween costume once a year, he said, "I escape myself."

By temporarily "escaping" himself through costume, Joseph, along with all the others in this book, arrives at a deeper version of himself, using the band as a marker of personal identity. Joseph is *not in disguise* when dressed as Chad Gray. At the end of our tape-recorded interview, Joseph admitted, "This whole Mudvayne thing, I suppose it's gotten to the point where—it's not even so much

Joseph Burnette as
Chad Gray from Mudvayne.
Bloomington, Indiana, 2007.

that I love Mudvayne that much. It's my signature. Everybody knows me as the kid that wears Mudvayne shirts." In his daily life, as a way to vary his look and add a sense of personal style, Joseph wears Mudvayne T-shirts. He also wears a belt buckle with "Mudvayne" engraved on it, and his backpack has a Mudvayne patch. For high school graduation, while adhering to the school dress code, he wrote "Mudvayne" on his shoes to retain his personal identity. His association with the band makes him stand apart from the thousands of other Midwestern young men around him and gives him an edgy, arty "signature."

IDENTITY THROUGH COSTUME

All dress is an expression of identity. Daily attire positions us within a social structure, within a frame of time and space. In everyday life people usually wear things that are appropriate and socially acceptable in accordance with their age, gender, and occupation. Daily dress fulfills personal functions as well, such as making the wearer stand out as particularly beautiful, or desirable, or stylish—as judged by mutually agreed-upon societal norms. But for many people daily dress functions to make the wearer *indistinguishable:* to *not* stand out, to go undetected, and, ironically, in disguise, passing as a generic version of some category. Dress is often an expression of our many social identities—age, gender, religion, socioeconomic class. This was one of the conclusions that I offered in *The Grace of Four Moons,* my study of daily dress in Modern India.[26] In the United States, for example, office attire is usually bland, conformist, uncreative, its aim being to erase peculiarities of personal style. It could be said, cynically, that the drab business dress code functions precisely to make the human worker into another interchangeable cog in the corporate machine.

When the identity being expressed is singular and significant, the clothing used for that communication is costume: *special dress that enables the expression of extraordinary identity in exceptional circumstances.* Costume is usually an intensification of the daily, a channeling of core values, explicit and insistent, a purposeful announcement through dress. This elaboration of dress into costume is formal—affecting in its aesthetics—and semantic, an intensifying alteration in its message. Formally, costume is the *extra*ordinary of ordinary dress; it is generally more extravagant in cost, materials, embellishments, structure, and mode of wearing (with a corset or an apron, for example). Many of the people I interviewed for this book describe their costume as "uncomfortable," which serves as a reminder that they are wearing special clothing. A woolen Civil War uniform is hot, itchy, heavy—the opposite of a loose, cotton sweat suit. Costume is also extraordinary in its semantic elaboration; it makes explicit references, whether political, social, historical, religious, aesthetic, or psychological. The communication is more sharply directed and its meaning is more intense.

Costumes have always been used for dress-up and to temporarily assume another's persona. Costume and fancy dress have been documented in ancient Rome, in rural Sweden, in Victorian England, and, by Cynthia Cooper, at fancy dress balls in Canada.[27] Following Shakespeare, Erving Goffman observed that human beings are always onstage, so different clothing can be used explicitly to express an adopted persona on particular stages.[28] Sometimes the camera—or even the mirror—becomes the proscenium for performance; in the nineteenth-century United States, "ordinary Americans," as Joan Severa documents, or Norwegian immigrants, as Carol Colburn argues, expressed self-conscious identities by deliberate poses in carefully chosen clothing.[29] People who dress for Halloween often strike the pose of their character when having their pictures taken. Civil War reenactors base their stance and facial expressions on the famous Mathew Brady photographs.[30] When stage actors first try on their costumes, they often mimic the posture in the costume designer's sketch. Costume is deliberately used to project an elected identity, specific to the time, place, and audience.

This book is not a generalized survey of costume throughout time and space. Rather, by focusing on specific case studies and featuring many individual voices, we consider the meanings and functions of costume for its makers, wearers, and beholders, exploring the spectrum of identities represented through costume use. In wearing costume we do not become someone else; rather, we become in some context a deeper or heightened version of ourselves. Costume provides an outlet for the expression of certain identity markers that do not have an outlet in ordinary life. Like ritual, costumed events are distinct from daily existence, and therefore they allow for extreme forms of dress to aid in the formation of an alternative identity. Dress grounds us in the daily social structure and in the essence of our personal identities. Costume, on the other hand, allows us to transcend the here and now, allowing for a deeper communication of meaning. This book explores the range of costume, and in so doing, offers a more complete understanding of the function of costume—and of dress—for human beings.

In this volume, I will explore the centrality of costume by concentrating on representative examples of special dress to decipher the phenomenological patterns of costume use. We will start in chapter 1 in Brazil, where race, politics, and resistance are communicated through carnival costumes. In chapter 2 we go to Sweden, where the folk costume is used as an expression of heritage, a connection to the land, its customs, and ancestors. Chapters 3–5 focus on historical awareness and education: the amateur garb of the Society for Creative Anach-

Baianas Sandra and Nina. Salvador, Bahia, Brazil, 2009.

ronism, the recreated military uniforms of Civil War reenactors, and the professional costumes of interpreters at Colonial Williamsburg. Chapter 6 centers on
the notions of collaboration and performance, analyzing costumes used in folk
drama and on the theater stage. The representative case studies move from grand
public spectacle and parade to instances where the audience shrinks is size yet
expands in knowledge. We also move from the social functions of dress, primarily as markers of religious, political, and ethnic identity, to the secular role of
dress as a communicator of personality and psychology. Each case study focuses
on the amplification of personality in particular contexts: the costumes exhibit
a series of intensifications of elective identity. Read as a group, the case studies
show how costumes are self-consciously and purposefully employed to express
basic human needs: for sociability, creativity, historical identity, heritage, and
personality. In each instance, individuals choose to express facets of their personalities in situated costumed contexts full of intention and meaning.

FESTIVE SPIRIT

Carnival Costume in Brazil

A
T THE POINT WHERE LATIN AMERICA AND AFRICA COME CLOSEST, Portuguese explorers landed on the shores of Bahia in 1500. Within half a century they had established Brazil's first colonial capital in the port city of Salvador and brought enslaved people from Africa to work the land. A Catholic country with the largest African population in the diaspora, Brazil has more people of African descent than any country except Nigeria, the most populated of the African nations.[1] The slave trade was officially abolished in Brazil as late as 1888, resulting in a large population of formerly enslaved and recently arrived people who entered the country largely through Salvador da Bahia. Intermingling in the New World, people of astonishing cultural diversity created the Candomblé religion: a syncretic mix of African and European faiths, gods, and practices. Yoruba *orixás*—many of them deified ancestors—became the African gods most often worshipped in Brazil, each one closely associated with a Catholic saint. The complex Afro-Brazilian identity—at once Catholic, African, and Brazilian—is on display in the public events of Salvador. Identity, history, race, religion, and political and social affiliations are all communicated visually by the clothing worn in festivals and by the costumes of carnival.

A spectacular sight in Salvador, one often reproduced in postcards and posters, is the "tapestry of white": a mass of men parading on the streets dressed in the all-white costume of the group Filhos de Gandhy. The men, ten thousand strong during the carnival parade, each wear a long white tunic, sleeveless and ankle-length; a terry-cloth bejeweled turban; blue socks and white sandals. Their ensembles are lavishly embellished with beaded necklaces, sashes, ribbons, raffia, and armbands of cowry shell. They are present at the secular carnival parades and at the sacred festivals that honor Catholic and Candomblé saints. The iconic costume is a text that appears in different social contexts, and it can be used to tell the complicated history of this place, signaling the solidarity, resistance, and defiance of the Afro-Brazilian population.

I observed and documented the summer festivals and the carnival of Salvador in 1996, 1997, and 1998, talking to many members of the carnival group (*bloco*) Filhos de Gandhy. In 2007 and 2009 I returned during the off-season for in-depth interviews with the leaders of the *bloco*. To deepen my understanding of the philosophy, aesthetics, and costumes of Filhos de Gandhy, I spoke with three principal members of the directorate: the fiscal officer, Ildo Sousa; the artistic director, Francisco Santos; and the elected president of the group, Professor Agnaldo Silva. Having grown up in Brazil, my first language is Portuguese, and I spoke comfortably with the three men during the informative conversations I translate below.

FILHOS DE GANDHY

The oldest and most respected carnival group in Salvador is the all-male group Filhos de Gandhy, literally "Sons of Gandhi," founded in 1949, the year after Mahatma Gandhi was assassinated in India. The *bloco* was started by a small number of unionized stevedores under the leadership of Durval Marques da Silva, known as Vavá Madeira. Gandhi's death inspired the dockworkers to form a carnival group and to name it after the great leader who fought racial injustice in India and who could serve as a model for the Afro-Brazilian struggle against discrimination, especially in Salvador. The *bloco* is currently headquartered in the historic center of the city, Pelourinho, literally "the Pillory," where slaves were once whipped. Memories of violence linger today; as the novelist Jorge Amado, who was born in Bahia and lived in Salvador, wrote: "These mansions of

Pelourinho, Salvador da Bahia, Brazil, 2007.

Pelourinho are full of tormented cries; this slope is full of grief, of a suffering that continues to this day among the modern slaves of this disenfranchised place."[2] Today Pelourinho is a UNESCO world heritage site, a place of glorious baroque churches, its streets lined with small Portuguese houses strung in rows, picked out with color—pink, peach, blue, green—and stylishly ornamented.

The group is now officially called Associação Cultural Recreativa e Carnavalesca Filhos de Gandhy, meaning they do more than parade during carnival. They also have a religious, cultural, and social presence in the city throughout the year that climaxes with the grandiose visual spectacle at carnival time.

Elsimar Lima buying sunglasses for the opening parade by Filhos de Gandhy. Carnival, Salvador da Bahia, Brazil, 1998.

The men of Filhos de Gandhy—exotic, beautiful, and bejeweled—are known for their flamboyant costume. The ensemble that Professor Agnaldo called a "*kit*" in Portuguese includes the garment, shoes, and accessories. The garment is an extra-long, white T-shaped tunic with that year's theme and motifs screen-printed in blue on the front. The design varies slightly from year to year, and it always states the year's theme and carries a drawing of Mahatma Gandhi with the attributes of the *orixás* around him. The participant—the *associado*—receives a pair of socks, usually blue, and a pair of plastic strappy sandals, usually white, with the word "Gandhy" printed on them. The tunic is tied at the waist with a blue sash, adjusted for the height of the wearer, and any extra fabric is puffed out over the belt. Also included is a pair of blue ribbons that pinch the fabric over the shoulder seams, tied into two symmetrical bows. The "costume kit" also comes with a white cotton towel, measuring two feet by four feet. Each member of Filhos de Gandhy will have the towel sewn into a turban. Right before the carnival, one sees dozens of men patiently sitting on chairs outside the headquarters having their turbans custom-made. A cotton drawstring bag, a handkerchief, and a white spray bottle of lavender-scented *alfazema* complete the kit.

Seeking to learn the history of the *bloco* from its current leader, in 2009 I met with Professor Agnaldo Silva in his office in the group's headquarters in Pelourinho for a long morning interview.[3] A retired teacher of chemistry, physics, and mathematics, he was at that time serving his fourth term as president of the group, to which he has belonged since 1976. Professor Agnaldo explained to me the social responsibilities of Filhos de Gandhy, including that of officially welcoming dignitaries—government officials and important national and international visitors. A small delegation of Filhos de Gandhy members, dressed in costume and playing instruments, is regularly dispatched to the Salvador airport to receive guests, and in August 2010 the president of India, Pratibha Patil, was welcomed to Salvador by a group from Filhos de Gandhy that included President Agnaldo Silva and Vice President Israel Moura.[4] The professor said that visitors to Salvador are charmed by the visual beauty of Gandhy, charmed by the rhythm of their instruments: the *atabaque* (drum), *agogô* (bells), and *xequerê* (bead-covered gourd). He said that Filhos de Gandhy is symbolic of Bahia, the *cartão postal* (postcard) of Salvador: "We have Filhos de Gandhy to represent Bahia."[5]

What makes Filhos de Gandhy appealing in the eyes of tourists and dignitaries is this mix of Africa and India. Africa provides the foundation for the *bloco* through music, dance, and rituals; India provides the ornamental charm through its fantastical costumes. In fact the Afro-Brazilian religion of Candomblé has always been basic to the *bloco*. Shortly after I had met him for the first time, during the first few minutes of my interview with Francisco Santos, the costume designer and artistic director of Filhos de Gandhy, he said to me, "We pay homage to Mahatma Gandhi, right, but there is a deep link between the history of Gandhy and Candomblé. The majority of the people who parade with Gandhy are people of Candomblé; do you understand?" Since its very inception, Candomblé has played a central role in the definition of the *bloco*. Ildo Sousa told me that the period of the founding of Filhos de Gandhy, in the late 1940s, was a time in Salvador when "the racial segregation was very evident. Very strong. And these stevedores, they, all of them, were practitioners of Candomblé." He explained that then, unlike now, Candomblé was a "persecuted religion, persecuted by the police" and hidden from view.

African cultural resistance is the deep message that the group communicates to the city and the world. By using the Mahatma as a peaceful foil, these men aggressively insert African religion into the cultural fabric of Salvador and Brazil. This is akin to the Mardi Gras Indians, who use their glitzy, beautifully beaded Native American regalia to expose the history and contemporary reality of African American life in New Orleans.[6]

A collection of oral history interviews with the original founders of Filhos de Gandhy—Anísio Félix's *Filhos de Gandhi: A História de Um Afoxé* (Filhos de Gandhi: The History of an Afoxé)—published in 1987, reveals that from its inception most of the original members were "people of the *axé*," practitioners of Candomblé whose aim was to spread the religion through the streets. Humberto Ferreira Café, stevedore and former president of the General Assembly of Filhos de Gandhy, frankly says, "Gandhy was founded with the objective of divulging on the streets the Candomblé religion."[7] During those initial years the group was classified by the carnival officials as an *afoxé* in acknowledgment of its religious rhythms and music. The Yoruba word "*afoxé*" translates as "powerful incantations."[8] *Afoxés* in Salvador are groups that chant in African languages; that play percussive instruments, especially the *agogô* bells, *atabaque* drums, and *xequerê* beaded gourds; and whose colors and symbols have meaning within the system of Candomblé. By parading in public, practitioners introduce and expose the unknowing to their religion, so *afoxé* is often called the "Candomblé of the streets." The first *afoxé* group paraded in Salvador in 1895, but they soon disappeared from public view as a result of the police persecution of Candomblé. (Candomblé gatherings in Salvador required prior registration to obtain police permits until 1976.)[9]

Professor Agnaldo told me proudly, repeating himself for emphasis, that the group is in the *Guinness Book of World Records* as the largest *afoxé* in the world.

He said the founders of Filhos de Gandhy wanted music to accompany their theme of peaceful nonviolence, but Indian music—the chants and clanking bells of Hare Krishna—did not seem suitable for carnival, so they chose to play the sounds of *ijexá,* whose slow, rhythmic and leisurely tempo went with the Indian costume and harmonized with their peaceful stroll.

> Ijexá is a nation of Candomblé. The beats of the *atabaque,* of the *agogô,* of the *xequerê,* is *afoxé,* meaning, Candomblé of the streets. *Afoxé* means Candomblé of the streets. Based on this Candomblé of the streets, they formed this *afoxé* and sang the songs of praise for the *orixás.*

> So, in truth, we have to associate Candomblé with India. That is why we call ourselves "Hindu-Africa." We are Afro-descendants, we are of African origin, and Candomblé is of African origin. And we follow the philosophy of Mahatma Gandhi and its advocacy of peace.

> For us, in the religious syncretism of Candomblé, it is Oxalá who is our chief god. Oxalá is he who wears white, who advocates for peace. And Mahatma was a pacifist who sought peace. So, together, we associate Mahatma Gandhi with Oxalá, who is the chief god for us.

Filhos de Gandhy venerate the Yoruba god Oxalá by playing *afoxé* music, bringing Candomblé sounds and praise songs out of the *terreiro* temple into the streets, and, in particular, by playing the rhythms of *ijexá,* a set cadence associated with specific *orixás,* including Oxalá. The chief god of the Yoruba pantheon, the creator of the world, known as Obatala in Nigeria and Oxalá in Brazil, gains visual presence through the possessed bodies of his worshippers—his sons and daughters—for the initiates consider the *orixá* their father, referring to him as "my father Oxalá"—*o meu pai* Oxalá. This principal god is always shown in white vestments, hunched at the waist, since he bears the burden of the world on his shoulders. He is committed to peace and renounces violence. In his hand he carries the *paxoró,* a staff resembling a multi-stacked umbrella, and his symbol is the white dove.[10] His association with peace makes the connection to Mahatma Gandhi obvious. In a large painting by Francisco Santos, Gandhi is held on the shoulders of the male *orixás* of war and thunder, Ogum and Xangô. Gandhi, as Oxalá, wears a white robe and the blue and white beads of Filhos de Gandhy; he carries the globe in his right hand, the *paxoró* in his left. Doves encircle his head, the central bird holding an olive branch in its mouth. Behind the Mahatma's right shoulder turbaned Filhos de Gandhy parade gleefully.

Oxalá is syncretized with Jesus Christ—at the moment of his death as Our Lord of the Good End, Senhor do Bonfim—who also happens to be the patron saint of the stevedores.[11] So Filhos de Gandhy pays homage to the great Yoruba god Oxalá and to the patron saint of Salvador's dockworkers. Both gods become linked to Gandhi in a sort of reincarnation of the great soul, the Mahatma. Francisco Santos told me that Gandhi's spirit passed to them to support their quest of peace on earth. This mixing, mingling, conflation, and association between different deities seems logical for the intersection between the Yoruba and Catholic religions—and even Hinduism. All are polymorphous iconically, with a large and diverse pantheon whose distinguishing features are predominantly vestments and physical attributes.[12]

Even the group's name—Sons of Gandhi—reflects their strong dual ties to Candomblé and Catholicism.[13] Brazilian Catholicism has kinship and family at its core: the young Mary as the daughter of Anne and Joaquin; Mary, the mother of God; Jesus as the son of both God and Mary. The familial model applies to Catholic confraternities—lay brothers—such as the Franciscan Brotherhood, whose male members see themselves metaphorically as sons of the same father. Confraternities, like Candomblé groups, offer mutual aid to their members, and in Salvador the lay brotherhoods devoted to Our Lady of the Rosary or to the black Saint Benedict of Palermo brought freed and enslaved blacks together. *Irmandades* (confraternities) allowed Afro-Brazilians to continue their African-derived religious practices within this social network, and they helped in the quest for *Resistência Negra,* Black Resistance.[14] In Candomblé one is initiated into a house, a *terreiro,* whose priest or priestess is called, in Portuguese, a *pãe de santo* (father of god) or *mãe de santo* (mother of god), and in Yoruba, as spelled in Brazil, *babaorixá* (father of god) or *iyalorixá* (mother of god). The initiate becomes a ritual offspring of this particular priest, a *filho de santo* or *filha de santo,* and the other members of the temple are seen as siblings. The *orixá* who rules your head, which is revealed during a cowry shell divination, is your father or mother, and the priest who initiated you is also your parent. If male, you are a *filho de santo*—the son of the "saint," the word commonly used in Brazil for the *orixá,* perhaps in linguistic accommodation to the Catholic saints who were already there when the enslaved Yoruba arrived. Filhos de Gandhy, like *filhos de santo,* linguistically forges familial and fraternal bonds among the members and the supreme power, be it Oxalá, Christ, or even the Mahatma. "*Filhos de Gandhy / Somos todos irmãos*" ("Filhos de Gandhy, we are all brothers") states one of their song lyrics,[15] and many men declare that they will remain a Filhos de Gandhy *até a morte* (until death).[16] The bond of family, religion, and community is strong and holds the group together.

Community was always one of the aims of the group founded by the friends and coworkers who were unionized dockworkers. Maintaining community and a peaceful coexistence led them to establish, from the beginning, the two rules that still govern the *bloco:* no women and no alcohol. The rationale was simple: if you introduce either—or both—into a gathering of men, there will be jealousy and fighting, defeating the purpose of this peaceful march.[17] Oral history accounts of the first parade in 1949 differ with regard to the group's size; individual memories range from twelve to two hundred men. According to Professor Agnaldo, sixteen thousand men pay their membership dues today, but only about six thousand participate in the carnival parade (others I spoke with estimate this number to be closer to ten thousand). Many believe that as the group has grown and multiplied, it has lost its original sense of camaraderie and friendship; the brotherhood concept in its name has been compromised as the group has expanded over the last sixty years. The old-timers agree: Eduarlino Crispiniano de Souza believes there should be a cleanup (*"tem que fazer uma limpeza"*) to rid the group of unsavory persons; Nelson Ferreira dos Santos feels that although Gandhy has acquired much quantity since its founding, it has lost the quality of moral character.[18]

COSTUME AND FESTIVE DAYS

During celebratory times Afro-Brazilians in Salvador achieve temporal and spatial dislocations and relocations through their costume. Jeweled turbans, beads, perfume, and raffia help the wearer escape the mundane, transporting him or her to another place, beyond the here and now. The Portuguese word for costume is *"fantasia,"* appropriate because the dress and the persona it represents are not attempts to replicate historical originals: they are exaggerated and elaborated, a fantasy expressed through material and trim, cut and silhouette, color, glitter, and shine. Yet the flashy costume intensifies the performing self more than it adds imaginary facets to the wearer's identity.

The Filhos de Gandhy costume, the most glorious of the local *fantasias,* epitomizes the beauty of the carnival of Bahia. It is more than a fun and frivolous garment; it is profound and filled with deep spiritual meaning. Yet carnival is only one of the many festivals in Salvador where Africa blends with Europe, where the Yoruba religion blends with Catholicism. Pride in a shared African heritage is expressed publicly in the festivals of Salvador through music, dance, ritual, spirit possession, and through costume.

The summer holiday season begins in Brazil with Christmas and New Year's Eve and culminates in the carnival celebrations of February or early March, at which point all festivities—Catholic or Candomblé—halt during the period of Lent. School is in recess until after carnival, and Brazilians travel their country

Festa de Yemanjá. Rio Vermelho beach, Salvador da Bahia, Brazil, 2007.

during the holidays. In Salvador two main citywide celebrations take place in the Brazilian summer: Lavagem do Bonfim on the second Thursday after Epiphany and the Festa de Yemanjá on February 2.

FESTA DE YEMANJÁ

In Brazil the Yoruba *orixá* Yemanjá is the goddess of the salt waters and associated with the Atlantic Ocean. She is passionately worshipped in Salvador partially because she watched over the slaves during the Middle Passage, ensuring their safe arrival in Bahia. The goddess, often depicted as a mermaid, also protects fishermen while they are at sea. Yemanjá is syncretized with the Virgin Mary; often called "Santa Iemanjá," she can be pictured as the Star of the Sea—Stella Maris—wearing a long blue dress with a starfish on her crown and shells falling from her outstretched hands.

The Festa de Yemanjá is a massive celebration in Salvador. Thousands of devotees gather on the Rio Vermelho beach before dawn on February 2, creating altars on the shore by sticking candles and roses in the sand alongside statues of Yemanjá and the gifts that will be dropped into the ocean.[19] Families, groups of friends, and members of the same *terreiro*—the Candomblé place of worship— celebrate the *orixá* throughout the day by dancing, playing drums, and singing. Many enter a state of possession on the coastline of the Atlantic Ocean.[20] In the Casa do Pescador people deposit gifts of combs, mirrors, perfumes, soaps, and notes to Yemanjá, which are taken in boats and dropped into the ocean. Devotees receive blessings from a Candomblé priest or priestess. The benediction comes in the form of scented water, in this case, *alfazema,* a store-bought lavender eau de toilette also called *água de cheiro. Alfazema* is used for ritual cleansing in Candomblé rites, and, as we shall see, members of the carnival group Filhos de Gandhy spray it into the air and onto those who request it as a form of blessing on the streets of Salvador.

The men of Filhos de Gandhy arrive late in the afternoon. But hundreds of Baianas are present throughout the event. "Baianas," literally "women from Bahia," many of whom are priestesses of Candomblé, are women, mostly of African descent, who wear white head wraps, white blouses, and multiple skirts of cotton eyelet and lace. They are distinct in their broad hoop skirts that evoke the European dress of the 1850s. At the Festa de Yemanjá there is an official stage where Baianas dance and musicians drum, but most of the action is scattered along the beach. Groups drum in circles while some participants achieve spirit possession. Families, praying beside the water, float floral offerings out to sea. Candomblé houses and groups of Baianas hire local fishermen to take them out to the channel, where they leave their own personal gifts: flowers, notes with wishes, plastic statues of mermaids and sailors, soaps and other beauty products, encased in makeshift miniature boats decorated with flowers and ribbons.

In the afternoon, in the heat of the day, you hear the *ijexá* rhythm that signals the arrival of the delegation of Filhos de Gandhy. About one hundred costumed men appear, several carrying on their heads huge packages wrapped in cloth, ruffles, lace, and ribbons, brimming with long-stemmed flowers. The arrival of Filhos de Gandhy is the climax of the ritual. Then at around five o'clock those who came for the religious event drift away, and the crowd becomes unruly and aggressive as the *trios elétricos*—gigantic trucks with deafening sound systems— roll down the street. The day devoted to the Goddess of the Ocean has transformed into a wild secular street party.

During the festival, young people wear matching T-shirts that grant them access to particular bars where they can dance and drink with friends.[21] The T-shirts often show Yemanjá as a mermaid; they vary greatly in artistic style and

Baianas at the Lavagem da Purificação. Santo Amaro, Bahia, Brazil, 1996.

bear the name of the bar and the date. The shirts become souvenirs of the day and are the festival version of the *abadá*—the popular costume T-shirt that the people will wear in a few weeks for carnival. Participation in the pre-carnival religious festivals and participation in the carnival parades and parties all center on a garment, often a T-shirt, worn enthusiastically on the day of the event, later stored in a closet to stimulate spirited memories of festive times.

LAVAGEM DO BONFIM

"*Lavagem*" simply means "washing," and several churches in Bahia have a ritualized *lavagem*—a day when devotees participate in a procession around the church with music and flowers steeped in perfumed water, eventually pouring the water outside the closed gates of the church in a symbolic cleansing of the sacred space. The festival varies in size and popularity; for example, the Lavagem da Purificação—the washing of the steps of the church of Nossa Senhora da Purificação in the Bahian city of Santo Amaro, birthplace of famous singers Caetano Veloso and Maria Bethânia—attracts thousands of revelers, most of them there for the all-night music and party.

Far greater is the Lavagem do Bonfim, a procession from the

Musicians. Lavagem do Bonfim, Salvador da Bahia, Brazil, 1996.

church of Our Lady of the Conception of the Beach—Igreja de Nossa Senhora da Conceição da Praia—through the city, then up the hill to the church of Our Lord of the Good End, Igreja do Nosso Senhor do Bonfim.[22] In this festival the Filhos de Gandhy "sea of white" is a dazzling site to watch. (I walked the five-mile route three times—in 1996, 1998, and 2007.) The slogan of the pilgrimage is *Quem tem fé, vai a pé* (Those with faith, go on foot). Thousands of men and women dressed in white, carrying flowers and pots of water, make the long, hot journey as a sign of devotion. Structured like a classic European Catholic procession, the pilgrimage ends at the principal church of the city that is named for the Savior, São Salvador. Yet the festival also carries Candomblé significance, for Jesus Christ is syncretized with the chief god of the Yoruba pantheon, Oxalá, whose color is white. Starting at seven o'clock in the morning, people begin to gather with bands of musicians who will make the trek as a unit. In 2007 the group Orishalá honored the Candomblé gods with large banners painted by Francisco Santos, the artistic director of Filhos de Gandhy. The Orishalá banner depicting Oxalá proclaimed *Deus Ama o Povo do Candomblé* (God loves the people of Candomblé). Another banner proclaimed *Salve As Casas de Candomblé* (Long live the Candomblé temples). Followers of the African religion have a public and central presence in this Catholic event.

The official program begins at around nine o'clock in the morning with a formal address by a Catholic priest who stands at the door of Our Lady of the Conception and greets us all, making a point of extending his welcome to the followers of the *cultos Afros-Brasileiros,* acknowledging the large population of the people *do axé,* as the followers of Candomblé are called. He told us that this

Musicians. Lavagem do Bonfim, Salvador da Bahia, Brazil, 2007.

Baianas. Lavagem do Bonfim, Salvador da Bahia, Brazil, 2007.

caminhada de fé (walk of faith) represents the washing of hatred and sin from our souls. The Catholic leader gave his speech surrounded by government officials, including three representatives of the carnival group Filhos de Gandhy, majestic in their white terry-cloth turbans. One of the delegates of Filhos de Gandhy took the microphone to reiterate his group's commitment to peace. Encircling the men were a handful of Baianas, and hundreds of Baianas will lead the three-hour procession to the Church of Bonfim, carrying on their heads or shoulders large

vases filled with long-stemmed white chrysanthemums immersed in perfumed water. Festival participants parade behind and among them, singing along with the amplified anthem of Senhor do Bonfim. At the gates of the Bonfim church, after speeches by the mayor and other government officials, some of the Baianas spill their scented water, *água de cheiro,* on the steps of the church, but most of them give the water to the faithful, pouring it on their heads or washing their faces with it. The Baianas act as priestesses, bestowing blessings on behalf of the god who remains behind the closed doors of his church. This *lavagem* is a symbolic washing not only of the church but also of the body and soul of the follower, who simultaneously receives the blessings of both the Catholic and the Candomblé deities, since many of the Baianas are associated with Candomblé as *mães de santo* (priestesses) or as *filhas de santo* (initiates).[23]

In the early afternoon, around three o'clock, the delegation of Filhos de Gandhy arrives, the "tapestry of white" making its way up to the Church of Bonfim, bringing up the rear of the parade. As at the Festa de Yemanjá, this unofficially marks a point of transition in the event. Although novelist Jorge Amado describes the entire day as a celebratory religious event filled with music, dance, and magic, there is a marked shift that occurs in the afternoon.[24] The older participants begin to leave, and the crowd thickens with young men and women who have come to party. The entire route of the procession, in fact, is lined with vendors of food and beer (and vendors of beads, including the white and blue plastic necklace of Filhos de Gandhy). Among the crowd there are many with matching T-shirts that serve as entrance tokens to the places where one can eat, drink, dance, and use the toilets. In dressing alike, people exhibit—as they do during carnival—temporary group membership and an affiliation with a locale where they will drink and dance until early morning. By the afternoon this religious pilgrimage has become a secular party, a *pre-carnaval* carnival.

Carnival revelers. Salvador da Bahia, Brazil, 1997.

CARNIVAL

When most people think of carnival in Brazil, they conjure up images of glistening *mulatas* atop floats, wearing scanty costumes of feathers and glittering sequins and beads. This image is correct for the flamboyant dancers of the carnival of Rio de Janeiro, where "samba schools," or *escolas de samba*—organized and rehearsed social clubs—compete with one another in a juried and televised spectacle of music, dance, and costume. Rio's carnival involves twenty-four samba schools that parade along the Sambadrome, a runway stretching almost half a mile, complete with permanent bleachers and luxury box seats that accommodate eighty thousand spectators.[25] Each samba school is allocated a strict span of stage time: no less than sixty minutes and no more than eighty minutes in duration. The pageant takes place on three consecutive nights and ends on Mardi Gras, with the winners announced on Ash Wednesday. The winning samba schools will parade again the following Saturday night during the *Desfile das*

Campeãs (Parade of Champions).[26] In her book *The Making of Carnival,* costume designer Rosa Magalhães details the long process of outfitting the hundreds of participants. Once the samba school's yearly theme is announced, sketches of the dozens of costumes are made, followed by the selection of fabrics and the creation of sample garments that are handed to the seamstresses. Eventually these outfits will be sold and fitted to the individuals who will wear them during the parade.[27]

In contrast to the unified carnival of Rio de Janeiro, the pre-Lenten festival in Salvador takes place along three simultaneous routes through the city: Barra-Ondina, Campo Grande/Avenida, and Pelourinho/Centro Histórico. Here carnival involves many groups, many *blocos,* with musicians and participants who strut and dance throughout the week. In 2010, for example, 260 *blocos* were listed on the official city schedule. In Salvador carnival lasts for almost a week, starting on Thursday afternoon and ending in the early afternoon of Ash Wednesday, with the band Timbalada's *arrastão* dragging along the coastal circuit of Barra-Ondina. That the party continues onto the first day of Lent causes constant displeasure to the Catholic Church.

Each *bloco* has a set schedule, parading from one to three times, each time for a period of six to ten hours. In Salvador anyone may purchase the right to parade with a group, acquiring a costume and access to the corded-off area around the *trio elétrico,* a tall, fifty-foot-long truck rigged with a powerful sound system, complete with dozens of speakers and a platform stage from which the band entertains the crowd. The costumes of the people who follow the parade change every year, signaling (financial) support and temporary membership in a particular *bloco.*

SALVADOR'S CARNIVAL BLOCOS

Filhos de Gandhy, considered an *afoxé,* is only one of about 250 parading groups on the streets of Salvador. The majority of the other groups are either *blocos de trio* or *blocos Afro;* the *blocos* divide into three main types. *Blocos de trio* are named for the massive *trio elétricos* musical trucks, and they feature *axé music*—the popular music of Salvador. *Axé* is the Yoruba word for "power," and in Brazil it has been diversely applied to designate the followers of Candomblé and a kind of popular music with no real connection to Candomblé. *Blocos de trio* are the groups that most people follow, the groups with the most costly costumes. Favorite *blocos de trio* showcase such popular acts as Chiclete Com Banana, Ivete Sangalo, and Daniela Mercury. The costumes of their followers consist of a pair of shorts and a T-shirt called an *abadá,* yet bearing no resemblance to the elegant

Nigerian robes that provide the name. Most of these outfits come in bright tropical colors—hot pink, orange, turquoise, or fluorescent green—with the band's name screen-printed on the front. During the carnivals of 1996, 1997, and 1998, I noticed that the outfit included a matching pom-pom that *bloco* participants could wave around. *Blocos de trio,* with their expensive costumes, attract a mostly Caucasian crowd of revelers, rich kids from São Paulo, Rio de Janeiro, and Salvador. *Blocos de trio* are known in Salvador as *blocos de brancos* (groups of whites).[28]

In 2010 the costume for the *bloco* Camaleão, one of the three *blocos de trio* of the band Chiclete Com Banana, cost participants almost eleven hundred dollars for the three days that the group would parade in the city. Photos posted on the website of Salvador's daily newspaper, *A Tarde,* show a large crowd of young people, with some of the women sitting on the shoulders of their male friends, cheering and hooting while holding cans of beer; the scene resembles spring break in Florida or a college sports pep rally. The photos also show some women displaying temporary tattoos of a stylized lizard's foot, the symbol of the *bloco,* since *"camaleão"* means "chameleon." The young women in the pictures resemble basketball cheerleaders more than they do the feathered dancers of the carnival in Rio.

Abadás for the *blocos de trio* are purchased from outlets such as Central do Carnaval and are available for pickup a few days before the group is scheduled to parade, allowing people a chance to employ seamstresses to transform their generic T-shirts into personalized garments. The 2010 website for Folia Bahia, another carnival outlet, tells its female reader why she should customize her *abadá:* to make beautiful what is already lovely; to attract the gaze in the midst of the crowd; to make sure her *abadá* is different from the thousands of others, its uniqueness reflecting her individual identity.[29] The website warns its readers that the *abadá* should be altered to ensure that the printed logo of the *bloco* is intact, for that is what grants the participants entry into the corded-off area around the trio and the band, where members can dance inside the secure area and use the restrooms inside the accompanying trailer, the *carro de apoio.* In this safe arena the *bloco's* followers are separated from the thousands of others who cannot afford the expensive costume, yet who trail the band's path, dancing beside the truck beyond the barrier of the rope.

Beauty is a goal; the *abadá* should fit tightly, and it should be sexy. Most customized female *abadás* turn into a version of a halter top, a short garment with an open back and plunging neckline, the shirt tying behind the neck and across the middle of the back. Many people in Salvador say that the *blocos de trio* attract the *gente bonita*—the "beautiful people"—a throng of affluent, young white men and women in shorts and tank tops, on display in the protected area around the trio while the city's black majority watches from the other side of the cord.

Besides the *blocos de trio* that play *axé music,* the other two types of parading groups are *blocos Afros* and *afoxés. Blocos Afros* are carnival groups that make explicit reference to historical and contemporary Africa and its diaspora in their percussive music, song lyrics, themes, and costumes (compare this to the *afoxé* Filhos de Gandhy, whose focus is on the old religion of Africa). Participation in the *blocos Afros* and *afoxés* offers an alternative to the popular music groups and provide an opportunity for Afro-Brazilians to express pride in their shared African heritage and to shape a united front in the struggle for equality in opposition to Brazil's racial prejudice. Among the most beloved *blocos Afros* are Olodum, Ara Ketu, and Ilê Aiyê. Their costumes are less expensive than the *blocos de trio* but more costly than the costume for Filhos de Gandhy, which is around $150. In 2010 it cost $194 for the costume for Ara Ketu and $216 for Olodum's costume (compare this to $1,087 for the costume for Chiclete Com Banana in the same year). The costume for Ilê Aiyê cost $250 in 2010 and featured long tunics for men and women, coming closer in look to the Nigerian robe called an *agbada.* Ilê Aiyê's *abadás* are made of stamped, printed cloth with explicit references, through slogans and images, to the heroes of Africa and its diaspora, such as Shaka Zulu, Nelson Mandela, Marcus Garvey, and Malcolm X. The male *abadás* are worn over pants; the female ones are worn with a long skirt. A profusion of beads, cowry shells, and especially bulbous turbans on women appear in this *bloco,* which prohibits nonblack individuals from buying costumes and participating.

Ilê Aiyê was founded in 1974 in the Candomblé house Ilê Axé Jitolu, with the belief that "the valorisation of the black population will promote the dissemination, in a positive way, of their culture and history." In its mission statement the group declares its goal to be "to awaken the self-esteem of the black people, to preserve Afro traditions and integration within the black community, and to stimulate the resistance and defense of the black race."[30] It follows that they have chosen the motto *Beleza Negra* (Black Beauty) and that attractiveness is a central goal, for feeling beautiful is a step toward self-esteem in this black city where discrimination against the majority population of African descendants continues. A month before carnival, Ilê Aiyê sponsors its beauty pageant, *A Noite da Beleza Negra* (A Night of Black Beauty), with the aim of electing a queen chosen for her beauty, dance, and racial persona, a model for the world, a "standard of black beauty."[31] The loveliest woman should also evoke the beauty of the *orixás*—the African deities—with reference to the "vestments, rhythms, dances, and gestures" of the gods.[32] The contenders wear costumes that evoke Africa: chest wrappers, several ankle-length skirts layered atop one another, accented with raffia, gold lamé, and sculptural turbans. The beauties dance barefoot (rather than in the high heels of Rio de Janeiro dancers), light on their feet, arms flung back in a rotating gesture, their bodies turning continuously, making their skirts swell and swirl. Their dance and costumes evoke Africa—whether in reality or in fantasy—in the same way the costume of Filhos de Gandhy evokes or fantasizes India. The winner of Ilê Aiyê's contest—*a Deusa do Ébano* (the Ebony Goddess)—will stand on display atop the *bloco*'s float during the three days of their carnival performance, gorgeous in her personification of Africa in Brazil.

Blocos Afros explicitly communicate their commitment to the struggle for equality and social justice for those of African descent in the diaspora. *Afoxés*—the type of carnival group to which Filhos de Gandhy belongs—take their message one step further, embodying a spirit of resistance by keeping the old African religion alive and relevant. *Afoxés* do this by playing the rhythms of Candomblé—the syncretized religion of Brazil that combines elements of various religions from West and Central Africa with Portuguese Catholicism. In their iconography, as we have already seen here, the traits of the Yoruba *orixás* are blended with those of Catholic saints. Both Catholic saints and Yoruba *orixás* are called *santos* in Portuguese; in fact, a common surname in Salvador is "dos Santos" or "Santos" (of the saints or gods), leaving ambiguous whether the reference is to the European or African religion.

The costume of the *blocos de trio* are simply called *abadás*—though not more than a T-shirt and shorts—but the costumes for the *blocos Afros* and *afoxés* are properly called *fantasias*—carnival costumes, extraordinary garments not designed to disguise or alter, but rather to highlight aspects of the wearer's identity. The costume of Filhos de Gandhy, unlike the fashionably transformed *abadá* halter top of the *blocos de trio,* cannot be cut or changed. In it we see Africa in disguise; through clothing that evokes India and the Orient, the customs and religion of the Nigerian Yorubaland are kept alive. Filhos de Gandhy, the oldest *bloco* featuring African culture, allows its members to escape Brazil temporarily and return to Africa via India, yet in the process they situate themselves firmly within the reality of Afro-Brazil, asserting at once a faith based in Africa and a political position in opposition to the dominant prejudices.

PUBLIC CELEBRATIONS OF HERITAGE

In public events the people of Salvador present their culture to themselves and to national and international tourists. Three main features unite these public celebrations: religiosity, spectacle, and fun. Carnival, the Festa de Yemanjá, and the Lavagem do Bonfim all combine European and African spiritual and visual components. In keeping with both Mediterranean Catholicism and West African religiosity, festivals in Brazil encompass the structures of procession and visual spectacle: there is a public walk to the shrine or church, signaling commitment to faith and community; the event involves paying homage and offering gifts to the deity as well as being seen by others who witness the act of faith. The celebration generally includes music and dance, food stalls, and sellers of religious tokens.[33] (The processions of Baroque Europe involved scattering money or jewelry to the spectators; in Salvador only the members of Filhos de Gandhy follow this tradition by giving away beads during the carnival, just as the krewes of New Orleans do at Mardi Gras.)

The procession involves walking to the place where the god lives—the church of Bonfim or the Atlantic Ocean, where Yemanjá resides. During carnival the procession also takes a set route, which for the *blocos Afros* and *afoxé* begins and ends in the neighborhood where the group is headquartered. In this way the carnival of Salvador resembles Mardi Gras in New Orleans, where the parade is a communal celebration of the neighborhood. In the carnival of Rio de Janeiro, by contrast, while the rehearsals leading up to the carnival parade take place in the specific locality associated with each samba school, the actual parade travels along the Sambadrome, a constructed, artificial route.

An unofficial configuration unites festivals in Salvador: they begin as religious events and end in a party. The morning involves prayers, procession, and spirit possession; the afternoon is given to dance, music, and alcohol. In this Catholic city named for Jesus Christ, "the Savior," Candomblé and expressions of Afro-Brazilian culture were forbidden, discouraged, and hidden from public view until the twentieth century. Afro-Brazilian groups were banned from public parading in 1904, though they were reinstituted in 1919, and until 1976 all Candomblé ceremonies required a permit from the police.[34] Ironically, Candomblé has now become a symbol of Bahia and an attractive selling point for tourists. The festivals of the city, often centering on glorious Baroque churches, have a public African dimension through music and drumming, *orixá* imagery, beads, and perfumed water blessings. In fact, all of these elements have a Catholic equivalent: liturgical music and chants, prayer cards depicting the saints, rosary beads, and holy water blessings. In this Catholic setting the African presence is nonetheless powerfully felt. Street food—in the historic district, in the downtown, at the beach—is West African, prepared on the spot by Baianas, whose cooking emits a strong aroma of fried *dendê* (pungent palm oil) that permeates the air and lingers deliciously throughout the city. Favorite savories include *acarajé* (black-eyed pea cakes), *vatapá* (bread, shrimp, and peanut paste), *abará* (steamed black-eyed pea mush), and *caruru* (okra stew), all eaten with red peppers, ideally washed down with cold beer.

The meshing of Africa and Europe is symbolically represented by the Baiana, a self-consciously designated emblem of Afro-Brazil in her white garments, head wrap, and jewelry. The composite ensemble has, as Daniel Crowley commented, elements that derive from post-contact Africa and simultaneously exhibit transatlantic influences.[35] According to art historian Mikelle Smith Omari-Tunkara, some pieces of clothing, especially the head wrap, were visual markers of "Africanness" in Brazil, and remain so, potently, in the ritual attire of Candomblé and, by extension, in the clothing of the Baianas.[36] The Baiana costume typically includes a *torço* (head wrap); a voluminous hoop skirt worn with several starched and embellished petticoats; a *camizu* (short-sleeved blouse); *pano da costa* (shoulder cloth); bead necklaces and silver bracelets; and *balangandās,* a cluster of amulets worn pinned at the waist. Yet, as Raul Lody's careful documentation of the variety of these amulets demonstrates, there is ample opportunity to personalize the "uniform" look of the Baiana.[37]

Filhos de Gandhy can be seen as male versions of the Baianas, in their white clothes, white turbans, and signature beads. The two can look remarkably alike, as shown in the gestural, impressionist draftsmanship of Carybé, a friend of the novelist Jorge Amado and Salvador's most famous visual chronicler.[38] The male member of Filhos de Gandhy and the female Baiana are the unofficial *padrinho* and *madrinha*—the godfather and godmother—of the city of Salvador. Filhos de Gandhy are the only carnival *bloco* present at all the religious events of the city. During carnival all Candomblé events halt and the Baianas are no longer visible. Filhos de Gandhy stand in for the absent Baianas, blessing the crowd with their lavender eau de toilette, inducing the presence of the African *orixás* through their music and iconography.

By unraveling the relationship between spectacle and religiosity, we acquire a key to the culture of Bahia. The Brazilian procession to the Church of Bonfim, like the Osun festival in Osogbo, Nigeria, for example, is mediated by the local government.[39] In turning a religious expression into a commodified spectacle for general consumption, art turns into heritage, the private becomes public. The strength of the African culture in the diaspora of Brazil lies in this visibility of the old Yoruba religion. Filhos de Gandhy, the oldest carnival group in Salvador, spreads knowledge of the *orixás* during the city's festivals by featuring religious iconography on painted banners and floats, and through songs, music, and costumes.[40] The Yoruba *orixás* are recognized primarily by their *indumentária,* their

Baiana. Lavagem do Bonfim, Salvador da Bahia, Brazil, 2007.

Israel do Carvalho,
Filhos de Gandhy.
Pelourinho, Salvador
da Bahia, Brazil, 2009.

ritual garments, attesting to the importance of clothing for religious communication. Through the costumes of Filhos de Gandhy—garments that ostensibly evoke the oriental exoticism of India—the group brings the Yoruba pantheon into relevance, amassing ten thousand men to sing and dance the praises of the African gods.

CARNIVAL FUN

Given a choice of joining one of 250 carnival groups in Salvador, I wondered why people chose Filhos de Gandhy, choosing to wear the iconic tunic and turban. I talked to many men who parade with the *bloco*; the non-directorate majority of men are called *associados* (members).[41] The costume is one of the reasons men gave for joining Filhos de Gandhy; they preferred to dress in the fantastical costume, to wear the turban and several strands of beads. The *abadá* shorts and T-shirt are less of a departure from daily dress than the Gandhy *fantasia*. There are temporary makeshift bars all along the carnival route. Part of the fun of carnival is to leave the roped-off area around the *bloco,* go drink with friends for a while, and then rejoin the group as it edges slowly through the streets. An advantage of wearing the Filhos de Gandhy costume is access to the restricted area of any carnival group, possibly because of the great respect the *bloco* receives, and also because of its close association with the governor of Bahia, the mayor of Salvador, and members of the police force. A poster hanging in the headquarters of the group features a drawing of a military police officer in uniform, looking in the mirror. In his reflection he is dressed in the costume of Filhos de Gandhy. His hard, dark-colored riot helmet implying violence is replaced with the soft, white terry-cloth turban of peace. I was told several times that a benefit of wearing the Gandhy costume is that you can enter any *bloco* to flirt (*paquerar*) with the pretty women. (Since no women are allowed inside Filhos de Gandhy, its members can flirt with women only by entering other carnival groups.)

I asked Professor Agnaldo what he thinks of drunken, aggressive behavior in the *bloco.* He said that those caught fighting are blacklisted and barred from parading with the group again, but he explained how hard it is to enforce this rule, because anyone can buy a costume and give it to someone else to wear during carnival. All you need to parade with the group is that year's costume, not an identification card. The professor also said it is true that a member of Filhos de Gandhy has access to any *bloco* during the parade: "Yes. He has access. It is because Gandhy is beautiful. And Gandhy has access, in any location that he chooses to enter; he is always well-received. The public admires the *bloco* because of its beauty."

Professor Agnaldo self-consciously alluded to the charm and beauty of his *bloco*. Beauty and visual spectacle are central to the current identity of this group, as they are for other *blocos* Afro such as Ilê Aiyê, since beauty leads to racial esteem, self-respect, and admiration from others. Two of the three interlinked themes of carnival I outlined above—fun and spectacle—converge; looking beautiful is part of the fun of parading with Filhos de Gandhy. Alberto Pita, the former costume designer for *bloco Afro* Olodum, told me that participants must wear the costume and feel attractive in it, and only then can they have a good time during carnival. "There is something about the costume that we perceive; that the costume is the act of feeling good," he said. "If you were to wear—even regular clothes, if you were to wear a costume, and if you don't feel good in it, then your carnival is ruined (*o carnaval já era*). If you don't *occupy* the costume, you are not going to enjoy the carnival."[42] A costume is not merely a garment to be worn; it involves a persona to be occupied, to be consumed and projected to its beholders.

Wearing the costume of Filhos de Gandhy and assuming the majestic persona can help a man exhibit self-esteem and confidence during the carnival parade and distinguish himself with personal touches from the thousands of other similarly dressed men he marches among. For many young people, carnival week in Salvador is a time to suspend a romantic relationship in search of temporary love conquests, a practice alluded to in several popular songs from Salvador. I was told by both women and gay men that Filhos de Gandhy provides the largest roving concentration of men in the carnival parade, all (presumably) unaccompanied and available. Jom Silva, a handsome young police officer, told me that one reason he parades with Gandhy is because "*everyone* looks better in a turban." The turban frames the face of its wearer, catches the eye of the beholders with its bright blue ornament, and adds several inches to the height of the man who wears it. Carlinhos Brown, a local pop star and celebrity, claims, "If I want to be beautiful in the carnival, I wear the costume of Filhos de Gandhy. I am certain that I will be beautiful."[43] If beauty is one of the goals of carnival, then the choice of Filhos de Gandhy is clear.

BEAUTY AND SPECTACLE: THE COSTUME OF FILHOS DE GANDHY

The purchased costume kit consists of the turban towel, the tunic, a pair of socks, and the sandals. Not included, but mandatory, are the turban jewel and strands of beads, sold at the headquarters and found in much greater variety at the nearby Praça da Sé in a religious goods store called A Conta: Tudo para Orixás, which translates as "Beads: Everything for the Orixás." The bead necklaces are blue and white plastic and fall in long loops to the waist. The size of the

Filhos de Gandhy president, Professor Agnaldo Silva. Pelourinho,
Salvador da Bahia, Brazil, 2009.

beads can vary. They are relatively cheap, less than a dollar for the thin ones, but twelve dollars for the heavy ones with multiple strands. Each member of Filhos de Gandhy buys dozens of them to wear and to give away, often exchanging them for kisses from pretty women. Evanildo Almeida Gomes, who works at the bead store, told me that in 2009 they ordered 120,000 strands of beads, 90,000 of which sold during carnival time.[44] Evanildo, who has paraded with Filhos de Gandhy for the last eight years, said that many of the members of Gandhy are, like him, "people of the *axé*." The secular carnival beads are sold alongside sacred Candomblé necklaces, and Evanildo said that many initiates wear their sacred beads underneath their costumes, exposing only the secular blue and white ones. But, he warned, sacred beads that have been "washed," that have undergone a Candomblé ritual, should not be worn for base activities like drinking alcohol or engaging in sex. The religious beads reinforce the two behavioral rules of the *bloco:* no alcohol and no women (both are allowed outside the demarcated confines of the *bloco,* but not inside).

Professor Agnaldo said that while the beads can be worn dangling down the neck or crossing the torso in Candomblé style, it is mandatory to wear them, for it is part of Filhos de Gandhy's *indumentária.* It is interesting that he did not use the usual word for costume, "*fantasia,*" choosing instead the word used to describe the sacred vestments, the ritual clothing of the *orixás.* Many of the old-timers, including former president Djalma Conceição, also use the word "*indumentária*" to describe the early rendition of the costume.[45] Some members, like Hamilton Ferreira Santos, claim that the blue and white plastic bead necklaces are linked to Candomblé.[46] Filhos de Gandhy's fiscal officer, Ildo Sousa, told me that the ornament was originally a Candomblé necklace, but then "it kept modifying, modifying, modifying, modifying, until today it turned into the carnival necklace of Gandhy." He added emphatically, "But it was originally a Candomblé necklace, because of the two *orixás* that are the *orixás* that Gandhy references: Oxalá who is white, and Ogum, who is blue. The necklace is blue and white." Professor Agnaldo sees the current version of the necklace as "a good-luck charm," helping the wearer look more attractive and helping him entice women. He made a distinction between the Gandhy beads and the ones he wears under his shirt, pulling them out to show me, telling me that those had a "foundation," those were "of the *axé.*"

Besides the bead necklaces, the other required accessory is the brooch that adorns the turban. The jewel, three inches in diameter, is made of blue and silver sequins, beads, and plastic gems, sewn onto cloth batting. There is some variation in design, allowing for individual expressions of taste. The jewel is a relatively new introduction to the costume. The old turban was literally a twisted towel, held together by its tight swirl, and tucked in. It was called a *torço*, alluding to the knotted and tied head wraps of the Baianas and the elegant, sculptural headpieces of women in Africa. Now the towels are sewn into a turban shape and can be taken off and put back on; they are called *turbantes*. The folded end of the towel, printed with the present year's slogan and an image of the Mahatma, hangs long down the back, like a neck flap, and there is a wide expanse of cloth on the top of the forehead, perfect for the display of a jewel. Ildo Sousa said the brooch is like the turban ornaments of the grand viziers of India. According to Professor Agnaldo, the plastic gem, the *broche,* was introduced in 1979 or 1980 and is a "star," concentrating power onto the head, for the head is of prime importance in Candomblé: it is the seat of the *orixá* and the seat of power. The head, he emphasized, holds the "force," the power, of the syncretism of Brazil. The brooch highlights the head; the turban protects it during the heat and confusion of the carnival in Salvador.

The beads, the brooch, and the turban are all fantastical costume accessories, yet each has significance within Candomblé. The eau de toilette, *alfazema,* likewise has a religious reason for being part of the costume paraphernalia. Lavender is widely believed to have healing properties. In Brazil it is used as a *calmante* to treat anxiety, as an antiseptic, and as a cleansing agent when diluted with water. *Alfameza* is used during Candomblé rituals as a purifier and cleanser, and like the Baianas during the *lavagens,* Filhos de Gandhy dispense squirts of *alfazema* as blessings, as a calming force in the chaotic streets of carnival.

I wanted to confirm with Professor Agnaldo that the *alfazema* is used to purify the streets, becoming another way Filhos de Gandhy are selflessly working toward peace in Salvador. His answer surprised me:

> In the syncretism of Candomblé, Yemanjá, she is the Queen of the Waters, she is the mother of all the *orixás,* she is the wife of Oxalá.
>
> In the syncretism of Candomblé, she is the mother of all the *orixás.*
>
> And so the *alfazema*—she, who is vain, Oxum, Yemanjá—they use the scent to attract lovers. And we use *alfazema,* the scent, to attract girlfriends.
>
> Yes, it purifies, but it cannot purify everything. But the *alfazema* is a reference to Oxum and Yemanjá.
>
> Because the men are perfumed for the ladies. A man—dressed elegantly, all in white—and with the scent to attract the ladies. He flirts with the beads and with *alfazema.*

Distributing aromas into the streets during carnival has a long history in Brazil. The Portuguese brought to their colony their practice of *entrudo*—of flinging either foul-smelling water at unsuspecting strangers or perfumed water at family and friends. A common courting practice was to fill wax lemons or oranges with perfume so that they would burst on contact and douse the recipient with sweet-smelling scents. The men of Filhos de Gandhy—through squirts of *alfazema*—continue the tradition of courting with perfume, a practice that Brazil's emperors Dom Pedro I and Dom Pedro II enjoyed.[47]

It is clear from Professor Agnaldo's explanations that in addition to its wider, communal function the costume has a personal purpose for the wearer. As the *bloco* has grown over the years, more embellishments have been added. The original costume consisted of a tied bed sheet and a white towel, both acquired from home and worn with cheap leather sandals called *malandrinhas,* literally "little rascals," as they cut up the feet of the wearer. The original costume was inspired by the 1939 film *Gunga Din,* which some of the stevedores had recently seen. The film, set in India during colonial times, is about an attempted rebellion against the British. The Indian characters, including the hero, Gunga Din, appear in white turbans worn with a flap hanging down the back of the neck, much like the current turban of Filhos de Gandhy. Pierre Verger's beautiful 1959 photos of Filhos de Gandhy capture the men in plain white tunics, a towel twisted on their heads. No beads, turban jewels, or accessories adorn the stark and crisp uniform. From the very first time they paraded, there was fear of police retaliation—a consistent theme in the early accounts. Professor Agnaldo also said that the originators of Gandhy were afraid their peaceful march could lead to an altercation with the police, for Gandhi himself, a peaceful soul, was violently murdered on the streets of New Delhi.

But as the years went by, the original assembly of working-class men—stevedores, bricklayers, masons, tailors, and printers—transformed into a gathering of politicians, policemen, lawyers, and doctors. An elevation of the social class and wealth of the individual members added to the group's social confidence, and Filhos de Gandhy began to depart from the simple costume and develop one with more flair, one that simultaneously celebrated the *bloco'*s history and praised the *orixás.* The tunic remained simple until 1978 or 1979, when, to commemorate thirty years of Gandhy, they introduced what Professor Agnaldo called in Portuguese *"design,"* featuring a cartoon drawing of Camafeu de Oxóssi, who was then the president of Filhos de Gandhy.[48] And since that time the tunic always features an image of Mahatma Gandhi screen-printed in blue.

Professor Agnaldo gave me the reasons for the addition of the color blue to the all-white costume, returning once again to the centrality of Candomblé for the *bloco*. He explained that white is the color of Oxalá, but there are two aspects of Oxalá: the older version, called Oxalufã and syncretized with Bom Jesus dos Navigantes, and the younger version, called Oxaguiã and syncretized with Bom Jesus da Lapa. Oxaguiã, the professor taught me, is a mixture between Oxalá and Ogum, the warrior *orixá* associated with Santo Antônio, so Oxaguiã is also called the warrior Oxalá. Further, he said, Ogum/Santo Antônio is the messenger of Oxalá. So white is for Oxalá, blue is for Ogum, and with the blue they also reference the boy *orixá* Oxaguiã, the youngster, because they are the *sons of* Gandhi. With the power of these male *orixás*, Filhos de Gandhy serve as warriors for peace.

DRESSING FOR THE ORIXÁS

I wanted to learn about the meanings of the distinctive costume of Filhos de Gandhy from all relevant participants—the men who wear it during carnival, the president of the *bloco* and its official spokesperson, and also, from the artist who designs it. With the help of Professor Agnaldo, I met Francisco Santos, visual artist and artistic director and costume designer for Filhos de Gandhy for the last twenty-six years.[49] I also spent time with his assistant Cristavam Correia dos Santos. Francisco's atelier, Panteon Galeria de Arte, is on the second floor of a building a few blocks from the Filhos de Gandhy headquarters in Pelourinho. Every wall surface of the small studio is filled with Francisco's paintings of the *orixás*, caught in exuberant dance movements, wearing the appropriate vestments, and carrying the characteristic instruments of identification. The *orixás*—as represented through the possessed bodies of their devotees—bend, sway, and swing in a flurry of lace, raffia, and colorful cloth.[50] Francisco's paintings of the *orixás* also adorn the large reception room of the Filhos de Gandhy headquarters, where the large murals—displayed amid small altars, clusters of candles, bottles of rum, jars of water, and bowls of manioc flour—are found as they would be in a Candomblé *terreiro*. In fact, his art ornaments the walls of the *terreiro* of the famous *mãe de santo* Mãe Menininha do Gantois, the *madrinha* of Filhos de Gandhy.[51] Francisco said that for years, until her death in 1986, a delegation of Filhos de Gandhy would make a trip to her *terreiro* to thank Mãe Menininha for her help and to ask for her blessing before a major event. They would also go to the churches of Bonfim and of Santa Luzia, something the *bloco* has been doing since 1949.[52] Filhos de Gandhy seeks the sanction of both church and *terreiro*—not separate entities in the minds of many people in Salvador. Francisco said they also regularly ask permission from the *orixás* to be able to play the religious music of Candomblé on the streets.

Filhos de Gandhy
artistic director,
Francisco Santos.
Pelourinho,
Salvador da Bahia,
Brazil, 2009.

Francisco is in charge of design for Gandhy because of the acclaim he has garnered as an artist working within the "Afro-descendant culture." He is someone who is always working within "the force" of Candomblé. To "divulge" the culture of Africa through his art is his mission in life: "Now, as I am faithful to my culture, I specialize in—and I insist on showing—the Afro-descendant culture." His personal mandate is consistent with the current attitude of practitioners and leaders of Candomblé: to take an active role in the dissemination of knowledge about the religion, as opposed to letting others (scholars, for example) speak on their behalf.[53] Francisco feels a duty to present the iconography of Candomblé on the walls of the Gandhy headquarters, on the carnival parade floats, and on the costumes that will clothe the bodies of thousands of men. Many of those wearing the costume might not grasp the deep significance and ideology that lie behind the design on their garments. But in time they will become accustomed, tolerant, or even initiated into the religion.

I asked Francisco about his method of designing each year's costume. He said the process begins when the officials of the Religião Culto Afro-Brasileira cast cowry shells in the tradition of African divination to determine which *orixá* will govern that year.[54] Based on the result, Filhos de Gandhy will incorporate aspects of that particular *orixá* into the costume, and that year's theme and design will somehow reference the *orixá*. Ildo Sousa explained that the directorate chooses a theme that will both propagate the mandate of peace and further the Candomblé ideology by paying homage to particular *orixás*. For example, previous years' slogans have asserted that Gandhy requests peace "with the force of the waters" or "with the force of the leaves." This, Ildo said, is a tribute to the *orixás:* "With the force of the waters means with the force of the feminine *orixás* of the water, who are Yemanjá and Oxum. With the force of the leaves, it's Oxóssi. And so we are always after this mission, this dissemination."

It is important for the allusion to the *orixás* to be made "discreetly," for the Culto Afro does not allow the *orixás* to be caricatured or impersonated. Professor Agnaldo said that the gods must be respected; they cannot be represented in a profane setting marked by frivolity and drinking. Francisco tries to "stylize" visual references, "symbolically" connoting the *orixás* without anyone dressing as them, avoiding explicit replication of the costumes reserved for possession in Candomblé when the gods descend to attend the ritual. The difference here is between representation and reference. During a Candomblé ceremony the person possessed becomes the god incarnate; during carnival the person is dressed in homage to the god through reference to his or her attributes, characteristic colors, or associated objects. In the secular parade people are not allowed to masquerade as *orixás;* this would be considered disrespectful and improper.

However, a local man, Raimundo Queiroz Lima, did impersonate the Mahatma when parading with the group during carnival. To look more like Gandhi, Seu Raimundo shaved his head and purchased glasses like the ones seen in photographs of Gandhi. This Brazilian impersonator even accompanied the delegation of Filhos de Gandhy when they went to India in 1999. There he was told that he looked like a "twin brother" of their compatriot, and he was taught to bow his head and bring his hands together in the gesture of supplication.[55] Some believe that Seu Raimundo received "Gandhi's spirit every year, for five days."[56] Professor Agnaldo spoke of Seu Raimundo as a "look-alike, an imitator, a copy" of the Mahatma. In 2007 Seu Raimundo passed away, and since his death, a life-size seated mannequin, a *boneco,* of Gandhi parades with the *bloco* and remains on display in the front room of the headquarters.

A doll now stands in for the dead Mahatma Gandhi and Seu Raimundo. But the African gods are alive and well in Brazil, and they shine through the costumes, music, and dance of Filhos de Gandhy. The costumes of the *associados,* and the costumes worn by the band members, the dancers, and even by those who dress to honor the *orixás* on the floats, are all designed by Francisco to emulate formal dress—*roupa de gala*—and to incorporate much "shine" with beautiful prints and rich fabrics that evoke both India and Africa. Francisco Santos himself appears each year on top of a float in elegant costume, dancing in praise of the *orixá.* At these moments he is unrecognizable to his friends, for "the shine" (*o briho*), the beauty, is so great that his identity is temporarily concealed in the brilliance of the spectacle; in this state, Francisco exhibits *axé,* the sacred life force of the Yoruba religion. And we have returned to beauty as an explicit goal of the costume of Filhos de Gandhy. Francisco explained:

> If a person does not have a beautiful face, when he puts on the *indumentária,* the turban, the perfume, he makes himself into a thing of elegance.
>
> And so the beauty of Filhos de Gandhy is precisely in this.
>
> You can observe, in any place, any poor place, a place where the people have less financial means—whether here in Brazil or in India—the people, if you observe, you might say: "He is ugly." "He is not beautiful." But when you put on the clothing of Filhos de Gandhy, the person— it's the same with Indians when they get dressed up—you see a sight of beauty. The shine is very strong. Very strong.
>
> And the beauty, the materiality, of Filhos de Gandhy is in this. Anybody in Filhos de Gandhy—maybe you are not beautiful, but when you wear the clothes, you make yourself into a beautiful person.

Siri Brasil, Filhos de Gandhy.
Pelourinho, Salvador da Bahia,
Brazil, 2009.

To design a garment that can transform an unattractive person into a beautiful person is Francisco's mission, his mandate. He elaborates:

> We know that in any country, there are ugly things, no? But when the artist—when there is an artist—he will reach deep and grab the beautiful things and specifically emphasize these, understand? The important purpose of the artist is this: he makes the ugly beautiful. And Filhos de Gandhy is this. It is happiness, beauty, and on top of it all, peace.

As the *bloco's* artist, Francisco designs a costume that will make its wearer beautiful. He does his part; the rest is up to the person getting dressed. He said that although the *bloco* cannot impersonate an *orixá,* the *associado* may do so by adding beads and representations of the *orixás'* jewelry and instruments, their *ferramentos.* And many men add specific symbols of their *orixás*—for example, a pendant of a bow and arrow to represent the hunter Oxóssi. Because the white garment is sleeveless, many men wear armbands and bracelets of metal or raffia. These are sold at the Candomblé supply store, and the *orixás*—male and female—wear metal armbands when they come out in the moment of possession. When the thousands of men get dressed before the parade, they ornament themselves, and in so doing, Francisco believes, they "complete" his costume design, entering into collaboration with the designer, who had envisioned complementary accessories. The wearer is adorned with sacred embellishments, and through dance he further incorporates the *orixá* into himself. While the colors of the costume—white and blue—are references to the male *orixás* Oxalá and Ogum, the *alfazema* perfume and the dance are references to the female *orixá* Oxum, the goddess of the sweet waters, of love, of beauty. Francisco explained that the dance of *ijexá* that Filhos de Gandhy do during the entire parade is a dance of Oxum: tranquil, as if one were swimming leisurely through calm waters. Dance historian Barbara Browning explains that "Oxum's rhythm is *ijexá,* a gentle four-four," and that *ijexá* is the "secularized version of the rhythm played for Oxum in the candomblé."[57] One can dance like this for hours, Francisco said, because the person's body accepts the rhythm, so it does not tire. In Alberto Pita's words, you must "occupy" the costume; Francisco Santos says you must "accept" the dance. Both of these statements can be seen as references to Candomblé possession, when the *orixá* becomes manifest through the body of the initiate, who embodies and accepts the god into the self. With the pop music carnival groups, one wears a pair of shorts and a T-shirt, what Ildo Sousa calls "just a piece of cloth," but with Gandhy, religious faith, or at least commitment to the ideology of peace, allows the wearer to shine through the garments, draped in the spirit of love.

Spectators are aware of the brilliance that radiates from members of Filhos de Gandhy, for the beauty of the costumed person is evident to both the wearer and his beholders. Francisco believes the natural beauty of the people who dress as Gandhy is enhanced by the costume, for the man is "transformed" in the clothing of Filhos de Gandhy. As a painter, he is particularly struck by the contrast of the white garments against the black skin of the wearer; that, along with the accessories, make for an irresistible look that women cannot refuse. "And then, the women especially, they are *enchanted* when they see Filhos de Gandhy," Francisco said. Cristavam Correira dos Santos interrupted Francisco to tell me that the people who watch the *bloco* pass are enraptured precisely by the "magic" of Filhos de Gandhy. Francisco agreed with his assistant, saying that viewing Gandhy parading on the streets is an "amusement" for the audience, a "dream" for the people.

Francisco assured me that spectators wait hours during the parade route just to get a glimpse of the *bloco,* and some lucky ones are rewarded with a bead necklace or a kiss. "When you see a thing of beauty, you want to embrace it," he added. "You want to embrace it, kiss it, right? It's a matter of wanting to get close." It is for this reason, for optimizing the visual spectacle of Filhos de Gandhy, that the *bloco* always parades in the afternoons: in the Pelourinho carnival circuit on Sunday at 4:30PM and Tuesday at 3:30PM, and on the Barra-Ondina beach circuit at 3:00PM on Monday. In the bright sun of the summer afternoon, the viewers can clearly see the beauty of Filhos de Gandhy streaming by in white, because the *bloco* parades in what Francisco called the "noble hour" that the group has been granted from the carnival scheduling officials (less popular groups are given slots late at night).

Visual spectacle is the aim of the carnival parade, during which Filhos de Gandhy may attract and recruit new members to join in their quest for peace, in their commitment to Candomblé and Afro-Brazilian resistance. In addition to the ten thousand men dressed in turbans, bejeweled and perfumed, the carnival parade includes a troupe of extravagantly dressed male dancers, a group of drummers (*a bateria*), flag bearers, and several floats that carry allegories of Mahatma Gandhi and the *orixás*. The front of the parade features stuffed or sculpted animal allegories. Professor Agnaldo explained that the elephant symbolizes peace (for it is associated with Oxalá), the camel stands for a spirit of resistance, and the goat is sacred in Candomblé.[58]

Spectacle connects Candomblé with the festivals of Salvador, including carnival. The extraordinary rite of the religious rituals, climaxing in possessions of the devotees by the gods, is a topic celebrated in anthropological writing, in literature, and in the visual arts. A number of Salvador's noted artists—including novelist Jorge Amado, photographer Pierre Verger, and painter Carybé—have richly captured the visual splendor of possession, of the initiation, the costumes, accessories, and body painting of the *orixás* present in the bodies of the initiates. In Carybé's splendid *Iconografia dos Deuses Africanos no Candomblé da Bahia*, based on thirty years of visual research, every step of the religious rite is beautifully rendered in its exquisite detail of ornament and vestment. His watercolors capture the full ensembles in each *orixá's* appropriate colors.

Festivals celebrating the *orixás* are successfully executed when the gods decide to come down (*descer* or *baixar* in Portuguese) to mount the bodies of the worshippers and make an appearance at their party. Participants wait in anticipation to witness the dancing, the sacred vestments, and the rhythmic movements of the sacred incarnate in human form. The climax of Jorge Amado's novel *The War of the Saints*, for example, features a dramatic entrance by the *orixá* Iansã at the *caruru* festival to honor her.[59]

Participants in a Candomblé ritual enjoy the display and beauty of the *orixás* as they "descend" to enthrall us with their sacred dance and beautiful costumes. For as anthropologist Roger Sansi tells us, "Nothing pleases them more than beauty: the beauty of offerings, the beauty of their house, the beauty of their dress and jewels, of the dance, music, good food. This is not an inner beauty, but a real, visible, material one."[60] We go to a Candomblé to see the beauty of the *orixás*, and they are, in turn, asked to descend to see the beauty of the human beings, dressed in the splendid costume of Filhos de Gandhy. As Gilberto Gil sings:

> Omolu, Ogum, Oxum, Oxumaré; Todo o pessoal; Manda descer pra ver; Filhos de Gandhi
>
> Iansã, Yemanjá, chama Xangô; Oxóssi também; Manda descer pra ver; Filhos de Gandhi
>
> Mercador, Cavaleiro de Bagdá; Oh, Filhos de Obá; Manda descer pra ver; Filhos de Gandhi
>
> Senhor do Bonfim, faz um favor pra mim; Chama o pessoal; Manda descer pra ver; Filhos de Gandhi
>
> Oh, meu Deus do céu, na terra é carnaval; Chama o pessoal; Manda descer pra ver; Filhos de Gandhi

In Gil's famous song "Filhos de Gandhi," he asks the gods—Omolu, Ogum, Oxum, Oxumaré, Iansã, Yemanjá, Xangô, and Oxóssi—to descend to see Filhos de Gandhy (*Manda descer pra ver*). The singer also asks Senhor do Bonfim to call the "gang," the *orixás,* down to see the *bloco.* In the last stanza he tells God in the sky that on earth it is carnival (*O, meu Deus do céu, na terra é carnaval*) and that He should ask the gang to come down to see Filhos de Gandhy.[61] The implication is that the procession, the "tapestry of white," is a grand sight not to be missed. The carnival parade of Gandhy is indeed a spectacular sight and regularly features the costumed and turbaned Gilberto Gil, a native of Salvador, Brazil's former minister of culture, and a longtime supporter of the *bloco.*[62] Every year during carnival Gil joins thousands of other men, calling us all down to see Filhos de Gandhy, to observe more than sixty years of heritage and resistance.

TRADITION AND SACRED RESISTANCE: AFRO-BRAZILIAN IDENTITY ON DISPLAY

In 2009 Filhos de Gandhy celebrated sixty years of peace on the streets. That year's costume was striking, partly because it incorporated a third color, gold, to enhance the usual blue and white.[63] The design on the front features a muscular Mahatma Gandhi, seated Zeus-like on a stone throne, wielding Oxalá's instrument, the *paxoró,* high above his head, held like a weapon ready to strike. The classical columns flanking the Mahatma, the doves encircling his head, and the *paxoró* are all rendered in gold. In his defiance and strength, the Mahatma sits tall, slightly confrontational, appearing unlike his usual humble, hunched self. Under the drawing of him there is a depiction of the main square in Pelourinho with the famous symbol of Catholic Afro-Brazil: the Igreja da Nossa Senhora do Rosário dos Pretos, a rococo church dating to the eighteenth century and built by slaves for their own worship.[64] The combined iconography of the drawings brings to mind at once Greek mythology, Indian politics, and the Yoruba and Catholic religions. To complete the ensemble, members received special commemorative sandals decorated with a silver lamé strap. This ostentatious version of the *fantasia* visually celebrated the great achievement of longevity enjoyed by no other carnival *bloco* in Salvador. Members of Filhos de Gandhy have preserved the tradition of the founding stevedores, and the collective vision is also personally meaningful to the members as individuals, for each has a personal tradition of parading with Gandhy and often a commitment to the ideals of Afro-Brazilian cultural resistance. Thus the carnival *bloco,* with its long history and collective force, ultimately allows for an expression of personal identity. As Ildo Sousa said to me, the tradition of the *bloco* and one's personal tradition of involvement in the *bloco* are "confounded"; it is difficult to discern the difference between the

Filhos de Gandhy fiscal officer, Ildo Sousa. Pelourinho, Salvador da Bahia, Brazil, 2009.

collective and the personal. In fact, it is through the collective that one defines and refines the personal.[65]

Ildo believes that Filhos de Gandhy has its long history because of its strong roots in Candomblé, the religion that served as a means for the retention and transmission of African culture in Brazil. This is of great appeal to many members, including Ildo, who has been with Gandhy for more than twenty-five years, fifteen of those in the directorate. He told me there is a discernible pattern for most of the directors, the almost one hundred men who occupy an elected position. They begin as a *folião*—a person who parades with the group—and then, as their commitment deepens, they join the administration of the *bloco*. The difference between Filhos de Gandhy and other carnival groups, Ildo said, lies in their degree of personal commitment, since most of the members of Gandhy have been with the group for more than ten years. (Unlike many of the popular music *blocos* that appeal to the youth, Filhos de Gandhy also attracts mature middle-aged and older men.) Ildo elaborated:

> In the other carnival *blocos,* the people join the *bloco* only to have fun during carnival, understand? And I think that in Gandhy, the people join for the emotion, for the pleasure of being, of parading. For me, this is the basic difference.
>
> The people [in Gandhy] are able to realize themselves, even spiritually. There is a spiritual component, no? I really believe that the basic difference that you could look for is this.

In fact, the costume often communicates commitment and time in Filhos de Gandhy. According to Ildo, a large number of people "live of Gandhy" (*uma gigantesca gama de pessoas vivem de Gandhy*), spending time embellishing and decorating their costumes: adding sequins, ribbons, and feathers to the turban; wearing additional strands of beads; and keeping the sash from previous years to accessorize the current ensemble. Ildo explained that each year's costume comes with only one sash, yet many men sport multiple sashes tied on either side of their shoulders and around the waist, even sewn onto the bottom hem of their tunics. This shows they have been with Gandhy for some time, accumulating pieces from many years and layering past carnival accessories onto their current costume. The turban, Ildo said, can be un-stitched and used in the house as a "normal towel," a personal reminder of Filhos de Gandhy in between carnival parades.

Ildo has kept all of his past garments, an amassed collection of twenty-five years of carnival costumes. I asked him if he feels different when he puts on the costume at the start of each carnival parade. He answered that he does, and that each member has his unique situation, objective, and feelings when getting dressed in the costume for the parade.

> At the moment that I get dressed in the costume, the first thing that I feel is accomplishment of my work. I spend the whole year working, and at the moment that I get dressed in the costume, the feeling is relief. The first phase is relief, like "Wow, we did it."
>
> So, it's like this. The first phase is relief. The second phase is the confraternity that I have with others. The happiness. And that takes care of us, the happiness.
>
> I get dressed at home, with my son, my two brothers, my nephew. The entire family goes out together—the men—no?
>
> This is what is so beautiful in Gandhy. This confraternity, understand?

Getting dressed in the costume of Filhos de Gandhy has deep significance for Ildo as it does for thousands of others, men who are able to "realize" themselves through the bond they create with other men, including their male family members. For Ildo there is yet another layer of connection. At the end of our interview he told me about his family's association with Candomblé: his mother is a *mãe de santo,* his brothers are all *filhos de santo,* and his family has a *terreiro* of Candomblé in Salvador. For Ildo the religious component of Filhos de Gandhy allows him to strengthen his ties to the Afro-Brazilian resistance movement as well as to continue the spiritual work of his family. And once again we are brought to the centrality of Candomblé.

There is an unfortunate history of police raids on Candomblé events, continuing through the twentieth century. As anthropologist Stephen Selka explains, in the 1940s some African religious and cultural expressions started to gain official acceptance, even though the Catholic Church denounced such practices as "superstitions" until Vatican II, in 1962, when the Church adopted a stance of "liturgical pluralism" and reached out to practitioners of African-derived religions, as

Selka says, "to capitalize on forms of syncretism it formerly denounced in order to extend its influence to the lower sectors."[66] One reason for the violent discrimination was because Candomblé was rightly understood to be the "central axis" of the history of Afro-Bahians, starting with slavery and continuing through various cultural and social subjugations. The religion went underground, still practiced in secret, and took on a quality of defiance and resistance.[67] Candomblé began to resurface again in the 1940s with the end of the military dictatorship of Getúlio Vargas. African political and cultural associations became more visible, and in 1945 the Bahian Federation of Afro-Brazilian Worship was founded.[68] As historian Paul Johnson tells, at this same time Afro-Brazilian ethnic symbols became national ones—*feijoada* (black bean and pork stew), Candomblé, and samba. This might have been a form of cultural appropriation to disguise further racial domination or a matter of actual acceptance. In either case Afro-Brazilian culture became more public. Candomblé houses of worship in Rio de Janeiro began featuring performances in the front room, where the dances, calls, chants, and incarnations of the *orixás* were visible for the first time to noninitiates, shaping a spectacle of the *orixás* that continues today.[69] It is in this cultural context of the 1940s that Filhos de Gandhy was founded.

At around this time Jorge Amado published his important novel about contemporary Salvador, *Jubiabá,* in which police officers crack down on secret Candomblé ceremonies throughout the city. The novel exposed the reality of Afro-Brazil: a place where the old religion and culture were powerful and beautiful yet under constant harassment. The book helped the elite of Brazil appreciate Afro-Brazilian religion and was the catalyst that brought French photographer Pierre Verger and Argentinean artist Carybé into Bahia.[70] Today anyone may attend a Candomblé ceremony, finding its location from the tourist offices in the city, and one can even watch a "folkloric" show in Pelourinho featuring music, dance, costumes, and pseudo-possession onstage, even while eating dinner.

Through Filhos de Gandhy, Africa is reenacted for the tourists, but primarily for the residents of the Afro-Brazilian city of Salvador. Hermes Agostinho dos Santos, an early participant, recalls the initial orientation of the group: "When we paraded for the first time, we knew nothing of Gandhi. We remembered Africa."[71] A memory of Africa is still kept alive by rituals—public and private—that Gandhy carries out during each carnival. By remembering and performing Africa in Brazil, Filhos de Gandhy participates in what João Jorge Santos Rodrigues, president of *bloco Afro* Olodum, calls the goal of a "re-Africanization of Brazil."[72] Before each parade that departs from Pelourinho on Sunday and Tuesday, a number of Filhos de Gandhy, including president Professor Agnaldo Silva, offer a *padê*, a gift of ceremonial food for the *orixá* Exú. Candomblé ceremonies (and *afoxé* functions) also begin with the *padê* for Exú, the trickster and messenger *orixá* who must be fed and appeased to ensure a smooth ritual.[73] The offering—which may include *farinha de mandioca* (manioc flour), *azeite de dendê* (palm oil), and a jar of *cachaça* (sugarcane liquor, harsh as moonshine)—is scattered onto the cobblestone streets of the square Largo do Pelourinho, a block from the headquarters. In the first years of Filhos de Gandhy, the *padê* took place at the doorsteps of the headquarters. Today it has moved into a more public place, becoming a spectacle that many watch and photograph. Some of the old-timers criticize this move from private to public,[74] but I believe it is part of the mission of Filhos de Gandhy to bring the hidden and forbidden parts of Afro-Brazilian culture into public view and toward general acceptance. By choosing a theme and a *design* that features each year's *orixá*, Gandhy disseminates the celebration of the *orixá* through the bodies of more than ten thousand men to an audience of millions. The founders of Gandhy countered the police persecution of *afoxé*—and violence toward Candomblé—by naming their group after a pacifist leader.[75] In the 1940s Filhos de Gandhy "returned Candomblé rhythms and music to Salvador's streets in peaceful protest against the continued regulation of Afro-Bahian religion."[76] As historian Scott Ickes says, Filhos de Gandhy "helped cement a place for the *afoxés* within the official structure of carnival."[77] By reintroducing African elements into carnival, Gandhy, along with the *blocos Afro* founded in the 1970s, is furthering the concept of negritude. Through a public assertion of Afro-Brazilian identity, Filhos de Gandhy hope that the old religion will come to new vitality.

But not everyone in Gandhy is an adherent of Candomblé. During our conversation, Francisco Santos said, "The majority of people who parade with Gandhy are people of Candomblé, understand? The majority likes Candomblé. The only ones that parade with Gandhy, the majority, are those that like the Afro-descendent culture." He went on to say that if the members of Filhos de Gandhy are not practitioners of Candomblé, they at least like and respect the religion. As the *bloco's* costume designer, Francisco emphasized the role of the garments:

> And so, the majority that parades with Gandhy believes in that white vestment. That is the vestment of our principal father Oxalá.
> And also the vestment of Ogum, who is another *orixá* that opens the path. He is the first *orixá* of Candomblé that opens the ceremony. He is a warrior. He is strong. He is like iron.
> And so this is the mystery of Filhos de Gandhy.

A delegation of Filhos de Gandhy offers a *padê*, ceremonial food for the *orixás*. Carnival, Salvador da Bahia, Brazil, 1998.

Ildo Sousa contends that many men parade with Gandhy for the beauty of the costume, for the fun of wearing strands of beads and exchanging them for kisses from pretty women. And that is acceptable, for there is no requirement that one must belong to Candomblé to parade with Filhos de Gandhy. Yet the entire directorate is comprised of followers of the Afro-Brazilian religion, and most, if not all, of them are Afro-Brazilians. The group's managers, organizers, and costume and float designers are all "people of the *axé*" who use Gandhy as an outlet for their spiritual conviction. As Ildo said to me candidly, "*Everything* in Gandhy— the symbolism—is *inside* Candomblé."

While the majority of carnival *blocos* in Salvador are the popular *axé music* groups, *blocos Afros* and *afoxés* are particularly visible and are celebrated by the local and international media for their extravagant and exotic costumes. All *blocos Afros* and *afoxés* make references to Candomblé, subtle or overt, because the religion has become the main symbol of Afro-Brazilian identity. The reference may be in the name of the group: for example, *Bloco* Olodum is named after the ultimate God who created all of the *orixás,* Olodumaré.[78] The reference may be in the bodily presentation of the band: Timbalada's musicians, for example, display white body paint—thick painted lines on their torsos, chests, faces—in oblique allusion to the painted bodies of the initiates of Candomblé when they leave seclusion and are officially presented to the larger community.[79] The reference may be in the rituals of the band: Ilê Aiyê officially starts their first carnival parade in their neighborhood of Curuzu with a Candomblé rite led by *mãe de santo* Mãe Hilda and the release of white doves into the Salvador sky. The reference can be iconographic: *Bloco* Ara Ketu has Oxóssi's bow and arrow as its symbol; the upturned arrow piercing the bow creates the "A" of the band's name. Filhos de Gandhy's homage to Candomblé and the *orixás* harmonizes with those of the *blocos Afros* and *afoxés* of Salvador.

Most of the carnival groups are music bands whose aim is entertainment, *blocos Afros* and *afoxés* stand in contrast to these popular groups by having a strong religious affiliation, and also a political and public service orientation. *Blocos Afros* and *afoxés* take to the public streets the political, social, and racial struggle.[80] They enact the "responsibility of black Brazilians to resist, to struggle, and eventually to construct a just society."[81] Through the spectacle of carnival, these groups are able to "dramatize social inequalities," as observed by Antônio Risério, a Salvadoran writer and social critic.[82]

African religions, Candomblé in particular, have always been an integral emblem of racial consciousness in Brazil, uniting people on the basis of a "shared sociopolitical identity."[83] The lyrics of many songs by *blocos Afros* cite the common struggle in northeastern Brazil—a fight for freedom, equality, and respect that is shared by those who are underprivileged by race and class. According to Brazilian actor and activist Antônio Pitanga, "The struggle of Brazilian blacks is not and cannot be isolated. It must be added to the struggle of all oppressed segments in the country."[84] The Afro-Brazilian movement gains strength by allying itself with the heroes and bandits of the Northeast, of the *sertão*. For, as the hero in Jorge Amado's novel *Jubiabá* declares, the stevedores are the slaves of today.[85] (Dockworkers, like bricklayers, washerwomen, and porters, labor in professions that are dominantly black.[86]) In building a political and confraternal alliance between those discriminated against because of class or race, the carnival *blocos*, including Filhos de Gandhy, engage in social criticism of current attitudes and policies that hold a faction of the population in slavelike status. A parallel political message is found in the carnival of Rio de Janeiro, though it is obscured by the extravagant costumes, floats, and glitz. All *escolas de samba* in Rio parade with an *ala*—a flank—of Baianas, a visual acknowledgment of Candomblé and Salvador as the source of Rio's carnival culture.[87] In Rio de Janeiro, as in Salvador, the carnival parade functions to broadcast the concerns and strengths of Afro-Brazilian culture by celebrating the religious and political heroes, including the *orixás*.

Carnival songs from Salvador or Rio de Janeiro often use the metaphor of travel; the *bloco* or *escola de samba* takes revelers on a mysterious journey.[88] Foreign themes and fantastical costumes carry them far away to reveal the reality of Afro-Brazil today. By traveling through space or time, the magical trip of carnival reveals the mundane and the local. Ultimately the social commentary is not about Egyptian pharaohs and "tribal mythology," but about the race and class struggles in the metropolis of Rio de Janeiro or Salvador.[89] Celebrants travel far, metaphorically, to see the near clearly. Filhos de Gandhy takes its members and spectators on a voyage to India, to Africa, in order to expose the reality of Salvador. João Jorge, president of Olodum, tells how Gandhy transported him away from the only reality he knew—Pelourinho, its colonial buildings and cathedrals, its black population—into a world he had not known before. Carlinhos Brown, founder of the musical group Timbalada, says that black people are seen as foreigners, as strangers (*estrangeiros*)—as non-Brazilians, as poor—and Filhos de Gandhy stresses this difference but turns it into a positive thing; its members are introduced to Africa, to African-derived religions, and to the Yoruba language.[90]

I asked Ildo Sousa, a deeply spiritual man who is currently working on his law degree, about the significance of Filhos de Gandhy. I inquired if the *bloco* represented Salvador, Africa, or India. His response, characteristically, was layered and thoughtful:

This is a complex question, because this question has to be answered with various answers.

First, does Gandhy represent the people of Salvador? It represents.

Why? Because carnival, in Salvador, is the main piece that is taken out from here, as entertainment for tourists. And the one element that makes the carnival of Salvador different is Gandhy.

Everyone knows that Gandhy is a *different* thing. It is a different *step*. It is a different form. The music is different, understand?

And so this is why I think it represents Salvador. Does it represent Africa? It represents.

Why? Because we sing the songs of Candomblé that have their origin in Africa.

Does it represent India? It represents. Because of the ideal of peace that accompanies us until today. So in reality it represents all of these elements.

In a quick follow-up question, I asked Ildo if Filhos de Gandhy also represented Afro-Brazilians and the ideals of negritude in his city. His face lit up and he said, "It represents. *That* is where it is at." I asked if that was because of Candomblé. He answered that is was not only because of Candomblé and then elaborated: "Candomblé is an enigmatic essence. It is there—deep. It may look like it is forgotten, but it is not. It is the principal piece of Gandhy. It *is* the principal piece of Gandhy, understand?" Ildo continued by telling me that the men who join Filhos de Gandhy for fun and parade year after year will begin to understand the Candomblé references through the religious symbols used in Gandhy. So the *bloco* is a tool used to maintain and recruit practitioners of Candomblé, a tool for proselytizing. The religion survived the Middle Passage and the horrors of slavery and endured through years of persecution. It was hidden from view until recently and is now exuberantly on display in the streets at carnival. As long as new people continue to join Filhos de Gandhy, the old culture will live to be rejuvenated and Candomblé and its African roots will remain strong in Salvador, the capital of Afro-Brazil.

At the end of our interview I asked Ildo if he had any questions for me. He seized the opportunity to talk to someone who is of Indian descent and asked me if in India the old religion is dying out with the proliferation of new technology. I said that it was not. Satisfied with my answer, Ildo said it is the same in Brazil. Candomblé, he predicted, "will never die. Because it is very connected to nature. To the forces of nature, understand? Our religion, it is very rich for this. The elements, the *orixás,* they are representations of nature, a symbolism. Our energy, everything is in this. It is a very simple thing. For being so simple, people find it complicated."

Carnival costumes symbolize resistance and the resilience of the African spirit. The costume of Filhos de Gandhy is a vehicle for expressing heritage identity, and it requires actors, dedicated individuals such as Professor Agnaldo, Francisco Santos, and Ildo Sousa. They taught me that carnival in Salvador, an event celebrated globally for its frivolity, has deep meaning for many participants. Through their commitment to the *bloco* Filhos de Gandhy, these men—and thousands of others—connect to their local community, to their families, and especially to their roots in Africa through the music, dance, the iconography of Candomblé, and through their collective worship of the *orixás.* What can be seen as trivial to a spectator can have profound meanings to the participants. Carnival in Salvador is more than a time of drinking and ribaldry; it is also a time when the *orixás* come down to witness the beautiful spectacle of their African-descended sons at a time of festive spirit.

HERITAGE

Folk Costume in Sweden

OLK COSTUMES IN EUROPE MATERIALIZE CULTURAL PRIDE AND resistance in the face of globalizing homogenization. Once worn as daily dress, beautiful garments have become symbols of heritage in many parts of Europe, particularly in the northwestern and eastern nations of the continent.[1] Traditions of folk costume are especially robust in Scandinavia, with Norway and Sweden as the prime locations for exuberant displays of elaborate clothing, generally marked regionally by form, color, and motif.

Afro-Brazilian carnival costumes developed out of a historic clash of cultures in a new locale, a place of imperialistic expansion, colonialism, slavery, and prejudice. By contrast, regional costumes in Sweden are set comfortably in place. Their journey has carried them forward in time, most notably in the parish of Leksand in the province of Dalarna, which has become the core of Swedish resistance and preservation of folk costume. The goal has been the *maintenance* of heritage through the purposeful acts of committed individuals: artists, museum professionals, church authorities, craft teachers, musicians, and local culture brokers. Through willed actions, the costume communicates aesthetics, identity, and community. The tradition of Swedish folk costume in Leksand is spearheaded by one extraordinary individual: Kersti Jobs-Björklöf. In this chapter Kersti teaches us about her famous costume: white linen blouse, laced bodice, wool skirt, and an assortment of colorful aprons.

DALARNA: INHABITING THE SWEDISH SPIRIT

The province of Dalarna, in central Sweden, occupies a special place in Swedish consciousness. Four features make it distinct. First is its architecture. Nordic in culture, Dalarna reaches through its log buildings toward Norway and Finland while southern Sweden connects to Denmark and Germany in its half-

Village of Ullvi, Dalarna, Sweden, 2007.

timbered structures. The second characteristic is the organization of agricultural settlement. Southern Sweden endured land reforms that transformed it into a landscape of separate farms, signaling values of family and individual industry. Dalarna, on the other hand, resisted the system of land reform, of enclosure, retaining its compact agricultural villages that foster a high sense of community.[2] Third, Dalarna's general agricultural prosperity produced a foundation for the flowering of folk art. By general consent, many of the fifteen modern parishes of Dalarna are famous for the arts created by the Swedish peasantry. Celebrated artifacts include furniture from Rättvik; clocks from Mora; paintings from Rättvik and Leksand; and costumes from Leksand, Floda, and Gagnef. And, finally, Dalarna's green rolling land with its silvery lakes has proved attractive to outsiders as well as the local farmers. Dalarna became a place where many city dwellers had summer homes, a common feature of Swedish society. Outsiders have long been drawn to its natural beauty and to the beauty of its handcrafted artifacts. The hand-painted "Dala horse" from Mora in Dalarna has become a tourist item and a national symbol of Sweden. Among Swedish Americans the whimsical red horse with its floral saddle stands for Dalarna and represents the whole of the country.[3]

For these reasons—a Nordic tone, a high sense of community, flourishing traditional arts, and a beautiful landscape—Dalarna epitomizes Sweden for many of the country's inhabitants. At the end of the nineteenth century, Artur Hazelius, inspired by his honeymoon visit to Leksand, set out to preserve Swedish tradition through its material culture. In the context of the romantic nationalistic mood, Hazelius embarked on a "pursuit of creating a visual record of Swedish national character."[4] His attempt to capture the essence of the country led him first to collect a costume from Stora Tuna, Dalarna, for his ethnographic museum, the Nordiska Museet, and then to collect a farmhouse from Mora for his magnificent outdoor living museum, Skansen.[5] The earliest objects Hazelius chose to represent Sweden came from the province of Dalarna (also known by its Latin name, Dalecarlia), a place believed to be "the most genuine representation of all that was truly Swedish."[6] Folklorist Barbro Klein writes that at Skansen Hazelius aimed to capture all the parts of the country, representing Sweden in miniature, but "of all the regions, Dalarna became the most valorized."[7] As Swedish anthropologist Orvar Löfgren explains, at the turn of the twentieth century Dalarna was seen to embody "the typical Swedish peasant heritage," in part because it fit "the middle-class mythology of 'the old peasant society.'"[8] The province still represents the best of what the nation has to offer: "In Swedish eyes Dalecarlia is some kind of Shangri-la, a problem-free oasis with the qualities romantically associated with the life of yesteryear."[9]

KERSTI JOBS-BJÖRKLÖF

The villages of the province of Dalarna surround an old parish church, often baroque in style. One of the parishes that encircle Lake Siljan is Leksand, and according to Ralph Edenheim, the former cultural director of the Skansen open-air museum, "Leksand can be fairly termed the cultural capital of Dalarna."[10] Outside the town of Leksand lies Tibble, a tight village of wooden houses. In one of these houses, painted Falun red like the rest of them, in the farmstead named Knisgården lives Kersti Jobs-Björklöf, whose family has lived in Tibble for many generations, the farm being in the family since the late sixteenth century.[11] Kersti's father, Verner Jobs, was the mayor of Leksand from 1951 to 1972. Her maternal uncle, Knis Karl Aronsson (known affectionately by his family as Kalle), was the force behind the founding of the local ethnographic museum, Leksands Kulturhus, which is part of the Leksands Kommun complex, which

Kersti Jobs-Björklöf. Tibble, Leksand, Dalarna, Sweden, 2007.

includes a library, an archive of local history, and an auditorium.[12] Knis Karl passed away before the museum was completed, and Kersti herself was its first director, implementing her uncle's ideas and occupying the post from 1980 to 2002, at which point she "became pensioned." Kersti's uncle Knis Karl is credited with reviving the rowing competition among church boats, with founding Dalarna's first folk musicians' union, and with introducing a course on the corner-timbering of log buildings in Leksand.[13] Kersti's dedication to the preservation of her heritage directly follows her uncle's lead.

My quest to learn about folk costumes in Sweden naturally led me to Dalarna. According to Inga Arnö Berg and Gunnel Hazelius Berg, authors of the popular book *Folk Costumes of Sweden*, "Dalarna is incomparably the most famous province for costumes in Sweden, and in many respects, the most interesting. Certainly it is the richest in preserved costume culture."[14] Ingrid Bergman, former head of the textile department at Nordiska Museet, wrote, "At the beginning of the 20th century, the wearing of folk costumes as an everyday practice survived only in the province of Dalarna."[15] Within Dalarna I came to Leksand, one of the last places where the folk costumes were used daily into the middle of the twentieth century, and the place where Artur Hazelius was first inspired—by the Leksand costume—to devote his life to the preservation of Swedish culture.

In 2007 I came to the Knis farm to learn from Kersti Jobs-Björklöf about the living tradition of her folk costume.[16] She told me she would teach me about the costumes in the same way she was currently teaching her nine-year-old granddaughter, Anna. Before any of the skirts, aprons, and bodices were brought into the living room where we sat, Kersti fetched the family photo albums. In order to learn about the clothes, we first had to understand her family and their history. Folk dress for her, as for many of the people I met in Leksand, is inextricably linked to family, to heritage, to place. Most of the old black-and-white and many of the newer color photos in Kersti's carefully labeled albums show men and women, young and old, in the Leksand costume.

THE LEKSAND COSTUME

There are more than four hundred regional folk costumes in Sweden today.[17] Most of these, like many costumes in Europe, follow a similar structural pattern.[18] The male costume consists of knee breeches, a long military-style coat, and a vest. The Leksand women's costume, following the common European style, has a blouse, a bodice, a skirt, an apron, a neck scarf, and, for married women, a cap. Accessories include a jacket, a silver brooch, a "pocket" purse, bonnet, hair ribbons, stockings, shoes, belt, and gloves. The costume of Leksand, like a few others in Dalarna, follows specific coded combinations, marked mostly by certain colors for the apron and bodice. These combinations are worn for different occasions and in different contexts, sending messages through the color as well as the material quality of the cloth. The various ensembles fall into two main categories—red and black—as Kersti explains in fluent English:

> You can divide it into red and black. So the red color is for all these happy occasions. Or for Sundays in church that are ordinary Sundays. And the black, then, it is for sad occasions, for widows, for mourning, for funerals, and for special periods during the church year.
>
> So if you divide into red and black, into happy and sad, then if you look at the material, on the red side, so to say, then these occasions—christening a child, confirmation, a wedding—and during the church year—Christmas morning, Easter day, and so on—the material is very often bought material, because they had a shortage of money. So therefore it was much more valuable.
>
> But if you look on the other side, with the black for mourning and for periods in the church—like Advent, preparing yourself for Christmas, and Lent, preparing yourself for Easter—then the material, then you have linen and wool and handwoven materials and the different things that they could make themselves.
>
> So also for everyday use at home they had these very simple materials, because they were so careful about those expensive things that they bought for money.

So I think it can be divided into these two fields [red and black].

And then the variations—I mean, you have the everyday life and what you use then. And if you start with a nice yellow apron with these black stripes that you have for a funeral—this was handwoven, you made it yourself at home—when you have used it in church, or for funerals for a long time, it could be used at home for every day. So it started in church, and in the end it was used at home for every day.

But that was never for the things that you bought. Because they were very, very careful about the clothes, because the clothes were so, so valuable.

Kersti explains the logical distinction that the people of Leksand made between clothes in the "black field," those that are handmade from wool or linen, fabric that was handspun, handwoven, and sewn at home, and the clothes in the "red field," those made from imported material, such as cambric cotton and silk, and often crafted by professional tailors.

Clothes in the black field are worn during periods of fasting and mourning, solemn periods in the Lutheran church calendar, as well as periods of personal loss, such as the death of a relative. This black group is signaled by the use of the black cotton bodice, laced up the front, worn with a yellow wool apron, handwoven with thin, horizontal black stripes. A heavy black wool skirt is worn with this ensemble. This is the proper attire at a funeral, and also what one wears to church on the three Sundays before Advent, the Sundays of Lent, and to the Good Friday church service.

The set of clothes in the red field is more varied. In this cluster one wears a red silk bodice, laced in the front, with embroidered medallions upon the bust. This bodice is also worn with the same black wool skirt, yet there are four aprons that signal different levels of specialness of the event. The aprons, called *raskmajd*, are made of a light wool fabric, "glazed" (they used to be waxed), and shiny on the front. The aprons, all made of the same material, are ranked in order by their color: blue, red, green, and yellow, a ranking that reflects the cost and availability of dye materials. When the traditional costume was first adopted, the blue apron was the most precious, because indigo (or woad) was rare and costly; the red apron was highly ranked because of the scarcity of madder root; the green apron was dyed with a mix of the pricey blue and the inexpensive yellow; and yellow was the color of the lowest-ranked apron and also the color of children's dresses in many parts of Sweden, since it was the easiest dye color to acquire, being made from birch leaves and moss.[19] Following the apron code, the most important celebrations—wedding, Christmas, Easter, or Midsummer Day—are celebrated in

church, colorfully, in the blue apron and red bodice combination. For Midsummer women also don a cotton neck scarf that is either checkered or printed with bright flowers.

There is another, more popular ensemble. This one consists of a wool apron with vertical stripes in a red, black, and white color scheme. The apron, worn with a black wool skirt, is matched with a striped bodice made of hand-loomed wool in a combination of red, black, and white thin stripes. A version of this outfit is what girls wear to confirmation in church, and this is the festive attire of the secular, public celebration of Midsummer.

This code of aprons and appropriate ensembles, while following an internally logical system, is complicated, and Kersti said that in the past "the knowledge was neglected or forgotten." Gustaf Ankarcrona, a painter from Småland and a great patron of the traditional costume of Leksand, thought it a good idea to write down this code, documenting it before it disappeared. He asked his friend Albert Alm, a lawyer, to record it. According to Kersti, Alm was sick at the time, convalescing in the clean mountain air of Dalarna and spending his time with the old women. He began interviewing the women around him about the use of the Leksand costume—since many of them still wore the clothes for regular daily use—and in 1923 he published *Dräktalmanacka för Leksands socken,* which Kersti calls "a help for the memory" and a "costume calendar."[20] Alm's almanac detailed the appropriate combination for every Sunday of the church year, guiding the villagers on what they should be wearing when they arrived at the parish church in Leksand aboard the famous church boats that carried people from their villages along the lake to town. Of all the costume almanacs in Sweden, the one for Leksand was the very first.[21]

The almanac was pivotal for the retention of the code of the Leksand costume. As Kersti explained to me: "This calendar was in a way a help, and also it helped for the revival of using the different aprons and so on in church. Because what you had during the different occasions in life—like christening a child, or confirmation, or a wedding—that was very well known and used." But, she continued, most people did not remember what to wear for the other, less celebratory events. The almanac reminded people that there was a code and with it a logical ranking of costume for the various liturgical celebrations and the various personal celebrations. While most people then, and especially now, did not own all the items necessary to adhere to the code, knowing that a code existed served to remind people of personal and religious events, marking the familial/domestic and the official/communal passing of time, differentiating between ordinary days and ritual times. Today the costume in Leksand still follows three different yet related temporal streams: the passing of the church year, the passing of the calendar year, and, with it, personal rites of passage. The third stream is the one in which fashion, and therefore historical time, is marked by changing fads, something that has always resulted in the costume of Leksand—and most folk costumes—to continue changing slightly while adapting aesthetically to current fashion. The general shift—in Sweden and in other parts of the world—from a self-sufficient agrarian economy to one reliant on industrial products has led simultaneously to change and to a renewed commitment to continuity.

In 1939 Alm compiled another almanac, for the parish of Floda in Dalarna, but this one did not contribute to a revival of the code of costumes in the way his Leksand calendar did. (He also made one, on commission from the Nordiska Museet, for the parish of Orsa, but it was never published.) Alm's 1923 Leksand book had been out of print for several years when Kersti and her mother, Karin Jobs, were asked to create another one, a commission sponsored by the Leksands Hemslöjdsförening, the handcraft association founded by the artist Ankarcrona. They published their *Almanacka för Leksandsdräkten* in 1978, and, unlike Alm's book, which contained only verbal descriptions, Kersti's calendar included color drawings by David Tägtström, showing men, women, and children wearing full ensembles, complete with jewelry, shoes, and other accessories.[22] Each Sunday of the church year has its own entry in this small book, and next to each description is a small color rendition of the specific bodice and apron to be worn on that particular day.

The book Kersti and her mother compiled has also gone out of print.[23] The code of bodices and aprons is now disseminated by the Leksand Handcraft store, centrally located next to the Kulturhuset ethnographic museum, across from the Leksands Konstmuseum, and a few minutes' walk from the Leksand church and adjoining graveyard, where Gustaf Ankarcrona is buried. Throughout the week the shop's vitrine displays the coming Sunday's complete ensemble, not on a mannequin, but folded neatly into an array. Every Monday, Ingrid Samuelsson, who works at the store, consults the almanac and changes the display, letting any passerby know what this coming Sunday's appropriate attire will be. The website of the handcraft shop also carries this information (only in Swedish), so that parishioners may go online and check the virtual almanac when deciding what to wear to church that weekend. The online description of appropriate ensembles, like the previous incarnations of the "costume calendar," emphasizes only the clothes for the women, since there are few variables in the men's costume. This web version of the almanac is illustrated with color photographs of women dressed in the different costumes. For each Sunday they offer two alternatives—

Klädsel i Högmässan, the costumes worn to church, and *Klädsel om man inte går in krykan,* the clothing a person changes into when she gets home or that she wears if she doesn't go to church on that Sunday.[24]

WEARING THE COSTUME: CODED OCCASIONS AND RITES OF PASSAGE

From the almanac we are able to identify the formal occasions on which the costume is to be used. The appropriate costume underscores the mood of every church service and every rite of passage celebrated in church—baptism, confirmation, first Holy Communion, wedding, and funeral. The most colorful combination—that of the blue apron, red embroidered bodice, embroidered leather half gloves, and cotton neck scarf with black embroidery—is worn for one's wedding and for baptizing one's child. For confirmation the striped handwoven apron is worn with the red embroidered bodice, a combination that occurs only once more, on the first Sunday of the New Year. For the first Holy Communion, girls appear in a version of mourning attire—with a short black jacket, the red embroidered bodice, the yellow apron of ordinary Sundays in church, and a headscarf tied under the chin. The funeral attire is similar, but a black rather than red bodice is worn, and the apron can be either the ordinary yellow Sunday one or the handwoven yellow apron with horizontal black stripes. Kersti told me there is one major yet subtle difference between the funeral and confirmation costumes: the headscarf tied under the chin for funerals is handwoven linen, in keeping with the "black field" of somber occasions; the one used for confirmation, used only once in a woman's life, should be a cotton scarf. Most people don't know this detail; Kersti has observed countless confirmation candidates take part in the procession wearing the "wrong" scarf.

The costume code described in the almanac tells us what should be worn at church, but not what was (and is) actually worn by people. Recall that Leksand is important because it is one of the last places where people wore the costumes on a regular basis. Some parts of the costume, especially the cap, were worn daily until the middle of the twentieth century. This is in contrast with the other centers, Hälsingland and Skåne, where the costume continued only as special occasion attire, not as daily wear. Kersti explained this to me by talking about the costumes illustrated in Berg and Berg's book *Folk Costumes of Sweden,* an encyclopedic survey of hundreds of regional costumes. The book is illustrated with color photographs of ordinary people wearing their own costumes and is consulted throughout Sweden and its diaspora, including the United States.[25] This is what Kersti said about the costumes in this popular book:

It is like a flora of Swedish folk costumes. But most of them are compositions from 1920 and later. So you have in Sweden special parts of the country—the south of Sweden in Skåne, and Lund and those parts—where they have old folk costumes. And you have a couple of them, in Småland, north of Skåne. And you have a couple not far from Stockholm. And you have Dalarna. And it's more the northern and western parts of Dalarna.

And here it has been used—and this is the only part of Sweden where it has been used in everyday life that long. And then in Rättvik the men used the folk costume as late as the women did here in Leksand. In Mora it was gone earlier, and in Gagnef, there the women also were using the costume very late. I think the very latest, and the very last, was here—women—here in Leksand.

The photographs in the local archives at the Leksands Kommun capture people wearing the Leksand costume into the 1950s and 1960s. There are pictures of old ladies and young girls in the vertically striped apron, worn over dark woolen clothes, each of the females with her head covered by a bonnet. The photos in Kersti's family album also show women in the local costume. One photograph, taken in either 1897 or 1898, depicts her grandmother Knis Johanna Danielsdotter as an unmarried schoolteacher with her pupils. Of the twenty-two students pictured, all fifteen boys wear ordinary clothes, and each of the seven girls wears a striped apron, just like the teacher. We know that in the past, teachers and (female) students wore the Leksand costume, at least the apron, to school daily. The costume was also used for special occasions, the kinds of occasions that warrant documentation in the form of a photograph, such as engagements, weddings, and baptisms. One framed photograph, taken around 1897, shows Kersti's grandparents Knis Aron Karlsson and Knis Johanna Danielsdotter, while still engaged, with seven friends. Again the four men pictured are in the dark suits that were generally conventional at the time, but all five women wear their fancy Leksand clothes—the striped apron with a front-laced bodice (without embroidery) and the neck scarf with fine embroidery. This scarf, *svartstickskläde*, with its black thread embroidery in geometric satin stitch, cross-stitch, and diagonal-line stitch, is one of the handcraft items, along with the woven band belt, for which Leksand is famous throughout the country.[26]

Finally, a picture taken on June 18, 1899, celebrates the wedding of Knis Johanna Danielsdotter to Hallmans Aron Karlsson (who would take the farm name "Knis" when he married and moved into his wife's farm). In this photo

Wedding portrait of Kersti's grandparents Knis Johanna Danielsdotter and Knis Aron Karlsson. Tibble, Leksand, Dalarna, Sweden, 1899.

Kersti's grandmother is wearing the proper wedding attire, adhering to the almanac—the blue "glazed" apron (recognizable in a black-and-white photograph by the ribbon appliqué on the lower part of all blue aprons), the leather belt, and the leather half gloves. Her groom wears a dark suit. This photo contrasts with the later photos in which both bride and groom wear the Leksand costume, a consequence of the recent revival, or reinvigoration, of the costume. The family albums also contain pictures of the wedding of Kersti's parents, in 1936, and her own wedding, in 1961, in which both bride and groom appear in Leksand costume. Both Kersti's father, Verner, and her husband, Sune, wear the Dalarna navy blue coat with embroidered epaulets low on the shoulders, which is the defining feature of the Leksand costume for males.

One of the proper occasions for wearing the Leksand costume comes during church services, as stressed by the almanac. Another photo in Kersti's album, from 1957 or 1958, shows Kersti's mother with three of her children all in their Leksand costume, sitting in the pews of the Leksands Kyrka. The almanac specifies that people should wear the Leksand costume to church, but that does not tell us *how* people wore them. But this photograph anticipates an important topic in the retention and revival of tradition: in order for the costume to continue to the present, it needed advocates, people who set an example by wearing the costume and kept its rich history alive. The Jobs family members—old and young, female and male—kept driving the costume forward, enacting Henry Glassie's definition of tradition: "the creation of the future out of the past."[27]

Today in Leksand the costume is seldom used for regular church services. Kersti is one of the few people who regularly wear their costumes on ordinary Sundays (many more wear the costume for Midsummer, Easter, or Christmas church services). Kersti has worn her costume for most of her seventy years of church attendance. "And I think I have not been in the church without my costume ever," she said, "just twice or three times, when I have broken my arm and I couldn't dress myself. If I go to a service, I can't do anything but use my costume." Kersti is one of eight "church wardens," two of whom are on rotating duty every fourth Sunday. This pair must prepare the church for Holy Communion, help to dress the vicar, and take the collection, passing baskets for the offering. These wardens, men and women, are representatives of the church, and they dress in folk costume.

In addition to the wardens, members of the church choir dress in folk costume, unless they are giving a formal concert at the church—singing a Bach Christmas oratory, for example, in which case they dress in the all-black clothing of classical musicians everywhere. Members of the choir differentiate between the folk/religious and the "classical" tone of their concerts by their choice of garments. Whether or not they wear folk costume depends on the organist, the leader of the choir. For the tradition to flourish, Kersti and others would like to see as many people as possible wearing the costume, so members of the congregation encourage the organist. As Kersti explained: "From the church side, we try to support those who are organists or the leaders of the choir. If we got a new one, as it is expensive to buy the costume, we pay, from the church side, we pay for his costume so that he will use it in church."

I asked Kersti if the organist would still be given a Leksand costume if he came from another region of Sweden. Kersti said yes, absolutely, and cited the example of a Japanese woman, an organist, who wore the Leksand costume every Sunday in church, carefully changing the apron color according to the costume almanac. In 2007 the organist and leader of the choir was Mikael Boström, who had recently secured the post and married Sofia Sandén, a singer in the choir. Mikael, originally from Stockholm, wore his Leksand costume as a church musician and as the husband of a Leksand native, debuting his newly acquired clothes during the Midsummer festivities and church service.

In church the costume is still worn for special celebrations, such as weddings. In many parts of Sweden, brides borrowed the bridal crown from the church to wear during the ceremony. By custom, only brides that were not (visibly) pregnant could wear this crown,[28] since the crown symbolized virginity, thus linking the bride to the Virgin Mary, who is often depicted wearing a crown. This is still the practice in Leksand. A gold and silver replica of the original brass crown, now in the Falun Museum, was gifted to the Leksand church in 1937 or 1938. The crown is worn with the folk costume—the blue apron version—and the bride wears several strands of glass beads around her neck. She is also festooned with silk ribbons and flowers. Customarily the bride would go to a woman whose task was to get her dressed for the event. Kersti believes that her great-grandmother Anna dressed brides in her house, which explains the antique full-length mirror that Kersti inherited from her. Sweden's first female Nobel laureate, Selma Lagerlöf, describes the ritual of dressing the bride in the nineteenth century in her *Memories of Mårbacka* and in her famous novel, *Gösta Berling's Saga*.[29]

In the past local women helped dress the bride for her wedding. Today the staff of the Leksand Handcraft shop dresses female confirmation candidates in rental folk costumes (the male costumes are rented from the Kulturhuset museum next door). The local newspapers publish a group photograph of the confirmation candidates, which is then kept by the church. Looking at the newspapers, one sees a group of people in uniform costumes, all matching. Most of these costumes are rented, so they appear brand-new, lacking the variety they would exhibit were they taken from family storage chests. The red, black, and white striped aprons worn by female confirmation candidates in Leksand range widely through subtle variation. In collecting samples for the Kulturhuset museum, Kersti gathered fifty different versions of the apron, displaying what her grandmother called "poetry": a poetic composition of widths reflecting the creativity of the weaver.

Starting with baptisms and proceeding toward confirmations and weddings, the folk costume is worn to celebrate a rite of passage. The last major event for which the folk costume is worn is the last rite of passage, the funeral. The costume almanac tells us what clothes are to be worn by those attending a funeral: yellow aprons and headscarves for women, and *rock* (or *kyrkrock*) black coats for men, which are long, plain, and collarless, more somber than the navy blue, military-style *blåtröja*, with its colorful embroidery on the shoulders, mimicking epaulets. Photographs of Gustaf Ankarcrona's funeral service at the Leksand church graveyard on September 24, 1933, illustrate male and female mourners in the appropriate costumes.[30] The mourning costume was worn not only for funeral services but also for wakes, and a version of it can be worn beyond the funeral ceremony. During the Tibble Midsummer festivities in 2007, a group of women wore black-and-white-striped aprons instead of the red, white, and black ones. Kersti told me they were in mourning for a dead relative, signaling their loss through the apron code.[31]

The mourners wore their prescribed costumes to attend services for the dead, and the departed one was also costumed. People were routinely buried in traditional garments. Men were buried in a linen shirt made for them by their betrothed, which was the shirt they wore for their wedding. Women were buried in a linen blouse, neck scarf, and bonnet—white with matching monochrome geometric embroidery. If the woman was unmarried at the time of her death, she wore the white bonnet of a married woman, since, as Kersti said, "in death you are the bride of Christ." In a farewell ritual, people wash, iron, and prepare the folk costume the deceased wears for burial. Kersti was asked to do this for her uncle Knis Karl when he passed away in 1980,[32] and Kersti's sister, Britta, was asked by their mother, Karin, to set aside and care for her bridal blouse, which she wore when she was buried in 1997. Museum costume collections have few examples of these items, Kersti told me, because the garments literally go to the grave with their owners.

When Kersti still worked at the museum, she gave tours of the permanent exhibition of costumes in the basement of the Kulturhuset. People were often skeptical of the meanings and validity of the costumes, and doubted the sincerity of their use, as Kersti explains:

> When I would show the dress at the museum, and they would say that nowadays you use the costume only for tourists, and for a presentation, and not for—I mean, what's real, what is strong? Is there any kind of tradition that is going and important, and so on? So some of them, I mean, they think that you do it to get more tourists coming, and I can say that, "You think that we dress our dear and near in Leksand costume in the coffin *for tourists*?" And they don't say anything more!

In fact, whether the costume is worn only for tourists, or for any outsider, is a point of contention at the center of the meaning of the Leksand costume today. There is a great difference between a staff member at Skansen donning a Leksand costume during a dance performance and Kersti wearing her great-grandmother's yellow apron to attend the funeral of a family member. For the former, the costume vaguely symbolizes national heritage; for the latter, it represents family, history, region, identity. For Kersti the costume cannot be separated from the individual family member who made and wore it.

One reason to wear the costume during public demonstrations is precisely to be seen by spectators, whether local or foreign tourists, because this intentional display helps keep the tradition alive. A costume worn only in the privacy of the home does not inspire others to adopt the tradition and push it forward. Kersti and many others do wear their Leksand costumes at home for family Christmas dinners and birthday parties; her grown children—Erik, Karin, and Anna—wear theirs for the public Midsummer festivities but not for family dinners at home. Most costume use today, in fact, takes place in secular public events. Formal dinners, including those associated with the Nobel Prize in Stockholm, specify on the invitation that one must wear formal wear—gown or tux—or folk costume. Many men I spoke with in Leksand told me they wear their folk costume whenever the occasion calls for a tuxedo. Like the tuxedo in the United States, the folk costume may be rented, or if owned it is worn as often as possible to recover the cost of its purchase. In the 1990s Kersti attended two museum openings in the United States: at the Museum of International Folk Art in Santa Fe and at the Field Museum in Chicago. At both events she chose to wear her Leksand costume instead of a formal evening gown. When I asked her which combination of the costume she wore, she told me that in Chicago she wore the festive version with the striped red, black, and white apron, but in Santa Fe she wore the somber ensemble of black bodice with the black-and-white-striped apron because, despite the celebratory mood of the opening, it was just before Advent and she was following the church calendar. Although Kersti wore her costume so that it could be seen by others, she continued to follow the costume code for herself in order to honor her religion and her tradition in a coded message lost on the American beholders.

MIDSUMMER

In 2007 I attended several Midsummer celebrations in Leksand—the official, parish-wide event in the town and several smaller gatherings in nearby villages. The routine was similar in all of them: women decorated the maypole with wreaths of flowers and birch leaves, fiddlers played, and then the pole was raised gradually while participants cheered and shouted encouragement. Once the pole was erected and secured, many people, men, women, and children, most of them in costume, joined hands and circled it, singing and dancing in celebration of the longest day of the year, when darkness falls but briefly before sunlight bursts out again. Midsummer Day is supposed to be celebrated on June 24, but since 1953 the holiday has been observed on the Saturday closest to that date. In the town of Leksand the spectacle of the 2007 Midsummer celebration began on Saturday morning at the river, where the fiddlers, folk dancers, and the choir gathered, together with the bishop and the vicar. All of these participants were in folk costume, most of them from Leksand, but other Dalarna parishes were also represented, such as Gagnef, Rättvik, Mora, and Boda. Many tourists gathered to watch the performers board the long, graceful church boats transporting huge heart-shaped wreaths. They were headed to the center of Leksand, where a stage and thousands of people, many already drunk, waited for the festival to begin.[33] While everyone onstage was in costume, a handful of spectators wore their costumes as well, including a young woman in a Saami skirt and blouse and a woman in a Finnish regional costume. Most of those in costume were women, with a few notable exceptions. Markus Kummu, the drummer for the rock band Dogday, wore his beautiful Delsbo costume with ostentatious rows of shiny brass buttons lining both sides of the short jacket and running down the center of the vest.

The Midsummer celebration in the village of Tibble, the day before, was a community affair. The speeches addressed local politics and were delivered only in Swedish, unlike the Leksand Midsummer remarks, which were translated into German, English, French, and Japanese. In Tibble not all of the performers were in costume, but most were. The fact that a few fiddlers, wreath makers, and maypole raisers were not in costume shows that wearing a costume is a manifestation of personal choice, not an obligation. They were not actors onstage, each outfitted by a costume designer and required to perform in folk costume. Many of the two hundred spectators who sat on the hillside in Tibble were also in costume, including Eva Erkers in her beautiful embroidered skirt from Floda and Barbro Tollerz in her Vingåker dress with the green apron she embroidered sixty years ago.

A summer rainstorm broke on the day of the maypole raising in Rälta, another village in Leksand parish. The announcer explained that, considering the inclement weather and the great cost of the folk costume, the participants would

be advised to change into ordinary clothes. Despite the weather and the announcement, the few who wore their Leksand costumes remained in them, some wearing transparent plastic raincoats that protected yet displayed their clothes.

Comparing the three Midsummer festivities—those in Leksand, Tibble, and Rälta—permits me to make a few generalizations. In some of them (like that in Leksand) the event is planned for a broad spectrum of viewers, for local people and for international tourists. At others (Tibble and Rälta) it is mainly for the locals. Folk costume in these places is worn not for spectacle so much as for

Mora folk costume (left) and three versions of the Leksand folk costume. Midsummer, Leksand, Dalarna, Sweden, 2007.

semiprivate celebration, for community and family. The event is not a staged performance, as the Leksand one is; it is a community event in which one chooses to wear the costume. While Dalarna is known for its tradition of folk costume, it is clear that within the province of Dalarna the parish of Leksand has a living tradition of costume use. But within Leksand that tradition is stronger in the village of Tibble than it is in Rälta. In Tibble a greater number of villagers were in costume, and the music was their own; in rich unison the musicians played "Leksandsvisan," the traditional Leksand fiddle tune that is performed on other important local occasions such as weddings, baptisms, and funerals.

ACQUIRING THE COSTUME: INHERITANCE, CRAFT, AND PURCHASE

Many people in Leksand have old costumes preserved in their family storage chests or storehouses. Others receive new pieces as gifts or they may make, buy, or rent them. While Kersti's storehouse contains many garments from previous generations, all of her children were given their own costumes to be worn during their confirmation service. She explained that her two daughters received handwoven ribbons or the fabric for the bodice or apron as Christmas or birthday gifts throughout the years. When they were ready for confirmation, all of these materials were taken to a seamstress to be made into a garment that would fit the child's current measurements. This system, described to me by many others in Dalarna, allows the parent to slowly accumulate all the pieces of the costume—like a wedding trousseau—offsetting the cost of the costume and allowing the parents to contribute gradually to their child's anticipated rite of passage.

Kersti's private stash of costumes includes some that are never worn because of their fragile condition; these are upstairs in the storehouse, a free-standing uninhabited building whose sole purpose is to hold the family's historical objects. The costumes that Kersti wears regularly are kept in a dresser in her bedroom. Another dresser in a large room in the adjacent guesthouse holds aprons, bodices, and skirts that are borrowed by visiting family members and even by neighbors and friends who have a need to wear the Leksand costume but do not own their own. In this way costumes may be the property of individual families, but they serve a communal function. Several costume pieces I saw were on "temporary loan," kept at the house of the current wearer, yet owned collectively by the family and associated with an individual because they bear embroidered initials and dates, making them easy to identify. In 2007 Kersti's nine-year-old granddaughter, Anna, wore the grown-up costume for Midsummer, the striped bodice and skirt, no longer the yellow dress of little girls. Her costume was put together by gathering pieces from her paternal and maternal family collections, a process similar to that of theater productions, where pieces are pulled from different storehouses, used, and then returned. One piece of Anna's costume had a nineteenth-century date embroidered on it. Kersti told me that this practice of relying on a large family network also works for those who have gained or lost weight, for those who are pregnant, and for visiting family and friends, since anyone can be easily accommodated on relatively short notice.

Commercial shops were prohibited in the countryside of Sweden until 1846, making it necessary for most of the materials and garments to be produced locally by the farmers and their wives.[34] Women wove and sewed the garments made of linen, cotton, and wool, yet many of the clothes, especially those for men, were made by professionals. Hired tailors have always made the men's and women's coats and the men's yellow chamois-leather breeches from goatskin. In the past many rural Swedes knew how to weave, cut, and sew their own garments, but these skills largely have been lost among the current inhabitants of Dalarna, as they have been among people in most parts of the Western world. Still, a few people, mainly women, continue to make the clothes, keeping alive the technical and aesthetic knowledge associated with the Leksand costume. Kersti's daughter-in-law, Ulla Björklöf, comes from a local family devoted to the Leksand costume, actively wearing and making the garments. Ulla's mother, Karin Gärdsback, and her two aunts, Britta Matsson and Anna Halvares, grew up in the village of Rältlindor, in Leksand parish. I had an opportunity to interview these women, now in their seventies and eighties, with Ulla, who served as translator, bridging the Swedish/English divide of that summer afternoon.[35]

The older women grew up wearing the Leksand costume to church on Sundays and on special occasions, because, as Ulla translated their words, "it is the most beautiful thing that they have, and it's also their tradition to wear it." In answering my question, they put aesthetics first and adherence to tradition second only to their desire to appear attractive, dressed in beautiful clothes. I was told that the three sisters learned textile arts from their mother, who in turn had learned to weave and sew from her own mother. In their village plot they grew flax for linen and tended sheep for the wool of the black skirt, but they had to buy the red-dyed wool for the bodice and apron. Britta, the oldest sister, and Anna, the second oldest, wove tablecloths and sold them to an agent in Stockholm, a business they were forced to abandon during World War II when the supply of weaving materials stopped. Anna taught weaving for years and has recently ceased doing the black embroidery on the white scarf, because her old eyes can't see the fine details anymore. Ulla's mother, Karin, continues to weave and sell her creations, making what many praise as the finest "glazed" apron, one that sheds raindrops better than the other aprons locally available for sale.

To make this blue apron, the most special of the aprons, Karin experimented with the wool for sale at the Leksand Handcraft store. She found the material inadequate, resulting in a stiff, uncomfortable garment that was not the right shade of blue. The three sisters came together, studied many old family pieces, and developed the perfect raw material. Karin has woven about fifty-five yards of this fabric, making approximately fifty-five blue aprons, some for the family, some for sale to local patrons. The striped aprons, likewise, are created by the sisters by analyzing patterns from old family pieces and then combining them, mixing and matching elements from different aprons to create what they called a "fantasy" design that adheres to tradition yet appears as a new composition, a woven poem. While these women rely on their own artistic skills and use their own family pieces for inspiration, they still must acquire the raw materials from the handcraft shop. There they buy buttons, the silk thread for the embroidery, the leather, and the paper patterns for difficult items, such as the men's vests. Karin explained that the shop plays a pivotal role in providing her with the supplies she needs for her artistic creations.

There is yet another option for those who are interested in wearing the costume but who have neither a family stock nor sewing skills. Sven Roos is from Gagnef parish, in Dalarna. He commutes to work in Stockholm from Leksand, where he has lived since 1980 after marrying a local woman, Britta Jobs, Kersti's younger sister. Sven is a master fiddler and comes from a long line of traditional musicians. He performs every year in many concerts and several Midsummer festivals. In all of these he wears his Gagnef costume: a long, dark blue coat; yellow breeches made of chamois goatskin; dark blue double-breasted vest; dark blue socks; and wide-brimmed hat. The Gagnef costume is similar to the Leksand male costume with two major differences: dark blue instead of white socks and the conspicuous absence of the embroidered epaulets. When asked to perform at weddings, either walking ahead of the bride and groom in the procession down the church aisle or at the reception party, he and other hired fiddlers are asked by the couple to arrive in their folk costume. Sven told me that he uses his costume while performing in order to pay respect to the audience and the occasion and to look good. He told me that while wearing the costume "you always feel well-dressed."

A long afternoon interview at Sven's house started in the living room with the tape recorder and ended in the room where the costume pieces are meticulously stored, separated by type.[36] I asked him to describe to me in detail how he acquired his costume. He started by telling me that many of the old pieces were bought at auction in Gagnef, such as a pair of suspenders with the date 1889 embroidered on them. At auction he has also bought old pieces that had never been used, such as the pair of woolen, hand-knit blue socks, thicker than the ones he could find in shops nowadays and therefore more real-looking and a better protection against the mosquitoes that bite through flimsy new socks. He showed me a small metal box he got at a farm auction; it came filled with an assortment of buttons and buckles (among other useless junk) that he has plundered over the years.[37] He commissioned a pair of goatskin pants and a vest, each from a different tailor who specializes in that particular garment. To each tailor he gave antique buttons to attach to his new piece, creating a composite new/old garment. This attention to detail makes Sven stand out among the others in Gagnef costume.

Since there is no handcraft shop in Gagnef, Sven had no help in locating tailors, weavers, and cobblers to commission pieces. He has often sought expert craftsmen and bought several pieces, including two pairs of handmade shoes, one pair ordered in 1974 from a cobbler in Falun, the other in 1990 from a cobbler in Orsa. Sven does not know how to knit or sew (although sewing is taught in Swedish schools to both boys and girls), so many of his pieces were made for him by his mother or his sister-in-law Sonja.

I asked Sven why he goes through so much trouble, spending time and money to find costume pieces for a collection that has been accumulating over many years. His reasons were mainly aesthetic. He explained that he haunts farm auctions "because the older pieces look better than the newly made ones. Because it

Sven Roos and his daughter, Kersti, in their Gagnef folk costume. Midsummer, Leksand, Dalarna, Sweden, 2007.

is a matter of the colors. Because the fabrics you can find today are not the same as those one hundred years ago." To prove this point he placed side-by-side an old and a new pair of blue woolen socks and an old and new pair of purple woolen gloves. In both cases the old pieces were more luminous in comparison with the new, garish versions. Differences in both wool and dyes create this significant discrepancy in quality and look. Sven also emphasized that the old woolen socks were made with a different knitting technique, using just two needles, which kept the seam visible on the back.

When recreating a traditional piece, in whatever medium, people tend to be strict in their definitions, choosing a date, a cutoff point for how they think that piece should look. It is natural to become conservative, since one is trying to retrieve the past from a few extant examples, and a newly assembled costume can seem lifeless. Sven told me:

> The costume hasn't looked the same all the time. Inspiration has always come from the outside. And what people saw, and what people could afford, they brought into the costume. Also, a hundred years ago, there was lots of inspiration, actually, from Dala-Floda, because they have fancy embroideries. And I have a pair of old suspenders from Gagnef, but they are inspired from the Floda embroideries.

A contemporary version of a Gagnef costume piece would likely adhere to a firm understanding of the costume's defining features. The modern maker would be unlikely to put Floda floral embroideries on Gagnef suspenders, trying instead to create a "pure" garment. Choosing old clothing allows someone like Sven to wear a more dynamic and aesthetically flexible costume, one that exhibits the right construction and materials, the correct color saturations, and even some influences from fashions of the past.

LEKSANDS HEMSLÖJD: THE HANDCRAFT SHOP

The Handcraft Association of Leksand, with its impressive store, was founded in 1904 by the artist and architect Gustaf Ankarcrona. It was the first handcraft store in Sweden to open outside of Stockholm. Ankarcrona believed that traditional artifacts possessed qualities that continued to speak to the sensibilities of modern people; his slogan was "Past ground for future cultivation."[38]

Floda Handicraft shop. Floda, Dalarna, Sweden, 2007.

The store sells a variety of Leksand crafts, yet it retains its emphasis on traditional costumes, providing customers with new and old garments and with the materials and patterns for the construction of the garments. Upstairs, in a room labeled "Textilkammaren," there is a small exhibition of the costume pieces and accessories compiled by Ankarcrona, with a goal to "educate visitors and increase sales."[39] The store also hosts classes in which community members learn to cut, sew, or embroider parts of their costume.[40] As Kersti told me, "Many women go to one course after another to make piece after piece," slowly assembling their folk costume. The handcraft store continues to be a tremendous force for keeping the tradition of the Leksand costume alive through these critical functions: displaying the appropriate clothing in line with the costume almanac in its front window and on its website; providing local craftspeople with the materials for creation; selling new and secondhand costumes; dressing confirmation candidates for the ceremony; and renting female costumes to brides and Midsummer revelers.

Entering the Leksands Hemslöjd store and turning left, one finds the store's costume section. A tall tailor's table stands in the middle, complete with measuring tape, scissors, and pens. On one side of the table are small boxes of buttons, metal eyelets, pompoms, threads, and ribbons. A wall holds colorful silk thread for the embroidery of the women's bodices and the men's faux epaulets. Behind the table are bolts of cloth—yellow for the children's dress, floral for the confirmation bonnets—and spools of ribbons. Beside the bolts of fabric, boxes and racks hold new and old costume pieces. A nearby shelf contains three-ring binders with paper patterns, photographs, and swatches of embroidered or woven fabric. In the far right corner there is a curtained dressing arena.

I had the good fortune to befriend and interview Ingrid Samuelsson, a textile expert who has worked at the store for many years.[41] Ingrid is the person who changes the store's window display every week, letting people know which costume to wear to church that Sunday. She outlined the process of buying a Leksand costume. A customer must first decide if she wants a readymade piece or a commissioned one. If she wants a readymade one, then the choices are between new and old clothes. New pieces—custom-tailored—are obviously very expensive. A complete Midsummer ensemble for a woman costs about US$2,500, and a man's ensemble costs around US$6,500. The secondhand garments vary widely in price and age as well as in fabric color, weight, and garment style. I saw, for instance, a new men's coat for 4,500 Swedish kronors (about US$750) while an old one was available for 900 kronors (about US$150). Fabrics change over time, even if purchased from the same manufacturer, and Ingrid can date a piece of cloth instantly by its weight and hue, knowing whether it was purchased in her shop five years ago or last month. She explained that the secondhand costumes are sold only on consignment, in a manner akin to the system used by vintage clothing stores and boutiques. Local antique stores also have certain costume pieces for sale, such as an apron or a "pocket" purse, but in order to acquire a whole ensemble—and most important, to receive expert advice about appropriate combinations and contexts of use—the handcraft store is the best place for the purchase of old pieces.

If one would prefer a commissioned piece, the first decision is the fabric, including choices about hue, weight, and technique—woven by hand or machine. For many pieces, such as the bodice, one must also choose the metal eyelets, the ribbon used to lace the bodice, and the silk threads for the embroidery upon the bust. The particular pattern of the embroidered motif is also selected from an array of designs. Once the customer has fixed on a design, she may purchase the pattern used to transfer the design onto the fabric. Accompanying instructions detail the color scheme of the embroidery, explaining which colors should be used for the different parts of the medallion. Ingrid told me that the advantage of commissioning a piece from the handcraft shop is that they carry heirloom fabrics and accessories and that they can professionally take the customer's measurements and have the piece made for her. Many people don't know how to sew, nor do they know seamstresses who can make the folk costume. The store, as Ingrid explains, acts as an intermediary, making the commercial connections between a customer and the tailor, embroiderer, weaver, or shoemaker.

Ingrid took me downstairs to another section of the store, a room with lockers, benches, and boxes of costumes. This is where female confirmation candidates come to be dressed by the store employees. This room is also used for dressing a bride in her rental Leksand costume. The store provides everything for them, except for flowers and the bridal crown, which are acquired from a florist and the church, respectively. The store's proximity to the Leksands Kyrka makes it a convenient place to get ready. The all-female employees of the handcraft shop, like one's female relatives, now dress brides and confirmation candidates, making them look pretty for their special day, giving advice, soothing their nerves, acting more like family members than like commercial agents.

Upstairs from the main floor of the store is the textile museum, and just next to it stand five mannequins dressed in the Leksand folk costume: an adult male in the long coat with the embroidered epaulets, a little girl in the yellow dress, and three adult women—one in the Midsummer festival attire with the red striped apron; one in the blue apron combination for weddings and other auspicious events; and one wearing the funeral garments with the white scarf covering the head and tied under the chin. When consulting with people in the costume room downstairs, Ingrid said, they often must take the customers upstairs to teach them about the history and art of the costume by showing them the mannequins and the old pieces in the museum display. In this way the employees act as teachers, as historians, imparting knowledge to those who want to buy a costume.

Even though the store window shows the ensemble to be worn for the upcoming Sunday, many people prefer to speak with one of the store employees, asking them to interpret the code for them, helping them negotiate and improvise. "So they want to have advice. *Good advice* from us," Ingrid explained. "So the phone is ringing the whole time, or next Sunday: 'Please tell me, is it the red or the striped apron, what is it?' So many questions; many, many questions. The whole summer is like that."

The Leksands Helmstöjd, although it is a store, also fulfills many important functions besides the obvious commercial ones, furthering Ankarcrona's original goals. Its employees act as saleswomen as well as museum docents, educators, and tradition bearers, like one's knowledgeable grandmother.

LEKSANDS KULTURHUS: THE ETHNOGRAPHIC MUSEUM

Kersti's uncle, Knis Karl Aronsson, a bachelor who dedicated his life to the preservation of Leksand traditions, had the idea in the 1960s of amassing a communal selection of men's costumes. Many women owned and wore the costume at this time, so he focused his efforts on encouraging men to use their costume as well. As Kersti told me, a man from their village of Tibble emigrated to Minneapolis, making a fortune for himself in America. He asked Knis Karl what he could do for his home place, and Knis Karl asked for a sum of money with which to purchase cloth and hire tailors to make the Leksand coats, vests, and breeches. Knis Karl believed that once somebody got used to wearing the folk costume he would become committed enough to buy his own. Knis Karl's opinion endures. Kersti told me that shortly before I arrived, the mayor of the city, who was about to travel to Japan on official business, wanted to borrow a costume to take with him overseas. Several community members thought that the costume should not be taken out of the country, and they also thought that since he was the mayor of the city, he should buy his own. Further, some people believed if the mayor owned his own costume, he would wear it more often and thus encourage its use by displaying it on his body during official occasions. In the end he bought his Leksand costume, and the newspapers published photographs of him proudly wearing it in Japan.

The men's costumes acquired by Knis Karl Aronsson were originally stored at Fräsgården, a characteristic early nineteenth-century courtyard farmstead with a two-room *parstuga* house that has been preserved as an outdoor museum and is administered as part of the Leksands Kommun organization. Kersti's mother, Karin, was in charge of renting the clothes, but when it became too difficult for her to make the long trip to Fräsgården, she decided to store the clothes in a house on the family property, in what is now Kersti's sister's home (which she inherited from their parents after their death). A small amount was charged for the rental, just enough to cover the costs of washing the clothes. The rental costumes moved to the Kulturhuset building in 1985 when the ethnographic museum opened, and Kersti's daughter-in-law, Ulla Björklöf, who works at the museum, now manages the rentals, keeping the practice within the family. Ulla told me that the museum owns the long blue coats with the embroidered epaulets and also the black funeral coats, vests, and the chamois breeches with the incised, subtle designs upon the thighs. More intimate apparel—shoes, socks, and shirts—need to be supplied by the wearer. Renters are usually grooms, confirmation candidates, and those attending baptisms and funerals. It costs 550 Swedish kronors (about US$93) to rent the complete ensemble of coat, vest, knee-breeches, and hat. Ulla has watched many men adopt a different posture—stretching out and standing up straight—when they have changed out of their slouchy jeans and into the Leksand costume. Seeing themselves in the mirror in the folk costume of their region, they are transformed, confident, tall, and proud. That is one power of costume.

PRESERVATION: IDEOLOGY, ARTIFACT, AND FUNCTION

Not all aspects of culture are intentionally preserved, but folk costumes, in many parts of the world, are thought to contain the history, geography, and identity of the people who wear them. Costumes are often selected to represent *heritage,* understood as those aspects of tradition that are self-consciously designated as worthy of preservation. Costumes, along with other forms of material culture, were an integral part of Hazelius's mandate to preserve *kulturarv,* or cultural heritage.[42] In modern Sweden, as in other parts of Europe and Asia, scholars are currently studying heritage, defined by folklorist Barbro Klein as "phenomena in a group's past that are given high symbolic value and, therefore, must be protected for the future."[43] Among recent immigrants to Europe, efforts at the preservation of heritage are essential for those displaced from their former homelands; this is also the case in the United States among those of Swedish ancestry who are eager to "make heritage" in the diaspora.[44] But within Sweden the displacement of the rural people is not geographic, but temporal. People in Dalarna want to retain a connection to their past and their ancestors, resisting the influence of "others" who are not foreigners, but contemporary versions of themselves.

Preservation of the Swedish costume has three major components: (1) the conceptual preservation of the idea of the costume largely through written accounts, paintings, and photographs; (2) the physical preservation of the actual garments; and (3) the functional preservation of the use of the garments in social contexts. While Leksand costume fragments have been found in excavated graves, the oldest book carrying images of the costume is C. Forssell's *Ett år I Sverge* (A Year in Sweden), a book published in 1827 and containing color plates of regional costumes, including four color illustrations of the male and female outfits of Leksand parish. These pictures show old-fashioned garments such as the rare black pleated wool skirt and the currently abandoned yellow bonnet, but they also depict the garments that are still in use today: both the male black and dark blue coats with embroidered epaulets and three different aprons—blue, yellow, and red-striped.

Another mode of the conceptual preservation of costumes lies in research, documentation, and presentation in scholarly mediums—museum exhibits and catalogs. This continues to be a principal goal of the Nordiska Museet and Skansen, following Arthur Hazelius's example. Knowledge of the Leksand costume is preserved by the efforts of such scholars as Anna-Maja Nylén, Ingrid Bergman, Gunnel Hazelius Berg, and Sigfrid Svensson. There are also picture books, such as *Folkdräkter och bygdedräkter från hela Sverige* and *Sockendräkter i Dalarna*,[45] that combine the encyclopedia with the how-to manual and feature real people dressed in their own costumes. In *Folk Costumes of Sweden* by Berg and Berg, published in 1975, Kersti Jobs-Björklöf, her brother, and her daughter model the Leksand costume.[46] Publications of this kind carry much information about costume use, illustrating the clothes themselves with old and new photographs of people wearing them, and they also include patterns for cutting and sewing and embroidery, as well as detailed diagrams.[47] By contrast, while current Swedish publications about costumes have contributed to the scholarly and popular interest in preservation, they do not match the impressive oeuvre of studies centered on the Norwegian folk costume, the *bunad*.[48] Of particular importance are the Norwegian costumes from the region of Setesdal, a picturesque destination where, historically, a large percentage of landed peasants have continued to wear their folk costume.[49] Setesdal parallels Dalarna in that the culture and costume have been valorized nationally: "In many ways the Setesdal costume has become the national folk costume."[50]

Costume books usually contain many historical and contemporary photographs of people wearing the traditional clothes, and photography is an important medium for keeping the idea of the costume in the consciousness of the people. Kersti uses the photographs in her family album to remember and to teach about the Leksand costume as well as to demonstrate her family's long commitment to wearing their folk costume. Kersti led the project at the Leksands Kommun archives to gather binders full of local photographs. The images—in the binders and in electronic form—await captions supplied by knowledgeable visitors or family members. The medium, and metaphor, of photography is indispensable in the preservation and dissemination of folk culture. Artur Hazelius, in his museum displays, tried to create "'snap-shots' of traditional life."[51] Orvar Löfgren argues that photographs, especially postcards, which miniaturize the large world into a small, portable medium, allow one to return to "a mythical past or a more authentic existence."[52]

Like photographs, paintings have always been indispensable in the maintenance of the idea of the regional costume, not only in Sweden but in many other parts of the world too.[53] Artur Hazelius commissioned several paintings for the Nordiska Museet, including one depicting a wedding scene in Dalarna, to preserve visually the costumes, customs, and home decorations—the folklife—of the peasants.[54] Many of Sweden's artists, such as Anders Zorn and Carl Larsson, spent their summers in Dalarna, producing art that featured peasants and their costume, locking it into the consciousness of the Swedish people.[55] Their paintings depict idyllic scenes of country life, celebrating and romanticizing the Swedish peasantry in a nationalistic spirit. While the details of the costume and ensembles are not always accurate, paintings do document the past in terms of its material culture: architecture, furniture, and clothing.

Written descriptions and illustrations of the costumes, whether in books, photographs, or paintings, all help to keep the costume—aesthetically—in the awareness of the local people, although many of these renditions, because of their artistic nature, do not contain accurate details about garment construction, materials, proper combinations, or use. For the costume tradition to continue, one needs more reliable texts: the tools and techniques of making and, most important, the garments themselves. Cutting and sewing, weaving and embroidery are taught and preserved in women's study circles,[56] by craft classes offered by the handcraft shop, and especially by the college of handcraft, Sätergläntan, in Dalarna. Knowledge of making is also preserved by individuals like Ulla's mother and aunts, who not only know how to cut, embroider, and weave but who also own the loom and the other tools of the trade.

The actual costume pieces exist, nestled in acid-free paper, in dark, cold storage rooms, in Leksands Kulturhus. These objects are well-preserved but not readily accessible to the average museum visitor. However, there is an exhibition at the Leksands Kulturhus that shows all the varieties of the costume, illustrating the various aprons, scarves, bodices, and organizing them into clusters according to occasion of use. All the costume varieties—defined by ceremonial use, work, gender, age, and season—are displayed in a long corridor with mannequins in dioramas. Kersti told me that in 1998 the museum mounted an exhibit and hosted an international conference on folk costumes. It was the most popular exhibit ever held at the museum. She also said the audience consisted mainly of local, elderly women who came to hear about their own traditions.

While the Leksand costume is so well exhibited in this local museum, the Nordiska Museet does not have a permanent display of the regional costumes of the country. The only permanent space devoted to clothing there is the "Fashion" gallery, which exhibits couture pieces from the permanent collection; its important assembly of folk costumes has been relegated to the storeroom. In this situation lies a general attitude. When a major exhibition of Swedish folk art appeared in Sweden, it featured postmodern departures such as tattoos, the customizing of cars, and new art made by Sweden's many immigrants. When the show traveled abroad, however, the objects chosen were traditional examples of folk art such as painted furniture and even costumes from Leksand.[57] These two exhibitions reveal a pattern: a national trend of fatigue with traditional folk art and a favoring of the contemporary and multicultural. For the last three decades, scholars of Swedish culture have also experienced a moment of national boredom with what some called "pompom research"—folklife studies that "celebrated trivial aspects of an agrarian society that was now gone forever."[58] (The "pompom" reference is from the little pompoms in the breeches of the men's costume; a detail of folk costume becomes symbolic of the breadth of traditional culture.) By contrast, in the international setting—and also at the local level—folk art and folk costumes are still at the center, admired for their beauty and history.

Costumes are preserved *visually* by artists and photographers and *physically* in the museum and in family storage chests. The only way they can be preserved in a *social* context—their meanings and communications intact—is through actual use, and this is the last major component of the preservation of a folk costume. The costume almanac, as we have already seen, is a force for documenting and disseminating the functional potential of different versions of the Leksand costume. But it is only a book (or website or store window display). It requires human actors to bring the costume code and performance into real life. Agents of the costume include the makers, wearers, and their beholders. Today folk costume is worn widely by musicians and folk dancers in Dalarna, as it is in many other countries of Europe. Kersti has worn her costume, carefully enacting the code written down by Alm, to church every single Sunday of her life. By wearing the Leksand costume, and displaying its variety and ensemble combinations, she helps disseminate knowledge about the garments—visually, conceptually, and socially.

Those who wear the costume, at considerable expense and hassle, need positive feedback and appreciation from others, for this keeps the tradition going. Kersti's mother always encouraged those around her to wear the costume. Kersti recalled that her mother would request that in lieu of a birthday or Christmas gift her family should wear the Leksand costume to the gathering; the sight of them in the Leksand folk costume was the best present she could receive. In 1954, when Kersti passed her school exams, she wanted a new outfit, as was the custom among her classmates. Her mother told her that she would get a new set of clothes, but requested that she wear the Leksand costume for the school ceremony. Kersti did this reluctantly, being the only one to wear the folk costume at the event. When she shook hands with the headmaster, who was also the headmaster at the time of her mother's exam, he told her that just that morning he had said to his wife, "I wonder if Kersti will wear the costume like her mother did back in 1922." Kersti said she did not appreciate standing out in the 1950s, but in the 1970s, during the revival of folk costumes in Sweden, she liked it. She was living in Stockholm at the time and proudly wore her Leksand costume, receiving much praise. Many people said to her, "I envy you," for having a traditional costume whose use had been preserved throughout the years.

In preservation there is a dilemma. One can choose to preserve the garment in a locked vault, keeping the fabric from deteriorating and the colors from fading. Or one can choose to wear the costume, keeping it circulating in the consciousness of the people, but perhaps damaging it during use. If it is kept, the clothes are safe; if it is worn, the clothes are alive. These opposed goals work against each other. The folk costumes at Stockholm's Nordiska Museet are safely locked in storage, preserved forever. Some of the Leksands Kulturhus costumes are displayed safely on mannequins but preserved less well than they would be if stored flat in acid-free packing. (The costume worn by an interpreter at an outdoor museum comes closer to Artur Hazelius's ideal of displaying objects in context, of presenting "folk life in living brushstrokes."[59])

The main difference between costumes stored in a museum and in a family clothes chest is that museum pieces are never worn. Kersti is the custodian of a large collection of family costumes, stored in various places: in the storehouse, in a dresser in the guesthouse, in her own wardrobe. In reference to a group of her great-grandmother's aprons, I commented that it seemed like a family museum, and she agreed, elaborating on this concept:

It is very difficult for me, because when working in a museum you know exactly how to handle things with conservation, with keeping it in boxes, with special silk paper. Using white gloves, everything.

So I said to my mother, "Oh, my God, we shouldn't use it; we shouldn't keep it like this." And she said, "It's not a museum. It's our family things. Go there; if there is something that can be used, use it. But you will tell your daughters that they must be careful, and try to tell them about my wonderful grandmother, and the stories about her. Just give them some nice stories."

And therefore, it's hanging there, and it's not hanging well. I have this bad conscience for not caring about it and so on.

In the summer of 2008, following the old Swedish custom, Kersti and her husband, Sune, planned to move out of their house into a small house in the village. Into their fine old house, inheriting the building and everything in it, will come her son, Erik; his wife, Ulla, who works at the Leksands Kulturhus; and their daughter, Anna. This eased Kersti's burden, the heavy responsibility of working for the preservation of the costumes—and traditions—of her family and her region of Leksand. "I am glad that Ulla and Erik will come here," she said. "And Ulla works at the Kulturhus. She is very careful, she is very interested in the costume, and she knows how to handle things. And so I think it will be in good hands. So now I am trying to teach Anna."

INNOVATION: CREATION, REVIVAL, AND REUSE

Change is manifest in folk costumes in many ways: the creation of a brand-new costume; the creation of a new version of an old costume, the revival of an old style, and during reinterpretation of the contexts of the costume's use. One way to control the costume and discourage unnecessary change is to impose restrictions on who can and cannot wear it, limiting the number of actors who might contribute to modifications. In Leksand pressures to change work against the conscious efforts at preservation of tradition; yet, efforts at innovation help keep the costume alive and relevant today while resulting in the loss of some of its social and aesthetic features.

Many of Sweden's folk costumes are recent creations, in contrast to the famous costumes of Dalarna that are celebrated partly for their long tradition. But even within the province of Dalarna, certain regions did not have a living costume tradition. One was Sundborn, in the mining region of Falun. The Sundborn costume, with its green vest, red apron, and striped skirt, was created by the district's famous artist residents, Carl and Karin Larsson, in 1902.[60] In fact, Carl Larsson, along with fellow artist Gustaf Ankarcrona, is often credited with creating the Swedish national costume in the early 1900s, even though its real inventor was Märta Jörgensen, whose role is generally downplayed.[61] The (female) national costume is a dress, with the bodice and skirt attached much like the Vingåker costume. It is a blue dress worn with a white blouse and a yellow apron, in the bright hues of the Swedish flag (this was not Jorgensen's original intent; she wanted muted versions of the two colors). White embroidered flowers appear on the bottom hem of the apron and on the front of the bodice. One may acquire the costume, readymade, for about one thousand dollars. Interestingly the only people I saw wearing this costume during Midsummer in Dalarna were women from Stockholm, who had no regional costume of their own, or tourists from Japan. Although the costume was created by artists to obliterate regional distinctions, as Kersti explained to me, ironically, the women who wear it now are those who do not have a strong regional affiliation—immigrants, tourists, and people from Stockholm. The most famous proponent of the national costume is Sweden's queen Silvia, who is shown in countless postcards wearing the costume along with her two daughters, princesses Victoria and Madeline, on June 6, the country's National Day.[62] Queen Silvia was born in Germany and grew up in Brazil, so the national costume is appropriate for her since she had no regional costume of her own. Beauty queen Yvonne Ryding also wore this dress as Miss Sweden in 1984 during the national costume competition segment of the Miss Universe pageant, the year she won the title.[63] The invented costume, worn by queens of all kinds, speaks aloud during national and international events yet remains obscure and silent on the regional stages.[64]

The instance of inventing a costume that never existed before, like the national costume, is rare. A more common practice is to make slight alterations to existing pieces or to revive forgotten items. The costume is always changing. Skirt lengths become longer and shorter depending on the current fashion. Anna-Maja Nylén, the late curator of textiles at the Nordiska Museet, wrote about fashion and the folk costume in her 1949 book, *Swedish Peasant Costumes*. She began her discussion of folk costume by writing, "Reaching back as far as we can, by the aid of actual garments, pictures, written records and oral information, we perceive that throughout many parts of the countryside, peasant dress followed the changes of fashion."[65] Innovation and change lie at the heart of the definition of folk costumes.

In the 1950s the Leksand skirt got shorter and "wider" with the addition of several underskirts that functioned as petticoats and changed the silhouette of the costume. At the end of the eighteenth century and the beginning of the nineteenth, the red vest was made of shiny damask cloth, with a high collar and a rolled hem, allowing the expert to determine the date of this style. Similar dating details exist for most costume pieces. Fabric, form, and method of construction exist in a state of constant, slight variation.

Self-conscious revivals of old pieces can also be seen as innovative acts since they alter the current costume repertoire. The green pleated wool skirt, worn under the apron in place of the black woolen skirt, provides an example. The green skirt, according to Kersti, ceased being used around 1860 but was revived in 1950. This skirt, when worn with the blue apron, warrants the wearer the use of red stockings, instead of the white stockings that are worn with the black skirt, since the red stockings were made of precious dye materials, madder root or even cochineal. The result is a celebratory mix of green, blue, and red, and a few paintings from Leksand depict this beautiful combination.[66] During the occasions when the blue apron is called for, most women wear the black woolen skirt, but Kersti wears her green pleated one (one of the three she owns), communicating a higher level of connoisseurship.

Kersti elaborated on the history of the recent revival of the green skirt:

> A teacher who was a colleague of my mother's, she wanted to marry and have a crown, and not the white cap, because she said that "it's such a day to be a bride and I want to use the crown."
>
> And so she was in discussion with my mother, and my mother said that in the old days when they were brides—and also for very special Sundays—they had a green skirt. "Shouldn't you have a green skirt?" Because when you combine the green with the blue it's much more beautiful than the blue to the black, and then you have red stockings.
>
> And then she got interested. And she said, "Yes, I will."
>
> And so she was dressed, a bride, I think it was 1950, like that, in a green skirt, and the crown, and with the ribbons and these decorations.

In this case the costume revival was motivated by aesthetics, for a bride wants to appear beautiful *and* special, in extraordinary attire. For Kersti's own wedding ten years later, her mother wanted to commission a special, handwoven green skirt, prompted, once again, by beauty. This is the story Kersti told me:

> And then there was an artist living here, and he was a textile man, and then my mother said, "You go up to this room where we keep our clothes, have a look at these old green ones—the ones used, from Anna, 1846, and the other one from Brita, 1870—and look what you think is the

Kersti Jobs-Björklöf dressed
for the Leksand church
Midsummer service.
Tibble, Leksand, Dalarna,
Sweden, 2007.

most beautiful color, and tell us what kind of color so that the yarn got the right green color together with the blue one."

So it was very much discussed between my mother—because she wanted a *beautiful* green color.

So there was a lady, who had woven many meters of this. So then for my wedding, relatives, they had made for themselves a green skirt.

The revival of the green skirt was provoked by aesthetics and inspired by old family pieces, continuing the family tradition while changing the course of current fashion.

Although the costume tradition, like all traditions, is flexible by definition, allowing for variation, it is a different matter when these variations are codified and made official—when they become heritage—as in the costume almanac. Kersti told me about a recent happening in Leksand that stimulated much debate among the city's tradition brokers. According to the almanac, one is to wear the "black tone" garments of black bodice and yellow apron at a certain time of the year, yet parents may schedule confirmations for their children during the same time of the year. The dilemma is this: should parents be allowed to bypass the general somber tone of the church calendar for the celebratory tone of their offspring's rites of passage and wear clothes in the "red tone" instead? Kersti describes the current situation:

> And people, they go to the handcraft shop, and say, "We have seen in the calendar, and we can see in the window that we should have black, and I haven't got a black vest. I only have the red one, because we use it for Midsummer, and weddings, and special occasions. What shall I do?"
>
> And they say, "As I haven't got that one, and this is a happy occasion—confirmation for my child—and what shall we do?"

Many in the community have appealed to Kersti, the author of the last published costume almanac and a leader in these matters, to help revise the official code and to help persuade the Leksand church to change its costume code. Kersti vehemently believes that people have the right to wear what they want to wear; the costume tradition continues because people wear the folk costume. But, she said, these kinds of decisions should not be made within the institution of the church. Flexibility is built into the code, and changes designed to accommodate a limited wardrobe should not be codified. She concludes:

> This is the tradition. If you don't have it, then use what you have. Tell the parents that if they have a red one, then be happy with their children and

use the red one. I am not going to blame them for not having—I am not a *police*! I think that it's better that they use it.

I think it's up to anyone to do as they like, so they feel happy. I don't blame them. I'm happy if they like to use the folk costume.

Kersti's statements show that even the most consistent champion of the folk costume is adaptable, believing that the costume code can be broken and that what really matters is that the costume continues to be worn with pride and love. The desire to police the clothes, however, is integral to the discussion of the Leksand costume, and it concludes our examination of innovation within the costume.

The first line of defense could theoretically occur at the handcraft shop, since the employees could be seen as gatekeepers to the tradition. This is not the case, as Ingrid Samuelsson told me. One female customer wanted to buy the red Leksand bodice to wear with jeans while riding her motorcycle. Ingrid felt it was not her place to prevent the woman from buying the garment for that purpose. She believes it is not the store's aim to "police" costume use, and she is not in the business of patrolling it. She will give advice, when asked for it, but will sell items to whoever wants to buy them. Ingrid also said that the costume is not a "uniform," that there is much room for variation, which is what we have seen throughout this chapter.

Ulla's aunts, elderly women of the community who are skilled textile artisans, also do not believe in reprimanding people or policing costume use. They recalled an instance when someone came to church for the Midsummer service wearing the black embroidered scarf with the red-striped apron, an inappropriate combination, according to tradition. When this woman saw what others were wearing and discovered her error, she felt "ashamed." She did not have to be told of her mistake. I asked Ulla's aunts whether they would tell someone if she were wearing the wrong combination. They said they would tell only if they knew that person; if it were a stranger or tourist, they would say nothing, reserving their counsel for those who were familiar. Kersti said that when she sees someone wearing the costume inaccurately—for example, with the belt tied on the wrong side—she says nothing. But if she notices that others in church snicker and laugh, then she takes the person aside and offers to help her, inviting the person to her house, where Kersti can instruct her, in private, about the costume. Ingrid, Ulla's mother and aunts, and Kersti are not interested in policing outsiders, for the costume means something different to a tourist than it does to a Leksand native. The code applies only to those on the inside, for whom the costume is a manifestation of regional heritage.

This brings us back to one of the central questions of this book: what is a costume? Is the Leksand folk costume a uniform, a performance outfit, or festive dress? The answer depends on who you ask, its contexts of use, and the goals of its nonverbal communication. During our conversations Kersti repeatedly told me that her costume is *not a uniform,* for a uniform is restricted in form and use and can be worn only by certain people who are allowed to wear it. In talking about the varieties of the striped apron, for example, she said that nowadays some people follow a single set pattern, "keeping every millimeter" the same, changing the costume into a "uniform," something it never was, since it always existed in a state of perpetual variation. In the Swedish diaspora, however, among a population less familiar and comfortable with its heritage, many view the folk costume as a "uniform" as Lizette Gradén shows in her study of Lindsborg, Kansas.[67] Kersti, a true insider, is more liberal about the costume tradition than others are.

Can outsiders wear the folk costume of a region that is not their own? Eva Erkers, who is from Dala-Floda, cannot understand why outsiders would want to wear her famous regional costume, coveted for its beautiful floral embroidery and singled out by Skansen and the Nordiska Museet for its excellence. Eva strongly objects to others wearing her costume: "You wear it to show where you come from. And if you aren't from a village, why to use it, why would you like to use it?" I offered the possibility that people might want to wear her costume because it is beautiful, as hers certainly is. She responded, "Yes, but you don't wear it because it's beautiful. You wear it to show where you come from; my opinion." Thinking for a moment, she continued: "I wouldn't have any problem if you would like to try it and take a picture for fun. But to wear it and use it to show where you come from, that's something else."

In Eva's wish to restrict the use of her costume, she reveals what the costume means to her—a manifestation of identity. This is different from Kersti's position, one that allows others to wear her costume as long as they do it "with love and respect."[68] Both positions are valid and indicative of what the costume means for people in Sweden today. The costume, like all forms of material culture, gathers meaning in context. Kersti told me of a couple, both members of the folk-dance troupe in Leksand, who performed in their costume but chose to get married in the conventional white dress/formal suit ensemble. When Kersti asked them why they did not marry in their Leksand costume, they said they would never do that; folk costumes are for performance, not for important rites of passage in the church (even though that was exactly the context for the costume long before folk-dance troupes were established). The Leksand folk costume can be a performance garment, a symbol of regional identity, or festive dress. However it is defined, the costume has always existed in variation, undergoing numerous innovations that have kept the garments dynamic, always changing, yet constantly traditional.

"ALL TRADITION IS CHANGE"

Traditions simultaneously exhibit continuity and change. Writing about tradition in the exhibit catalog *Swedish Folk Art* (subtitled "All Tradition Is Change"), Henry Glassie expands on the idea: "Though a force for continuity, tradition is not the antithesis of change. Tradition lives only in individual minds as part of the adaptive process of daily life, so it exists in a steady state of change."[69] He continues, describing the patterns in tradition, among which are intentional replication and revival: "Since tradition is a temporal process, all creations result from selections made among precedents, so all are, in some measure, the products of revival."[70] Many other folklorists have also usefully addressed the idea of tradition: Lauri Honko describes it as "cultural potential or resource"; Dan Ben-Amos defines it, in part, as "knowledge that is secured in the minds and memories of the people, only to be performed on appropriate occasions."[71] We have seen that for the Leksand costume to continue, some of its aspects have been carefully preserved, such as the general look and types of garments and the code of aprons, and some aspects have been changed, abandoned, or revived, such as the green pleated skirt. Inga Arnö Berg and Gunnel Hazelius Berg, in their *Folk Costumes of Sweden,* explicitly discuss change and variation with regard to the folk costumes of the country, explaining how new ideas and innovations were either speedily incorporated or slowly accepted: "Thus variations arose; old forms were mixed with more modern expressions, and differences among rural regions appeared more prominent."[72] A perusal of their book, with its four hundred folk costumes, reveals that regional variations can be great or subtle. Berg and Berg describe how throughout the country, in any given region, diverse versions of the costume existed, allowing for the expression of individuality and regional affiliation at once.[73]

FOLK COSTUME AND THE MAINTENANCE OF HERITAGE

In speaking about the tradition of the Leksand folk costume, Kersti said, "When my mother's generation is dead, I think that it's gone." This declaration shocked me, and I was dismayed until I understood what she meant. Kersti's statement can be understood as part of a hyperbolic rhetoric of preservation, not descriptive, but rather prophetic, a jeremiad.[74] Her subversive, critical opinion of the current state of affairs is meant to ensure the preservation of creativity for the future. She states hypothetically what she hopes to avoid in order to encourage those around her to work against her forecast of death for the Leksand folk costume. I asked Ulla's mother, Karin, and her aunts, Brita and Anna, if they thought the tradition of making and wearing the costume was dying. After Ulla translated my question to them, they responded in unison with emphatic cries of "Nej, nej, nej, nej!" Ulla's translation of their subsequent collective statement was "No, not dying. They think it is going up and down. Now it is down."

The costume tradition in Sweden, like all traditions, has gone up and down. A balance of preservation and innovation—both are aspects of tradition—is necessary to keep any custom alive, flowing along through history, experiencing robust and lean moments. For a tradition to survive, such as that of the folk costume, it requires actors—ideological and visionary outsiders as well as motivated, dedicated leaders from within.

Mats Hellspong and Barbro Klein, in detailing the history of folklife studies in Sweden, generalize a pattern of outsiders' interest in the folk cultures of their country.[75] In the sixteenth century the elite were attracted to folk customs in part to highlight for the rest of Europe the uniqueness of their Nordic culture. During the next century Sweden experienced the glory of a superpower, taking pride in its antiquities, using archaeology and history as vehicles of propaganda for imperialism. In the eighteenth century the country turned back into itself, with a renewed appreciation of its flora, fauna, and folk culture. Botanist Carl Linnaeus, among others, traveled the nation, documenting what he saw, including the life and customs of the country people. It was during the nineteenth century that romanticism inspired many to collect from the peasants their songs and tales, and Artur Hazelius launched his collecting of the material culture of the peasants—starting with costumes from Dalarna—for what would become his monumental and hugely influential museums, Nordiska Museet and Skansen. At the turn of the twentieth century, Hazelius and other members of the Swedish bourgeoisie held sentimental notions of the peasants. In *Culture Builders* ethnologists Jonas Frykman and Orvar Löfgren provide the cultural context for the collecting, and valuing, of folk arts and lifestyles—an attempt to delineate middle-class identity in relation to both the "declining peasantry and the emerging working class" of Stockholm—giving us an understanding of the audience for Hazelius's museums.[76]

The sequence of outsiders who helped to further the costume tradition of the local farming people begins with scientists and scholars, Linnaeus and Hazelius, and continues with artists. Carl Larsson, influenced by William Morris and the Arts and Crafts movement, wrote in *Ett Hem*, in 1899: "Therefore, oh Swede, save yourself in time. Return to simplicity and dignity. It is better to be awkward than elegant. Dress yourself in skin, fur, leather, and wool. Make yourself furnishings that suit your heavy body, and on everything put bright colors."[77] Through ideology, practice, and art, Larsson helped to bring the folk costume into the twentieth century. With his wife, Karin, he created the famous Sundborn costume. With artist Gustaf Ankarcrona (and Märta Jörgensen) he invented the national costume, worn by people who have no regional costume of their own and eminently displayed since 1983 on the royal body of Queen Silvia. Ankarcrona's contribution to the preservation of the Leksand costume continues today in the pivotal role that the handcraft store (that he established) still plays in the dissemination and maintenance of the folk costume tradition. It was Ankarcrona who persuaded Albert Alm to document the costume code in the almanacs he created for the parishes of Leksand and Dala-Floda.

Hazelius, Larsson, and Ankarcrona all lived in or visited Dalarna, and while technically outsiders, they worked closely with the people whose costumes they strove to preserve. Their efforts led to institutional support for folk costumes through handcraft stores, craft study circles, colleges of handcrafts, and museum displays and collections. We can add another institution that has always played a role in the continuation of folk costume traditions: the church.[78] By fostering the custom of attending services in folk costume through its almanac of acceptable coded ensembles, the church remains a source of rules that are enacted and enforced by local people. Any institutional drive for or against the costume tradition, however, must be furthered by local people.

Folk costume in Sweden experienced a great wave of revival in the 1970s and is now, according to many experts, at a low ebb. In this chapter I have argued that outsiders were influential but that the main agents for the preservation of the costume have been insiders, dedicated local leaders. Hazelius and Ankarcrona were crucial; their ideological mandate remained the political and aesthetic aim of Leksand's people long after these men had passed away. Studies of European folk costume constantly credit influential individuals—kings, scholars, and artists. Although folklorists such as Barbro Klein, Dorothy Noyes, Regina Bendix, and Thomas Dubois have called for ethnographic study of identity and costume in Europe,[79] the practitioners and leaders from within the culture remain anonymous in the scholarly record. The application of performance theory to the study of costume in Europe would reveal the willed decisions these insiders make in shaping their own heritage.

One important component in the preservation of heritage is the family unit. Kersti continues to work on the trajectory set by her uncle Knis Karl and her mother, Karin. Ulla's professional affiliation with the ethnographic museum and its collections was inspired by the years of artistic dedication given to their community by both her mother and her aunts. With Ulla's marriage to Kersti's son, Erik, two devoted families have joined forces in the maintenance of Leksand customs. Beyond these key families, individuals working alone and in groups operate within the institutions initiated by the outsiders, keeping the heritage going, at the handcraft store or the ethnographic museum. Many individuals, such as Kersti and her brother-in-law, Sven Roos—through their personal connoisseurship, dedication, and good taste—rescue old pieces from obscurity and wear them, inspiring revival, keeping the garments fashionable, or at least visible.

In analyzing this system of heritage maintenance, we identify some actors as outsiders and others as insiders. How accurate a distinction is this? In the case of folk costumes in Leksand, we categorize the artists and scholars from elsewhere as "outsiders." But many of them summered in Dalarna, including Artur Hazelius, whose house in Ullvi stands about two miles from Kersti's farm, Knisgården. Kersti and her uncle Knis Karl are considered "insiders," born and raised within the tradition, but both served as directors of the local ethnographic museum, and they engaged in scholarship and public programming, much like Hazelius himself. There is a pattern, not just in Sweden but in many other parts of the world: outsiders often respond to movements that have started on the inside. They choose a particular locale—in our case Leksand, Dalarna—because it contains a living tradition that attracts these outsiders in the first place. (It is not a coincidence that Hazelius, Larsson, and Ankarcrona all came to Dalarna from beyond.) So outsiders help energize and mobilize the local people who become involved in carrying forward the mandate of preservation and revival, but this process starts from within, emotionally, and borrows power from the intellectual and political aims of progressive artists and scholars. Revivals of folk traditions are generally credited to outsiders and their formal institutions, but it is the insiders, the local creators and leaders, who populate these institutions—the museums, schools, and stores—who accept the responsibility of local action and actually make things happen.

By giving the credit for a revived tradition to an outsider, we steal the power of the insider; we obscure the acts of those who make, sell, and use—of those who, in Leksand, by wearing their costumes, commit to the preservation of heritage.[80] Artur Hazelius helped his country resist international forces by celebrating the national. Kersti Jobs-Björklöf helps her community resist national forces by celebrating the familial, the local, the regional.

Kersti taught me generously about her tradition of folk costume during many long interviews while I was in Sweden, and then through follow-up emails and explanations upon my return to the United States. She has been generous with me, but she places her hopes, and her tradition, in the hands of her granddaughter, nine-year-old Anna. I am an outsider, a scholar of folklore and dress; I can write and teach about the tradition. Her granddaughter, Anna, is an insider; she can live it. Both of us are necessary for the survival of the costume tradition. We are both committed: my obligation is ideological, intellectual; Anna's duty is emotional, familial, personal, and primary.

PLAY

The Society for Creative Anachronism

HISTORICAL COSTUMES ENABLE THEIR WEARERS AND BEHOLDERS to travel in time, to imagine or inhabit the past. During historical reenactments, accuracy and authenticity are valued, for meticulous costumes grant their wearers the right to represent the past, often in critique of the present.

The next three chapters examine distinct categories of historical reenactment: first, the Society for Creative Anachronism, an amateur association whose primary focus is in-group entertainment with no spectators in attendance; second, several groups of American Civil War reenactors, semiprofessional historians who strive for both personal enjoyment and public education; and finally, the Colonial Williamsburg living history museum, a professional institution whose mission is to educate a paying audience of visitors.

Each example of historical costuming centers on the premise of time travel, of transporting oneself and spectators to another time and place. The specificity of time and place vary, as do the degree of authenticity, the levels of tolerance of inaccuracy, and the skills of performance. All three examples of living history involve people impersonating others—nobility from the Middle Ages, Civil War soldiers, or residents of Williamsburg in the eighteenth century. Unlike our examples from Sweden and Brazil, in which history was gathered into the costumed individuals, in historical reenactment the individual is gathered into history, as these studies consider the expression of identity through the clothing of someone from another time and place. Personal heritage, however, remains a major motivation. In each of these examples we find historical costumes used as a means of social commentary. In each, dedicated individuals combine artistry and a notion of accuracy to make, wear, and perform historical costumes, achieving personal fulfillment while working toward the creation of community.

In 1966 Diana Paxson, a graduate student studying medieval literature at the University of California, Berkeley, hosted a gathering in her backyard where friends came dressed as medieval "knights and ladies" and engaged in competitive combat. According to Paxson, "everyone was more or less transformed" that night and the event felt "incredibly real."[1] After the tournament the group of twenty-four formed a costumed procession and marched down to Telegraph Avenue and back. As Paxson explained, "It's the thing to do in Berkeley, protest—we were protesting the 20th century."[2] And so the Society for Creative Anachronism (SCA) was formed, a group that now boasts thirty thousand paying members whose collective goal is to relive the "current Middle Ages," to experience the Middle Ages as they "should have been."[3] Members recreate the past by choosing a fictional persona who lived between 476 and 1600 in Western Europe. By selecting the attractive parts of a bygone era—chivalry or magnificent clothing—and incorporating them into their modern lives, SCA members continue to protest the present.

The SCA is officially a "non-profit educational organization dedicated to researching and recreating the customs, combats and courtesy of the Middle Ages."[4] Members volunteer their time and invest much money in their fighting and camping gear and costume, so the events must be appealing and comfortable. The biggest annual gathering is a two-week battle held at a campground in Slippery Rock, Pennsylvania, called the Pennsic Wars. In 2011 almost twelve thousand people attended the event. The SCA's website explicitly states that the campground is equipped with bathrooms—showers and flush toilets—and with shops selling ice, food, and drinks; a food court; and laundry facilities. Everyone at Pennsic must be in costume—called "garb" by the society, for here, as in every SCA event, there are no spectators, only participants. Some people consider playing in this "game"—as it is often called—akin to being in a theater production, but unlike a play, with the SCA there is no stage, no script, and no audience. Costumed participants operate in the arena, choosing to enter and exit their assumed personae, passing in and out of historical engagement and accuracy. Entertainment and amusement, however, are central goals for most of the group's members. Patrick O'Connell, in his book *The Knights Next Door,* refers to Pennsic as "a camping version of a costumed fraternity party," a "medieval-themed spring break."[5]

Historical accuracy and amusement seem to be contradictory pulls for those in the SCA. Eleanor Ide, writing as Lady Alura the Twinn, in her article "How to Get What You Want Out of the S.C.A.," observes that there are "two major factions" in the group—the "Authenticity Mavins" and the "Fun Mavins"—implying that people can be authentic or they can have fun, but still the two connect even if they are difficult to reconcile.[6] This unresolved tension, along with the name of the group, allows for acceptable inauthenticity, or *anachronism,* since this is a voluntary hobby, not a job. Being in the SCA is a personal investment of time and money, and having fun is a major goal, but for some people their personal pleasure is derived precisely from the fact that accurate costumes are made, worn, admired, and ultimately rewarded with official recognition.

For each of the groups of historical reenactors discussed in this book there is some sort of a guidebook, a set of recommendations about dress, accessories, and behavior. For the SCA it is *The Known World Handbook,* a 250-page volume with instructive articles about the society, how to choose a persona, and how to make your own clothes and armor, among other pieces of useful information. (There are two other SCA publications: the unofficial and out-of-print guide, *The Pleasure Book,* and the pamphlet "A New Members' Guide to the Society for Creative Anachronism," which is given to new participants.) A do-it-yourself attitude prevails in the society. The handbook describes, as the SCA's website does, exactly how to make a T-shaped tunic and assures you that "with a minimum of sewing skills and a lot of imagination" you can create your own garb.[7] An article on the uses of clothing patterns tells the novice that "some sewing knowledge is helpful but, with a little time, even beginning sewers can make period-looking garb in which they would feel comfortable at a society event"—comfort, I believe, being defined as both historically passable and physically bearable.[8]

At all SCA events, including the few I attended, most people look comfortable. Participants are asked only to make "a reasonable attempt" at historical accuracy, wearing clothes they made following the handbook instructions. The majority of the participants wear some version of a T-shaped tunic, what is called the "workhorse garb of the SCA,"[9] because it can suit, with slight modifications, both male and female personae who lived anytime between 600 and 1200. Looking better than others, therefore, can become a private goal, and many people strive to meet a personal standard of excellence and authenticity within the loose and flexible frame of the SCA, which allows for diversity of quality. The SCA merely requests that its members "capture the spirit of medieval Europe." In a group defined by the premise of "creative anachronism," some members choose to express their creativity by *not being anachronistic,* by wearing and making historically authentic garb, constrained by the chosen persona, and appropriate within the hierarchal rules for clothing within the SCA.

Sarah Lash as Sybil Sevenoak and P. J. Schultz as Don Michael St. Christian. Constellation Academy of Defense of the Shire of Mynydd of the Midrealm, Bloomington, Indiana, 2009.

Many members pass through developmental stages: the longer they are in the SCA, the more time and commitment they have invested in the organization, the higher their personal standards of authenticity, and therefore the better their costumes become. Sarah Lash, a young academic originally from California, who now lives in Wisconsin, began in 1998 as a patron of the Renaissance Faire.[10] She quickly learned that attending the fair in costume was more fun, so she bought herself a long chemise and a bodice from one of the vendors. When she got a summer job at a Renn Faire in California in 2004, a committee charged with approving the costume of every employee rejected Sarah's entire outfit, forcing her to make modifications and new purchases; what was good enough for a visitor to wear was not authentic enough for an employee. Years later she joined the SCA, where there is no costume inspection committee. As Sarah said, "There is no one to check. The standards for authenticity are lower at the SCA than they were at the fair." In the SCA she retained a Renaissance persona, partly because she loves the costume of the period between 1515 and 1545—bodices, skirts, pearls, snoods, flat caps—and partly because of its aesthetic fit: "I have picked a period that is very flattering on my body type." Sarah went from being an employee at the Renaissance Faire to enjoying her created persona, Sybil Sevenoak, transforming herself from a "Renaissance wench" to a "middle, upper-middle-class Elizabethan lady."

In a span of ten years Sarah's costume progressed from a visitor's purchased set of garments, to a Renn Faire employee's uniform approved by the commercial venue's board, to a self-monitored wardrobe of authentic garb in a society that condones and encourages anachronism. In March 2008 Sarah attended an event in the Midrealm, the Midwestern kingdom of the SCA. The event commemorated the coronation of Sarah's friends, Lutr and Tessa. She made herself a fitted velvet gown with "ermine" (white rabbit fur) trim. She used Ninya Mikhaila and Jane Malcolm-Davies's book, *The Tudor Tailor,* as her guide, taking the pattern for the "Fitted English Gown" from pages 78–79, and substituting the plain sleeves from page 77. The motivation for authenticity was internal: to look good, to honor her friends who were being crowned the new king and queen, and to push herself artistically by constructing an accurate set of garments.

Part of the fun of playing a persona is the opportunity to wear, and also make, your own garb, as Sarah did. In contemporary American culture few people are taught crafts, few young people know how to make things with their hands, including how to sew. I was told repeatedly that gaining the ability to make your own clothing is one of the pleasures of the SCA. Jarett Diamond, at the time of my interview with him in 2009, was a medical device engineer who worked in a "corporate atmosphere," which, as he explained, "is not a place where personality shines. I'm creative, and I'm a critical thinker."[11] The SCA allowed him an outlet for the expression of his artistic abilities. As Miguel de Santiago, his Spanish Renaissance persona, Jarett found the SCA to be a site where his skill was honed and valued:

> This is a place where I can actually create something with my hands, a beautiful thing, and bring it to somebody and say, "Hey, look at this thing I made," and most likely there will be an appreciation for it.
>
> Or I can wear this thing I made, and someone will come up to me and ask, "How did you make that?" or, "What is your source and documentation?" and you start a conversation this way.
>
> This is not something you really see in everyday life too much.

Many members of the SCA follow an evolutionary path. They begin by relishing the pleasure of making and wearing a garment of their own creation, as Jarett did. Then their commitment and standards change, and they often commission or buy a more authentic and professional set of clothes. At this stage the pleasure of wearing a beautifully crafted item takes over. Appreciation shifts from one's own amateur creativity to the excellent, professional products of others, as Jarett described in a narrative of the moment when he abandoned his objection to buying "fancy garb."

> It changed at Pennsic War. A couple of years ago I walked into a store— there is a very famous tailor by the name of José. Yes, and he stopped selling. He put all the rest of his work on consignment at another shop. I walked in and I found this doublet.
>
> So I saw this doublet, and it looked about my size. And I put it on. It had this beautiful brocade under-doublet which I put on. And I put it on and something happened.
>
> I felt stronger. I stood up straighter. I felt a more self-assured bearing just come upon me.
>
> And I said, "I need to have this." Because it made me feel like a million dollars in gold. Just the way it felt on my body. And that was—I've never experienced anything quite like that before. This was made by a master tailor. And it turned out that it was actually his. And it turns out that actually he and I are very similar sized. So I bought it.

Jarett Diamond as Miguel de Santiago. Constellation Academy of Defense of the Shire of Mynydd of the Midrealm, Bloomington, Indiana, 2009.

Jarett told me that a few months later he had gained a few pounds and the doublet "did not fit quite as well," prompting him to lose the weight, because he owed it to himself—and to the garment—to look good in it. Jarett initially joined the SCA to practice his fencing and combat skills, yet he developed a reciprocal relationship with the clothing, learning of its power to transform the self, to become a marker of personal identity. The costume gives Jarett license to be artistic and creative, to escape the corporate, scientific frame of his work life.

The SCA is founded in a realm of imagination and romance, and adventure, and bold acts of chivalry. Some of the more flamboyant aspects of my personality certainly come out.

I feel—when I put on my garb—I feel empowered. I'm constructing the fun and the adventure of the period as I imagine it, certainly not as it may or may not have existed at the time. That's an important part of making it real for me, looking around and seeing people taking time and effort into their appearance.

One's garb is linked to one's SCA persona, and sometimes the association can become overwhelming. P. J. Schultz, through his Renaissance persona, Don Michael St. Christian, wears elegant sea captain coats, two of which he said are "super well-known."[12] During a long interview, P. J. repeatedly told me that his persona had become so huge that it was a burden: "My SCA identity is actually so large, it's bigger than I am. Sometimes whether I want to be Michael or not, I have to be." P. J. continued, saying, "My persona is one hundred percent my clothes." He pointed to a stuffed squirrel a girlfriend had dressed for him and declared, "My identity is so caught up in my clothing that you can dress a squirrel up and it still looks like me."

Michael St. Christian was a sea captain, twenty-one years old at the time of the Spanish Armada in 1588. Since the SCA does not allow a persona to have been either a historical or a known fictional character, P. J. loosely based his creation on Sir Francis Drake, hero to the English, pirate to the Spanish. "I mimic the romantic notion behind who he was," P. J. said. "The idea that he was truly just a sea adventurer. A pirate in every other nation but his own." In choosing his garb, as in choosing his daily clothing, P. J. likes to stand apart from the crowd, to be well dressed and stylish. He chose to model his outfits in line with Drake's reputation: "I wanted a pirate persona because I wanted an excuse to take my clothing in that direction." Some of the garments Michael St. Christian wears are "identical" to what Drake would have worn, such as a doublet and an under-doublet, with a particular style of pants. The pirate character allows P. J. to move freely within his persona's time period. He explained, "I'm English, but I travel. If I'm rich, I have my own tailor, and I have seen the world." Since his persona has his own tailor, P. J. has collaborated with master tailor José to create his famous black sea captain's coat. He designs his clothes by mixing and matching styles, rationalizing that a traveling pirate would have been able to do the same: "My clothing does not appear in history *specifically,* but all the parts of it do." The length of P. J.'s famous coat, for example, is not documentable until 1601, and most of his clothes look like they are from the seventeenth century, stretching the limit of the SCA cutoff date.

P. J. stands out among the thousands of other SCA members who wear simple T-shaped tunics. By being slightly out of the time frame, by wearing well-tailored clothes, and by designing his own garb, P. J. has crafted for himself a unique personal style. He studied paintings and photographs of historic clothing, lifting ideas from different sources, and "created a style around them." He explained to me that his black coat has a collar from Spain, cuffs from England, and yet the basic cut is Russian, making it a unique garment crafted by the master tailor José for approximately eight hundred dollars. Civil War reenactors, P. J. said, have a greater "purchasing presence"—many sutlers and outlets supply them with authentic gear and uniforms. Those in the SCA must be more resourceful and inventive, engaging in their own research and setting their own standards for accuracy and personal flair. P. J. moved from the usual reenactors' "ten foot rule"—things must look accurate from ten feet away—to complete precision: "I have the right jewelry. I have the right way to tie my socks. I have the right type of way that I garter over garter. I have all kinds of things that just make it perfect."

SEWING THE GARB

This "perfect" costume reflects both its wearer, P. J., and his tailor, Master José, for the two enter into a creative collaboration. Carolyn Jenkinson is an expert seamstress, but unlike José, she does not make clothes professionally. In her early twenties at the time of our interview, Carolyn had been sewing since she was in high school.[13] In college she directed and acted in plays; she also took classes in theater costume and modern pattern drafting. She defines herself like this: "I consider myself a seamstress first, and then more of a historian and an artist." In 2014 Carolyn will enter the graduate program in Design Studies at the University of Wisconsin, specializing in the study of textile. Her initial draw to the SCA was the costumes. She chose for herself a fourteenth-century French persona, Ysabel Verdelet, and wears gorgeous kirtle and *cotehaire* inner and outer garb, sleek and elegant, with buttons all the way up the torso and along the long, tight sleeves.

Carolyn's exceptional dress must be set in the context of thousands of other amateur costumes. "Eighty percent of people do not dress period," she explained. "They just throw on a T-shaped tunic, and they do their thing. Twenty to ten percent really try and look good. And you really can tell. One of these people walks by, and you're like 'Wow!'" Carolyn is young and has not yet moved up through the SCA ranks, achievable through competitive combat, or demonstrated excellence in a period craft or service to the society. But her professional garb makes her stand out: "I feel like because of what I'm wearing I automatically look so important. I look so much more important than my status in the society really is, because I can really make these things." In an organization of thirty thousand

Carolyn Jenkinson
as Ysabel Verdelet.
Bloomington,
Indiana, 2009.

people, in which most make their own garb, wearing a well-crafted outfit bespeaks dedication, vision, and talent. But it can also indicate social networks and achieved social status. Many people, Carolyn included, do not make clothing for sale, but they will construct garb for close friends. Carolyn observed that "the better you look, the more you know somebody who is really good" at making clothes. Social responsibility extends to serving the elected king and queen, who will occupy their positions for six months. The vision of a king in jeans and a T-shaped tunic would be unacceptable, Carolyn told me: "It would be scandalous to see a king and queen on the throne in something less than outstanding. If that king and queen stepped up and had no money and no garb, the populace would make them garb, they would donate, just so we have the image of a gorgeous king and queen."

Because of its particular historical orientation, the SCA is a social organization in which prowess and chivalry are rewarded, where study and craft are publicly acknowledged, where people meet and work to form a community. Accuracy and history are judged as they pertain to the forty-five-year history of the organization, and not necessarily to the one-thousand-year history that the SCA has set for its frame. Carolyn observed, "It is not about the history; it's about the social elements." The history recounted by SCA reenactors whenever they gather for talk or song is that of the SCA. The personae the members select lead no life beyond their invention, but past encounters at Pennsic and memories of events within the society make for rich topics of discussion. Sarah Lash analyzed the ballads of the SCA and found that the episodes the bards commemorate in song celebrate the society and its members, not the historical events of long ago.[14] That is also generally the case with the costumes; most clothing adheres to a vocabulary that is specific to the SCA, due to the factors of convenience, cost, environment, and comfort. In the article titled "Basic Costuming" in the *Known World Handbook,* the author says of a particular modification to a sleeve, "It's not in period, actually, but it's most useful."[15]

Carolyn Jenkinson explained that the proper clothing of her time period starts with a white linen, sleeveless shift undergarment, plus two outer layers: a kirtle, an extremely form-fitting dress that laces up the front and has long sleeves, with buttons up the sleeves; and the *cotehaire,* the outermost layer, with short sleeves and buttons up the front so that the long sleeves of the kirtle show beneath the short sleeves of the *cotehaire.* It is beautiful and striking but heavy and hot, and many SCA events take place in the summer. Further, many people can't afford all the layers. So a new garment has been developed, a "heraldic *cotehaire,*" which, as Carolyn said, meshes all three garments—the shift, the kirtle, and the outer garment—into one. She said that actually a long-sleeved garment (kirtle) should always be worn underneath the buttoned garment (*cotehaire*); one would never see a long-sleeved garment that also had buttons up the front. But according to Carolyn, this has become the "staple fourteenth-century SCA dress: long sleeve with buttons down the front and buttons on the sleeve, all in one dress." The dress, like the ballads, communicates to its members a shared history of the society. It speaks about the internal bond these people have chosen to forge with one another, not about the history of Europe between 600 and 1600.

While many members of the SCA feel it is their duty to criticize an inauthentic costume, to teach the wearer to attend to history, Carolyn and other seamstresses I spoke with are more forgiving about the do-it-yourself attempts at garb, perhaps because they understand the passion and commitment—and difficulty—of making clothes. Carolyn has seen the wide range of garb that exists within the society and believes people need to be tolerant. "I've seen so many people crushed going to an event. They've made something, and they don't know; costuming is not their thing," she said. "So they've made this dress, and they're really proud of themselves for making it, and somebody is all, 'Oh, that's not period.' That's a shitty thing to do. People do this for fun."

The pair of individual goals—fun or accuracy—organize things socially. Some people are in the SCA for fun, for exercise, and to develop skills in combat. For this segment of the society, amateur or inauthentic garb might be a way to signal that they are *not* in it for the clothes; beautiful or accurate clothing is not an important desire. But for others, joining the SCA awakens the pleasure of wearing and, eventually, making or designing clothes, as Sarah Lash, Jarett Diamond, and P. J. Schultz have done. For others still, like Carolyn Jenkinson and Aimee Formo, their participation in the SCA enables them to perfect their sewing skills. For the tailor and seamstress the SCA provides an artistic venue for creation, a place to display personal talent and garner praise for excellence.

Aimee Rose Formo accepts commissions for clothing from members of the SCA. When she was four years old, her grandmother taught her to sew. By the age of six she already knew how to use a sewing machine. At the time of my interview with her, she was living in Indiana and pursuing a master's degree in history, but earlier she had joined the SCA when she attended Randolph Macon Women's College in Virginia.[16] While in college Aimee worked at Thomas Jefferson's Monticello. Her sewing skills and interest in history led her to join the SCA in 2005—taking on the persona of a fifteenth-century Spanish woman she named Ysabel de la Zarza—in order to perfect the craft of making historical garments: "I saw the SCA as a way to sort of force myself to become more historically accurate with my clothing construction." She holds high personal standards of excellence and believes she will never realize the degree of accuracy she strives for. "The more historically accurate you get, and the more involved in the SCA you get, I think, the more, just desperate you are for one hundred percent historical accuracy," she said. "You can never actually get there. But you try. Like, every year I think, 'I'm just going to throw out my old garb, get new garb, start over,' because some of it just isn't up to par anymore. But I never do."

She uses period materials—silk, linen, wool—and cuts her cloth using patterns from Simplicity, Rocking Horse Farm, and *Tudor Tailor*. Although Aimee uses a sewing machine for the internal stitching, she uses hand stitching for all the parts that will show. She makes her own eyelets, and she is currently taking bobbin lace classes to be able to make her own trim. Still, Aimee acknowledges that there is some "cheating" involved in the SCA, that some level of compromise will always be present: "It is cheating, but to some extent, I am okay with it in the context of the SCA. We all have busy lives. If I were going to be that involved, I would start by making the fabric, and I would never be able to go to an SCA event for six or seven years, because I'd be busy knitting and weaving fabric, dyeing, sewing."

Aimee sees compromise in the SCA as a necessary consequence of limited time and money. She gives her customers a choice of machine- or hand-sewing, explaining to them the difference in cost and completion time. Being so knowledgeable about fabric and construction, she has a subtle understanding of authentic garb: "If store-bought buttons were available then, maybe they would have bought it if they could afford it. So it's a departure from accuracy in object, but I don't think it's a departure in attitude of construction."

THE "MAGIC MOMENT"

I asked Aimee—a trained historian, currently on the staff of a historic house museum—if she thought costume enables the wearer to travel in time. She said that wearing costume is an active way to experience another era: "It's like theater rather than attempting to time travel. And the only difference is that you are actually involved in the theater instead of just watching it." I asked if, while wearing period dress at an SCA event, she was able to transport herself in time, to achieve "the magic moment." Her response was frank and sensitive: "I am a little skeptical of the magic moment itself. It seems polite to me to keep up the illusion for everyone else." Many historic reenactors yearn for the "magic moment," an intense feeling of authenticity, of being momentarily transported in time and space.

P. J. Schultz described for me one of these fantastical moments that, although he experienced it twenty years ago, remained vivid in his memory: "I think that that particular war, that particular site, when all those guys go in motion, and the dust rises up, and everything that's real isn't in your vision anymore. This moment could truly be in the Middle Ages—it was awesome!" Lady Alura the Twinn describes in *The Known World Handbook* her own magic moment as a novice SCA member: "During a feast, when the glow of candles soften the hard edges of reality, during court, when the ceremonial language and beautiful garb make everything seem special, I can become, for a moment, the person I am pretending to be, the person the mundane world won't let me be."[17]

The magic moment for SCA members—and for Civil War reenactors, as we will see in the next chapter—is often induced by visual cues: accurate clothing and weapons, a particular configuration of people, and environmental factors. For a visually oriented person like Aimee Formo, it is not the inaccuracy of cut or trim or sewing of garb that prevents the prospect of a magic moment, but the scene of the entire ensemble, the anachronistic mix of time periods and cultures that the SCA encompasses. "My biggest moment of 'Wait a minute,'" she said, "is always the fact that on the left is a guy in a toga, on the right there is a geisha, and I'm wearing Elizabethan garb. And I'm married to a Viking who wears Elizabethan garb because he wants to match me."

SCA events take place in public parks or high school auditoriums and gyms. The Europe of medieval times is recreated in the United States, usually in a rented facility, mainly in the summer months. Regardless of the accuracy of the material culture, the surrounding location will never be right. In Civil War reenacting the events often take place on the actual battlefield where the war was fought 150 ago, in the same season and with similar weather. At historic sites such as Colonial Williamsburg, Jamestown, or Plimoth Plantation, the setting, the buildings, and the roads are real (or fastidiously recreated). Accurate clothing helps the visitor and the wearer move into the past, but clothing is not the sole vehicle of transportation. Compromise is basic to the SCA, for reality is not what the members are after. They aim for an impression, "a reasonable attempt" at the past, in order to enjoy fantasy in the present, "these current Middle Ages." In Aimee's opinion the SCA "is historically accurate—at least somewhat."

THE SOCIETY AND A SENSE OF COMMUNITY

Authenticity and accuracy are defined differently within the SCA, depending on social and personal factors and on the motivation of the players. One function the SCA fulfills is that of sociability, of the formation of community. Within the larger national organization there are varying scales of social union: kingdoms, principalities, baronies, shires, guilds, households. Details of the garb—colors, heraldry—signal allegiance to one or more of these units. While everybody is "presumed to be minor nobility," there are achievable goals based on fighting prowess, skill in arts and crafts, and service to the organization. Earned SCA ranks—kings and queens, knights, squires, laurels, pelicans—are also indicated by clothing: color of belt; wreath, crown, or coronets upon the head; medallion or embroidered patch upon the garb. There are no external judges policing the accuracy of the costumes (as there are in Colonial Williamsburg, for example), and there are no spectators or bystanders (as there are in Civil War reenactments and at historic museums). All judgments—reprimand or praise—within the SCA are internal. One may choose to dress according to a period or to throw on a simple tunic. Authentic garb is not a requirement, and it is not essential to social functions, to camaraderie, physical exercise, feasting, dancing, and having fun.

In addition to the social function of community building, the SCA serves personal desires for pleasure, beauty, creativity, and pride. An individual might make her own garb and receive praise for it; she might experience a magic moment, engage in an exciting mental journey to another time and place. The society provides a venue for the validation of one's identity. The SCA started in the 1960s, in the period of the civil rights movement and heightened awareness of ethnic and racial diversity within the United States, and the organization—with its focus on Western Europe—permits its members to celebrate their heritage. As Carolyn Jenkinson said, "Most people in the SCA are Caucasians, of European ancestry. So it's like, 'This is the cool part of our history.' For most people in the SCA that's the coolest thing about their heritage." The SCA allows its members to reconnect to the lands, customs, and history of their ancestors, recreating Europe on American soil. This is unlike societies for recreation in Europe—Spain, the United Kingdom, Sweden—where access to the specific geographic area where events occurred and the continent's relevant (archeological) material culture makes for more direct and intimate historical reenactments.[18]

The SCA provides an outlet for creativity, aesthetic delight, and psychological release, achieved partly through the mandatory donning of historic garb. For some it offers the only chance to express a suppressed version of themselves. "In the SCA . . . we try to recreate ourselves as we should have been, in a fantasy world where nobility, honor, and courtesy are the ideals of everyone. . . . The SCA lets us play at being our best selves, the selves we could be in a perfect, fantasy world, perhaps the selves we really are and never dare to show." These are the words of Lady Alura the Twinn of *The Known World Handbook*. In the SCA one can escape the confines of daily life during costumed events. She continues: "SCA members don't like to use the phrase 'the real world.' The SCA is the real world. That other place where we have to live between events is only the mundane world, the everyday, dull world where nothing we do means anything, where they don't let us be heroes, where we can't be the people we really are."[19]

The internal personal motivation is dependent on a social motivation, for one can express this truer version of oneself only within the communal context of an SCA event, with other members present. I asked Sarah Lash if she believes that some members of the SCA are, like Civil War reenactors, driven by a sense of living history. Laughing, she responded:

> We're more an emphasis on the living, and less on the history.
>
> There is a lot of historical interest; there is a lot of history that goes on, but we're—I think in general—we're more interested in making it livable. Making compromises. Making it so that we can just be, really, a different version of ourselves. We're not versions of a historical person.
>
> I mean, there's a few people who really play persona. There's a few, maybe one percent of the SCA, actually play their persona. And the rest are playing their modern Middle Ages persona. We call it "these *current* Middle Ages." And that's who most people are playing.

SCA members escape the mundane world to enter a fictional space where personal achievement and a fictitious persona are performed and celebrated. The SCA is a recreation society, not a reenactment.[20] Members strive to live the Middle Ages as they should have been, not as they were.

4

REENACTMENT

Reliving the American Civil War

FIFTY THOUSAND PEOPLE, MOST OF THEM MEN, REENACT THE events of the American Civil War in locations across the country. Some interpret the life of a common soldier; others assume the persona of a famous general. All of them yearn to experience a piece of American history, and many also take on an educational task, since all the events occur on public ground before an amassed audience. Reenactors and self-defined living historians, these people are not interested in enacting a fictional European persona as the SCA players are, but they aim to impersonate actual military heroes on both sides of a divided United States in the nineteenth century.

I met Wayne Brunson at the Turning and Burning Festival in Gillsville, Georgia.[1] Amid booths selling handmade crafts—pottery, baskets, quilts—his stand displayed a hand-painted sign reading, "Civil War Life / Just Talk / Nothing for Sale." Brunson, an Alabama man who travels to Georgia's public schools to demonstrate aspects of the life of a Civil War soldier, usually dresses in a Union uniform, despite having several Confederate ancestors. He has been a Civil War reenactor for more than twenty years, but he also spent time in the SCA, so he was able to compare the two activities for me. He began by telling me, "Civil War reenacting is trying to recreate the past and present it in a way that the public can see and visualize how things were in 1860s." The SCA, he told me, is a private organization whose main activities take place in restricted spaces for an audience composed solely of SCA members. He admitted that the SCA "has contributed greatly to the knowledge of how life was in Renaissance and medieval time periods." But Civil War reenacting, according to Wayne, is more interactive: "It's more hands-on, it's more public. We're out here on display for the public. Most people don't know—at Civil War reenactment events soldiers pay to get in too.

We pay to be the attraction at a Civil War event. Some people do it for the fun of dressing up as a soldier, shooting at other folks. Other folks do it for the sense of history that it gives you, and your interaction with the public." Civil War reenactors are on display in the presence of a discerning public, the uniforms, weapons, and accoutrements must look real, because, as Wayne said, "what the public sees is supposed to be nothing but what is authentic."

Reenacting groups, like military units, are under the command of a particular individual—a private, colonel, general—who acts as the leader. There is an annual membership fee (thirty dollars or so) to offset the costs of insurance. The fee that reenactors pay to participate at events subsidizes the cost of the medical staff and the water and ice that the military park provides to the hobby soldiers, sometimes swelling to tens of thousands. Money raised at reenactments can also support the preservation efforts of the battlefield.[2] Reenactment venues require participants to sign a consent form or waiver, and to register for participation. The registration form usually includes information about the appropriate attire, containing some version of the following: "All uniforms, including footwear and equipment, must be of proper period materials and construction" or "All re-enactor clothing, uniforms, accessories and accoutrements must be of the appropriate style, cut, construction, and fit of the 1860s era."[3] Some venues,

Union soldiers on the march at the reenactment of the Battle of Gettysburg.
Gettysburg, Pennsylvania, 2010.

particularly those on major battlefields, have stricter rules of authenticity. For
the 125th anniversary reenactment of the Battle of Gettysburg in Pennsylvania,
for example, the official regulations stressed tight standards: "Shoes and boots

Confederate soldiers on the march at the reenactment of the first Battle of Bull Run.
Manassas, Virginia, 2011.

must be of period style and construction. . . . Footwear is one item which has been allowed to slide in the past but will be closely monitored at Gettysburg." The regulation guidelines continue with an official call for authenticity in the camps: "Anachronisms are forbidden from view of the authentic camps and on the field. . . . Proper period dress must be observed at all times in the encampment."[4] Maryland's Antietam National Battlefield Park Military Living History Uniform Guidelines provide friendly advice to its reenactors: "So, when buying, remember that fabric, cut, and construction are all important to achieve a proper period look." Yet the park is strict about its regulations: "Unless it is absolutely necessary for you to function, we discourage the use of glasses. If glasses must be worn, they must be of midnineteenth century style. No modern metal or plastic frames. No exceptions!"[5] These rules are unlike those of the Society for Creative Anachronism. Here inauthenticity is not tolerated, and there is usually a person or committee charged with inspecting and approving the accuracy of uniforms and weapons on the battlefields. Some concessions are necessary, of course. At the sesquicentennial of the first battle of the Civil War, in Manassas, Virginia, in July 2011, we were promised the "sights, the sounds and the smells of the battle as only our forebears in the quiet communities of Prince William County could have otherwise experienced 150 years ago," yet we were told that "the only accommodations made to the history of the battle are to modern safety considerations for reenactors, spectators and due to the limitations of the site itself."[6]

The SCA's *Known World Handbook* explains the rules of the game, recounting the history of the organization and providing instructions on how to make your own garb. The details of the American Civil War are available in thousands of history books. Reenactors' handbooks inform participants about specific uniforms and weapons and often where to buy them. The situation is unlike the SCA in that garments and weapons are generally not made by their users. They are available in abundance from commercial suppliers, and there are a host of published guides to assure authenticity. *Uniforms of the Civil War: An Illustrated Guide for Historians, Collectors, and Reenactors,* by Robin Smith and Ron Field, efficiently organizes photographs of the uniforms and of men in uniform—the Union Army by infantry, cavalry, artillery, generals, special units, zouaves, and militia units, and the uniforms of the Confederate Army by state. R. Lee Hadden, a veteran living historian, has written a step-by-step guide titled *Reliving the Civil War: A Reenactor's Handbook,* in which he stresses, unequivocally, "Reenactment is a re-creation of an actual historical event that is both representative and historically correct."[7]

ACCURACY

The historically accurate uniform does more than comply with official battlefield regulations; it does more than follow the rules in the handbook for reenactors. It responds to internal motivations for authenticity, signals respect for the hardships and deaths of the hundreds of thousands of men who fought, and is unofficially monitored by those in the reenactor's immediate social circle who are apt to apply the negative term "farb" to anyone who is not attired in historically accurate clothing.[8] (There are many explanations for the term; two of my favorites hold that it derives from "far be it from me to criticize" or from "fast and ruthless buying."[9]) The reenactors in Tony Horwitz's *Confederates in the Attic* use the word "farb" for "reenactors who approached the past with a lack of verisimilitude," people who were observed "wearing a wrist-watch, smoking cigarettes, smearing oneself with sunblock or insect repellent—or worst of all, fake blood."[10] The opposite of "farb" is "hard-core," the term for a reenactor whose uniform, look, and speech patterns are as real as possible. A hard-core reenactor eats hardtack and semi-rotted meat and sleeps on the ground—all for an authenticity of experience, for the "period rush."[11] The hard-core reenactors contrast with the "motel militia," those who spend the night, comfortably, in an air-conditioned hotel room and come to the battlefield only for fights.[12] Whether one is a farb, hard-core, or a member of the motel militia is an in-group judgment, which can build into peer pressure to stay within an acceptable range of authenticity. Reenactors include individuals who are self-appointed monitors of accuracy. Mark LaPointe, a Union reenactor from Massachusetts, described these people to me:

Union Army reenactor Mark LaPointe. Bloomington, Indiana, 2010.

> Some are so into it that it's almost crazy. We call them "Stitch Nazis." They come and tell you that your uniform is wrong. They are just pompous enough that they can say things that sometimes are not necessary.
>
> But then I also look at them and say, "Well, you're fifty pounds overweight, and you're about thirty years too old for doing this, so if you are that interested in historical accuracy, you should probably be home, or doing something else, because you don't fit either."[13]

The clothing and accoutrements for reenacting the Civil War are expensive, and given the degree of internal and external pressure for accuracy (including that of body type[14]), most beginners borrow gear until they are committed enough to make a serious financial investment. Mark LaPointe, who has reenacted with both the Twenty-eighth Massachusetts and the Nineteenth Indiana regiments, told me that fifteen hundred dollars is the average cost for the basic uniform: coat, shirt, pants, hat, musket, "leather" (belt, cartridge box, cap pouch, haversack), canteen, and tent.[15] Individual reenactors must research their own uniforms, learning the history of the particular styles of their regiment by looking at photographs, extant garments in museums, and by relying on the expertise of sutlers and quartermaster retail stores. In the town of Gettysburg, Pennsylvania, the Regimental Quartermaster is a place where one can purchase every piece of necessary gear: weapons (muskets, pistols, bayonets, swords, and scabbards), tinware, canteens, leather goods, and the uniforms of both armies—hats, hat brass, hat insignia, shirts, vests, trousers (infantry and mounted), great coats, Union jackets, Confederate wool shells, footwear, and accessories. The owner of the store, George Lomas, told me he can outfit anyone, from novice to expert, from private to general, and that the uniforms are now machine-stitched because the handmade ones have become too expensive. Similarly, the store Abraham's Lady, a few doors from the Regimental Quartermaster, supplies women's Civil War–era clothing and accessories, selling readymade dresses as well as custom-ordered ones made from their selection of heirloom fabrics, buttons, and dress patterns. They also provide a "Personal Shopper Service" to their customers. The proprietor, Donna Abraham, owns an extensive collection of period garments and *carte de visite*, featuring photographs of people she calls "real Americans," and has published a two-volume book called *The Way They Were: Dressed in 1860–1865*. Her sales associate Elizabeth Atkins, a trained historian, shares expert advice on the authenticity of garments and accessories. The shop provides its customers with a catalog containing instructions on how to dress accurately and "How to Avoid 'Farbiness.'" I noticed that both Abraham's Lady and the Regimental Quartermaster had booths on the sutlers' row at the Gettysburg and Manassas reenactment events during the summers of 2010 and 2011.

IMPERSONATING GENERALS

Many of the men I spoke with began this pastime by reenacting as privates and then moved to portraying generals. This seems to be a natural progression in (reenactor) rank based on age and level of experience. I was told several times that reenacting battles is a "young man's hobby" because of the physical exertion required by drills, marching, running, and charging while wearing a hot wool uniform and carrying bulky gear and heavy weapons. After years of reenacting battles, some dedicated people ease into the role of living historian, engaging in active education and direct communication with the public, explaining life in the 1860s, and describing (and interpreting) the tactics and strategies of the generals they portray.

Dressing as a famous general can be both easier and more difficult than playing a private. Much information is available on specific generals—including photographs and preserved uniforms—but the audience is also more knowledgeable about these men of history, so errors of accuracy are easy to detect. The

Niles Clark as Confederate major general George Pickett at the reenactment of the first Battle of Bull Run. Manassas, Virginia, 2011.

Dwight Hensley as Confederate major general Richard Garnett at the reenactment of the first Battle of Bull Run. Manassas, Virginia, 2011.

amount of historical data on particular Civil War generals varies, and there is a wide range of accuracy on display. Dwight Hensley, for example, portrays Confederate major general Richard Garnett. I asked Dwight, when we spoke in the shade of Major General George E. Pickett's tent in Manassas, about his specific uniform choices.[16] He told me that General Garnett once commanded the Stonewall Brigade; he had served with General Thomas Jonathan "Stonewall" Jackson and was killed at Gettysburg. The photograph of General Garnett in the history books, according to Dwight, is actually a photo of his cousin, so Dwight has had to guess what Garnett looked like. He created his persona by essentializing the style of that period—long hair and a beard—and deducing that Garnett would have worn the standard issue uniform because he was "a twenty-year military man, a veteran soldier." In Virginia, while depicting the first Battle of Bull Run of 1861, Dwight wore his blue uniform, leftover from Garnett's days as a U.S. Army officer, and at the reenactment of the Battle of Gettysburg of 1863, he wore the gray Confederate uniform that Garnett would have had by then.

The uniform Niles Clark wears to impersonate General Pickett also reflects changes in the life and rank of his persona, the "dandy" and flamboyant Virginia officer. Niles explained that Pickett's attraction to "frills," including the embroidered French knot, or "chicken guts," on the sleeve, made him a shooting target during battle.[17] "But when he got shot at Gaines Mill, he knew why," Niles said. "It's because of all the braid. So he decided to go more subdued. So he had a design around the cuff only, instead of going up the sleeve. So they always look for the one with a lot of the braid—to shoot at." Niles told me that his different coats track George Pickett's escalating rank, a coded way of communicating the officer's particular standing at each battle. He said that a major general's coat has two rows of three sets of three buttons, for a total of nine per side, eighteen in total; the brigadier general has two rows of four sets of two buttons, for a total of sixteen, eight on each side.[18] A lieutenant general will also have the same number of buttons, but the actual buttons will be in the drooped eagle design. Niles's understanding exemplifies the kind of research living historians do to get their uniforms right and to impart knowledge to the assembled crowd, many of them military men and women, detectable by the T-shirts, sweatshirts, baseball caps, and pins they wear. Living historians and spectators alike proudly communicate their military affiliation.

Dwight Hensley knows little about General Garnett; Niles Clark knows much more about General Pickett, and continuing on this line we come to Jay Vogel, who has amassed a tremendous amount of information on Confederate lieutenant general James "Pete" Longstreet, which he uses to perfect his impersonation

Jay Vogel as Confederate general James Kemper at the reenactment of the Battle of Gettysburg. Gettysburg, Pennsylvania, 2010.

of the famous Georgia officer.[19] There are no existing uniforms worn by General Longstreet; they were burned in a house fire, Jay said. But by colorizing photographs of the general, Jay was able to get a sense of the hue of the wool, even though he admits having to "take some leniency on certain things." Jay follows

Bonnie and Frank Orlando as Mary Custis Lee and Confederate general Robert E. Lee. Gettysburg National Military Park Visitor Center, Gettysburg, Pennsylvania, 2010.

the military regulations of the time, wearing the standard blue trousers with two gold stripes down the side, and he wears a frock coat, though Longstreet preferred a tunic coat, a frock coat with a shorter skirt. But Jay could not find a pattern for it, so he wears the standard frock coat, inaccurate for Longstreet but accurate for Longstreet's rank. Jay knows the exact measurements of the man he portrays and is proud of the similarity of his build to Longstreet's. According to Jay, Longstreet was six foot two and weighed 200 pounds; Jay is six foot one and weighs 198 pounds, and he has grown a full beard like Longstreet's. To perfect his impersonation, Jay has gone beyond appearances and obtained Longstreet's curriculum at West Point and has read all the books the general read. As an amateur historian, Jay relies on his research skills to approximate the clothing and personality of the general. He said to me, "I can't be General Longstreet. I know that. All I am really doing is interpreting history. Everything I am presenting is based on *fact,* on actual documentation of the period."

Like Jay Vogel, Frank Orlando relies on his own extensive research to interpret Confederate general Robert E. Lee, arguably the most beloved figure in the American Civil War.[20] Those who are reenacting common soldiers must rely on generalized knowledge, but there is a vast bibliography on General Lee, and Frank has read many historical books and biographical sketches, because, as he told me, "In order to do this, you have to understand the human being. I don't think a day goes by when I'm not reading two books on Robert E. Lee."[21] Frank and his wife, Bonnie, who interprets Mary Custis Lee, are both deeply committed to accuracy. "We refuse—we refuse to walk around here and be inaccurate, historically," Frank said. "Because we're doing the tourists here an injustice. We're doing ourselves an injustice as well. Because if we want to get into the persona, into the character, then—and think like them—then we have to look like them as well." When Frank and Bonnie appear before the public at Gettysburg National Military Park, they are also transporting themselves back in time: "When we put this clothing on, you know, we feel like we get to immerse ourselves in the 1860s."

Jay Vogel's body measurements are similar to those of General Longstreet, and Frank Orlando told me that Robert E. Lee was five foot eleven and weighed 170 pounds, exactly Frank's own height and weight. He said that General Lee was "a very fastidious dresser; very specific. He didn't wear all the gold braid on the arms and everything. He wore a colonel's uniform; he didn't wear a general's uniform. He thought the highest rank he ever earned was as a colonel in the United States Army. So that's what he chose to wear." General Lee, according to Frank, wore a particular shade of wool called "cadet gray," a color closer to blue than "Confederate gray." After five months of searching for the right seamstress, Frank settled on someone he thought could guide him toward authenticity. She helped him order the wool fabric from the same factory in Richmond, Virginia, that made General Lee's original uniform during the Civil War. The fabric had to be custom made, and it took six months, but Frank believes that "it was well worth the wait, so now, when I walk, when I do impressions of Lee, I know that what I'm wearing is historically accurate." Frank's attention to detail extends to the muffin buttons—Virginia state, not Confederate States of America—and to accessories as well. "I also have a belt, presentation belt, that is accurate," he said. "It's an exact copy of the one that Robert E. Lee wore; it was made by a gentleman—a leather maker—in Arkansas. And then the belt buckle was actually cast from Robert E. Lee's belt buckle, at the Museum of the Confederacy, in Richmond, Virginia. So you try to be as accurate as you possibly can."

PERSONAL IDENTITY THROUGH REENACTMENT

Accuracy—whether as precise as Frank Orlando's or as generalized as Dwight Hensley's—enhances the experience of the visitor; it also aids the reenactor in his quest to ground himself firmly in his character, often serving a psychological function. Many of the men I spoke with are proud of their resemblance to a historic figure. John Schlotter is "a spitting image" of General John Hartranft. Niles Clark has been endorsed by the George Pickett Society and makes appearances at the general's gravesite to commemorate the anniversary of his death. Jay Vogel looks like General Longstreet, although he resembles Tom Berenger, the actor who portrayed Longstreet in the film *Gettysburg*, more than he does the real Georgia general.[22]

Looking like a famous general can help the living historian find his "calling," help him achieve his "mission." Mike Sipes's story captures the experience.[23] Mike was in Memories Past, a sutler shop in Gettysburg, being fitted for his Maryland cavalry reenactor's uniform, when Robert E. Lee impersonator Phil Carpenter approached him and told him he looked like Confederate lieutenant general Jubal A. Early. Phil went to his car, brought out a frock coat, asked Mike to put it on, and showed Mike a portrait of Early, "and there is a lady standing behind me. And she looked over my shoulder, looked at the picture, looked at me, and, 'May I have your autograph? No, may I take your picture?' I says, 'Yes, ma'am, you may.'" Mike was surprised by the resemblance, saying, "God works in mysterious ways." Then, years later, on Remembrance Day, Mike dressed as General Early to accompany Phil Carpenter as General Lee to a ball. At a restaurant in Gettysburg, while Mike waited outside for Phil to join him, he had his second moment of personal revelation.

> I walked outside. There were three Confederate soldiers standing there.
> And they had their backs turned to me.

Mike Sipes as Confederate lieutenant general Jubal A. Early at the reenactment of the Battle of Gettysburg. Gettysburg, Pennsylvania, 2010.

And they were all facing away from me. When the door opened, it made a creak sound, and they naturally turned to see who had come out. As soon as they did, I stood there. It's nighttime now. The lights are on. And the soldiers immediately came to attention, said, "Good evening, General Early"—just by looking at me. I had no idea who they were. They had no idea who I was. But they recognized me as General Early.

At that point I realized I was on a mission. I was on a mission.

So, time being what it is, that was my calling. That was my calling. Time being what it is, I had to give up my Second Maryland. Because really, I didn't want to be out there. I wanted to be here.

By "here" he meant among the generals who are living historians, not out there among the privates in battle.

Many living historians heed the personal call to devote a considerable amount of time and money to achieve an accurate look by acquiring detailed historical information. The challenge is to look like the real person, and to think as he would have thought, in order to accomplish an accurate impression. As Robert E. Lee impersonator Frank Orlando explained:

> I cannot throw a different slant on history just because I'm thinking from 2010 and I have access to all the different strategies that Robert Lee did not. There's so much conjecture involved in history. So you just have to say what Robert E. Lee would have said, what he would have thought. He wasn't a complicated human being. We have a tendency to complicate iconic people.

By looking just like him, and also by thinking like the leader of the Army of Northern Virginia, Frank humanizes a historical figure, entering the persona from the outside, just as theater actors do who follow the Stanislavski method: starting with the clothes, the weapons, the mannerisms, and then moving into the psychology. Living historian Kent Courtney calls this "method reenacting."[24] The result is an amalgamation of the actor with the historical persona, and Frank Orlando reflected: "It gets to the point where I have a difficult time differentiating between Robert E. Lee and myself. You know, it almost meshes. And so that makes it quite interesting."

THE PERSONAL JOURNEY BACK IN TIME

Accuracy of uniform can welcome the reenactor into the life and thoughts of his persona and can carry him back in time, perhaps to experience a "magic moment," that fleeting, intense feeling of being dropped into another era, a rare instant that relies on authenticity.[25] Union private Mark LaPointe, like many reenactors, has experienced some spiritual moments on the battlegrounds where thousands of men died and where their ghosts might remain. In Gettysburg, at McPherson's Woods, Mark and his friends saw lights that responded to the sound of their voices, and at Little Round Top they smelled tobacco smoke. Mark told me, "These spirits are drawn to you, perhaps because you look familiar. You're wearing a uniform that they relate to. They think that you are a comrade, so they are coming up to say hello." The way reenactors look can enhance the experience of visitors to the battlefield; it can even fool the ghosts of slain soldiers. But visible anachronisms can prevent the magic moment for the visually oriented reenactor like Mark LaPointe. When I asked him if he had ever had a magic moment, he said,

> Yes. Absolutely. What works best for me is to not actually see what is going on. They call it taking a hit, when you decide to be killed now. I always fall face-first, 'cause it's safe. But then I just listen. I close my eyes and I listen to everything—all the gunfire, the cannons, the horses, the people screaming, the bugles going. And that, for me, it transports me back, more so than looking.

I asked if visual stimuli contributed to the transportation, and Mark replied:

> Not so much anymore. Because you look down the line, the visual line, and you realize that half the people who are doing it don't belong there, because they're too old, or too fat, or they just don't fit. They don't have the right stuff on. They're just—it just doesn't look right to me. It sounds more accurate to lie down on the ground and just listen.
>
> And to me, really, I can't imagine what it would've been like, because if you are down, you are either wounded or you are dead. But I can hear, so I'm wounded. And I can lie there, in the heat, dying, listening to what is going on, asking for help perhaps, and people are just running by, no one is paying attention. And you're just thinking, "This is how I'm going to go, this is it. I'm never going to see my home again, my family, my wife, my kids." Whatever it might be. You can really put yourself into that, what that must have been like.
>
> So, for me, that's how I get my buzz, as they say.

Achieving the magic moment in Civil War reenacting is often a deep and meaningful experience precisely because one is transported into a real situation—not to a fictional fantasy land, but to a gruesome time of war, death, and civil unrest.[26] For some reenactors who are military veterans, the journey through history to a war of the past can return them to their own combat experience. Jay Vogel, the reenactor who impersonates General Longstreet, said that with special permission from the National Military Park, he and others have been able to retrace the steps of Pickett's Charge on July 3, the anniversary of the famous Confederate march when more than ten thousand Civil War soldiers were killed or wounded. "Once we cross Emerson's Pike," Jay said, "we know what's happening to the men at this time. They are starting to come under musketry fire." The group gets quiet while they walk, somber in light of the real lives that were lost here. "As we

Jay Vogel as Confederate lieutenant general James "Pete" Longstreet at the reenactment of the first Battle of Bull Run. Manassas, Virginia, 2011.

cross, it's like a total release of emotion happens," he added. During the charge Jay uses history to connect to his own military experience, channeling the feelings of those doomed soldiers: "For me, it brings back memories of my past in the military. That's when I truly understand what is going on." He told me that when he was in the Marine Corps, he lost four friends in Beirut, and he is reminded of that time during reenactment. Pickett's Charge "carries extra emotion" when Jay recalls his own losses, and he limits how often he seeks the experience. "I can only handle doing that so often," he said. "I do it about once every two years now. If I need it any more—emotionally—I would. I couldn't probably handle it. It's emotionally draining." Far from being an exciting endeavor for the seeker of thrills—as some SCA magic moments can be—these episodes in Civil War re-enacting are profoundly moving because of the reality of the circumstances and because of personal ties to dead ancestors, as is the case for Jay: "I had relatives that fought on both sides of this war. Both got wounded on the Peach Orchard on the same day. Ties me back to the past, my family."

CAMARADERIE

Reenacting the Civil War gives thousands of American men a feeling of historical involvement, teaching them about their country's past and the struggles of their ancestors. But in reenactment there are social consequences as well as personal ones. Like members of the SCA, Civil War reenactors build communities among themselves, using the excuse of historical war to camp, drill, sleep, and eat together, to interact, sharing information and joining together through their interest in the past. Several of the men I spoke with specifically said they value reenactment for its camaraderie. For Jim Opdenaker, who impersonates Union general William Tecumseh Sherman, this is an opportunity to spend quality time with his family: his wife, Chris, interprets women's fashion of the period; one daughter, Rachael, demonstrates Civil War–era children's games; and his oldest daughter, Hannah, portrays Tillie Pierce, a fifteen-year-old girl who wrote the book *At Gettysburg; or, What a Girl Saw and Heard at the Battle*.[27] Jim said, "That kind of makes it a whole family thing for us. For me, it's a family thing first. As long as they are happy, I'm happy."[28] For others it is an opportunity to bond with their male friends and fellow veterans, as exemplified by John Schlotter, who portrays Union general John F. Hartranft: "My buddy—we're both retired army—he convinced me to join up." A native of Pennsylvania, John is currently the postmaster for Gettysburg (coincidently, General Hartranft was the postmaster for Philadelphia). When I asked him why he reenacts, he laughed and responded, "That's a good question. It's funny. We get together, we have a good time, you know, talking war stories. And I never, really, had an interest in Civil War history. I did have an interest in history. So I'm learning as I go."

Camaraderie, sociability, personal pleasure, and self-education are among the reasons why these men spend thousands of dollars and hundreds of hours in hot wool uniforms on battlefields, portraying the men who fought and died in the American Civil War. But there are other purposes for Civil War reenacting, social functions that are dependent on achieving an authentic persona and accurate interpretation: heritage, ideology, and education. All three of these motives run throughout this book, but they are particularly poignant among Civil War reenactors.

One way to express heritage is through the choice of a unit in the Union or Confederate army. Mark LaPointe, who is originally from Amesbury, Massachusetts, would never impersonate a Confederate soldier. For Mark, reenacting on the Union side is partly about connecting to his regional heritage. "I have always been drawn to the North," he said. "Maybe it's my roots too. I'm from the North. That's where I grew up. So I can relate to the history, the people that lived there at the time, and I can get to know their stories. You know, my heritage is Northern." Mark told me that personal history, a direct connection to ancestors and family, "has never been a driving force" for him; he is "drawn to the time period" and the particular history. He continued, "I'm a huge Abraham Lincoln fan, so I think it would be a disservice to his memory to fight for the Confederacy. They were doing what they felt was right for them. I don't believe or condone slavery in any way, and I'd hope to think that if I were alive during that time period, I would also feel that way."[29]

For others heritage is about a direct connection to one's ancestors. Niles Clark, who portrays Confederate major general Pickett, is from Indiana, but he has "on my dad's side, forty-nine Confederates; three Union on my mom's side." Dwight Hensley, who portrays Confederate general Richard Garnett, likewise, is from Indiana. Dwight started reenacting as a Union private with the Nineteenth Indiana Brigade and said, "I did Yankee for about ten years, and that was to pay tribute to my mom's side of the family, who is from Kentucky. They fought at Lookout Mountain, Chattanooga, Tennessee, for the Yankees." But his father's side is from North Carolina, and they fought with the Gallan's Brigade, "in the cornfield portion of the Battle of Sharpsburg, or Antietam. And five of them went into the battle and none of them walked out. And all for state's rights. They were fighting because they thought that the U.S. government was taking their rights away, and they were." Impersonating Confederate general Garnett at reenactment events enables Dwight to connect to the patriotic ideology of his ancestors and his current family as well.

> Soldiers nowadays are willing to give their lives and actually die for the Constitution and our freedoms. I know when I went in, I almost died in the army. I would have been more than glad to die for my country. Consider it an honor—to die for my country.
>
> My ancestors, they fought for the country too. All the way from the Revolutionary War, all the way to now. My nephew just got back from Afghanistan, fighting over there. My family is still fighting in wars. That's the way they did back then.

Confederate lieutenant general Jubal Early is portrayed by the pleasant, chatty, and extroverted Mike Sipes. Mike is originally from Maryland but now lives in Hanover, Pennsylvania, twelve miles from Gettysburg, where I first met him. For Mike, as for Dwight Hensley, the Civil War provides a way to connect to his ancestors and through their impersonation to act on a personal political ideology. When he was a child, a trip to the battlefield of Gettysburg "spurred" him on to want to learn about history. He eventually found an ancestor, Nicholas Owens, who had fought in the Confederate Second Maryland Battalion. He discovered other ancestors, from North and South Carolina, and so "to honor my ancestors' heritage, I joined the Sons of Confederate Veterans, the Maryland division." He found a unit in Baltimore that portrayed the Second Maryland Cavalry (dismounted) and joined in. He enjoyed the activities: "I was making smoke. I was doing a lot of yelling and screaming. And I was honoring my ancestors at the same time: Second Maryland Cavalry."

Three years ago Mike was asked to become a member of the group of living historians called Lee's Lieutenants, under the command of Al Stone, who interprets General Lee. In the group, Mike portrays Jubal Early alongside Jay Vogel's James Longstreet, Niles Clark's George Pickett, and Dwight Hensley's Richard Garnett. For Mike, being a living historian enables him to interact with the public throughout the reenactment events, and he is usually found in the area where the horses are tethered, laughing and joking with visitors in the shade of the trees. He told me how satisfying it is to be able to teach about history for its connections to the present:

> There are certain things that need to be pointed out. There is so much of a parallel with 1861 and 2010. So much of a parallel going on, in fact. When you change history, it becomes a lie. And there are so many lies lately. The fact that I don't have the opportunity, or am able to, openly, openly, honor my ancestors, and the flags of my father, really hurts me. As an American.

Many of the men I spoke with—especially at the anniversary of the Battle of Gettysburg in 2010 and at the sesquicentennial of the Battle of Bull Run at Manassas in 2011—lamented that they could not openly express their true sentiments. I was told that the "politically correct" climate of today prevents the celebration of the Confederacy, its flag and ideology.[30] This is, in fact, a driving force for many Civil War reenactors: to use history as a way to criticize what they perceive to be the growing power of an expanding central government. It is one reason to don the authentic uniform. As Mike Sipes says, "When people come to

Members of the Twenty-first Georgia Volunteer Infantry at the reenactment of the first Battle of Bull Run. Mark Sloane is second from the right. Manassas, Virginia, 2011.

me and they say, 'Why, how do you put on a wool uniform, stand out in ninety-five degree weather?' I go, 'This is why. History needs to be taught.'"

Mike is one of many living historians who volunteer their time, money, and expertise in the belief that history is not properly taught. Their aim is to impart an alternative view, shedding light on the past and on the present state of society, politics, government, and civil responsibility. Ideology, in fact, often trumps regional affiliation. Most of the men I met who impersonate Confederate generals were actually Northerners. Mark Sloane, a reenactor I met during the military parade at Manassas, referred to himself as "Southern at heart."[31] Originally from Pennsylvania, Mark read voraciously about the Civil War, and the more he learned, the more he was "drawn to the Southern side." In a long follow-up email message to me, he wrote:

> In most cases the South were vastly outnumbered in men, arms, and supplies. Yet being led by General Lee, Jackson, Hood, Longstreet and others, the army of Northern Va. won battle after battle. So the South went into the battles as so to speak underdogs, not a chance in hell as to pulling off a victory. Yet they came out victorious.
>
> So that's what draws my inward being to the South. Plus the uniforms were many times what their wives and sweethearts made for them. The Militias were well dressed and by 1862 most of the men had a shell jacket or coat of sack cloth. I like the many styles of uniforms the South wore.[32]

Mark Sloane's motivation is ideological, but the uniform is also a draw. He told me that many of the men who portray Confederates are Northerners like himself. He first became a member of the Tenth Pennsylvania Reserves but then immediately joined the Fifth Virginia, which is made up of men from south-central Pennsylvania. Mark also joined the Eighth Georgia, whose members are from southeastern Pennsylvania, as well as the Fifth Texas, whose men are also from south central Pennsylvania. And during the parade in Manassas, Mark was with the Twenty-first Georgia, made up of men from New York. As he wrote in his email to me, "So many Southern units are portrayed by guys who live in the North. On the other hand, you will find very few guys from a Southern state portraying a Union soldier. They mostly will dress Confederate. Still a lot of ill feelings about the war even though it was 150 years ago." Mark has observed that many of the Southern reenactors he knows are "die hard Rebs. Not many will wear the Blue."[33]

Donning the uniform—whether gray or blue—can materialize an ideology during a forceful act of engagement with history that enables interaction with other, like-minded fellows, as it is for Mark Sloane and thousands of other reenactors. In closing, Mark wrote:

> Personally I am proud to wear both uniforms, Union and Confederate. We were all Americans fighting for what they believed in. Most of the North fought to preserve the Union. As on the other hand most of the fellows of the South fought for their State. Believing in State rights. Believing in fighting for their towns and homes. They were tired of being taxed higher and higher and the industrial North was getting richer and richer while the agriculture-based South was getting poorer and poorer.

LIVING HISTORIANS AND EDUCATORS

Costumes—in this case the uniforms of Civil War reenactors—develop, like all varieties of material culture, out of diverse, mixed motivations. They can be used as part of an ideological rhetoric, and they can express a personal admiration for a particular individual and the values he or she embodied. This is the case for Frank Orlando, who admires the leadership skills of his persona, Robert E. Lee. Through his impersonation he hopes to "impress upon people—today's people—how important duty was to the people of the 1850s and 1860s." Frank feels a double responsibility—one for truth and accuracy to the visitor, the other for honesty to the memory of General Lee: "I wouldn't want to slight Robert E. Lee by doing something in public—you know, he is not with us anymore; Robert E. Lee died in 1870—that he would be ashamed of." Frank, a retired schoolteacher from Pennsylvania, admires General Lee as a religious and moral man, a loyal and loving husband, and a much admired leader who sent out specific orders to his men not to rape, pillage, plunder, or steal while in the North. According to Frank and many others, the Southern leaders were more charismatic, chivalrous, and ultimately more interesting men to portray at living history demonstrations.

The same historical individual can be both admired and reviled by current living historians and used as a vehicle for an expression of the reenactor's philosophy. Recall Mark LaPointe's reverence for President Abraham Lincoln and his affiliation with the Union Army as a reflection of his loyalty to the memory of Lincoln. But at the same time, Jay Vogel, a man from Minnesota who portrays Confederate general Longstreet, finds President Lincoln to have been "quite an evil tyrant as far as I am concerned, because he violated the Constitution." Niles Clark, an Indiana man who portrays Confederate general Pickett, feels the need to educate those around him about Abraham Lincoln, who is viewed—erroneously, according to him—as "God's gift" to humanity, "until the truth came out;

then the real Lincoln" was revealed. Niles sees his mission as educating those around him. "See, there's truths out there," he said. "People will look for them, and that's the main thing about learning anything—you got to look for the truth. You can't just take what someone has written or put in a movie for granted. We search. And I read." And he works to educate the visitors as one of Lee's Lieutenants, encamped at the living history village on the battlefield, sitting in front of his tent, alongside generals Lee, Longstreet, Jackson, and Early, and President Jefferson Davis, talking to thousands of visitors who want to learn about their country's history.

Ultimately the goal of most living historians is education: of the self and of others. Like actors on the theater stage, a topic we will examine later in this book, living historians must go beyond perfecting a look: acquiring the right clothing, accessories, and mannerisms. They must learn about the people they are portraying—their values, attitudes, and worldviews. Members of the Society for Creative Anachronism, and many theater actors, portray fictional characters, but Civil War reenactors, because they represent real people and historical facts, feel they are doing the real men a disservice if they do not adhere to high standards of accuracy with regard to biography as well as uniform. Many of the living historians with whom I spoke participate in school programs when they are not on the battlefield. Dwight Hensley and Niles Clark participate in School Days— an event mounted for about three to four hundred eighth graders in Montgomery County, Indiana—wishing, according to Dwight, to "try to teach the kids what really happened. And not by some sugarcoated history lesson they learn in school." Talking to students enables these men to offer their angle on history. Niles wears the uniform of Major General Pickett at the event, telling "the Southern side of the story" in this Northern state, to "fix what they are learning wrong."

For adult visitors to the battlefield, Niles Clark and Dwight Hensley, dressed as Confederate generals, argue that the federal government was taking away states' rights that the Constitution granted, so Lincoln's actions were in violation of what the Constitution guaranteed each state. In talking to me, without regard to my political beliefs, the two men extended their analysis to the present day. Niles said, "We can even look at the powers that be now. They're trying to undermine the Constitution. It's our rights being taken away. And that's not what we formed this country for." Dwight chimed in: "It's not what Lincoln died for. It's not what the Yankees died for. None of that. 'Cause nowadays, they're still trying to tramp on the constitutional rights to this day. It might not be an outright battle, warlike. The war is still going on." Wearing uniforms of the Civil War era and talking to visitors about the nineteenth century is a way to comment on the current situation. Contemporary men dressed as the officers of the Civil War can pass judgment on the Obama administration while speaking ostensibly about Abraham Lincoln's presidency.

Every year Niles Clark tells the Confederate version of the Civil War by enacting a famous general for grade school students. Wayne Brunson visits public school classrooms in Georgia and Alabama, interpreting the common soldier, focusing on daily life, believing as he said, "You need to portray more the common, average, than the extreme." He owns both Confederate and Union uniforms, but "ninety percent of the time, when I do reenacting, I do it dressed in blue" for the Southern schoolchildren he visits. He does not adopt a persona, nor does he speak in the first person. He prefers "just talking to folks. Showing them what I have. Showing them how I dress. What men wore. How they lived their lives." Although all of Wayne's ancestors fought in the Confederate Army, he does not believe in the "mystique" of the "lost cause." He takes a broader view of the war, one he tries to impart to the students he visits. "But for us, as Americans," he said, "the American Civil War brought us together, [and] drove us apart, but it made us what we are today." By portraying a common soldier, Wayne does not emphasize the causes and consequences of the war, and he explicitly wants to provide education, not political ideology:

> I really keep the politics out, but you can't do this hobby without having a very clear understanding of some of the causes of the war. And even though I don't discuss it, really, unless I'm asked, and even if I'm asked, I'm not a reincarnated Confederate soldier. I understand how they lived. I try to understand their politics.

Education through reenactment happens in the classroom, and it happens at battlefields, museums, and private Civil War events, where thousands of people gather for a chance to discuss the war and the politics of the 1860s with the (impersonated) key players. Soldiers engaged in skirmishes appear at a great remove from the spectators and do not interact with the public, but the living historians, on both the Union and the Confederate sides, are available for long chats. They are clustered in two groups: the Union officers and politicians of the Federal Generals Corps, and the Confederate leaders portrayed by Lee's Lieutenants. These men look like historical figures—in appearance and in uniform—and they are able to engage visitors in conversations about history. They serve as educators, augmenting the facts taught in schools and gently correcting misconceptions derived from popular media, from films like *Gettysburg* and *Gone with the Wind,* both of which were based on fictional books—Michael Shaara's novel *The Killer*

Jim Opdenaker as Union general William Tecumseh Sherman, with
wife, Chris, and daughter Rachael, at the reenactment of the first
Battle of Bull Run. Manassas, Virginia, 2011.

Angels and Margaret Mitchell's *Gone with the Wind*—popular
works that have fed attitudes of affection for General Lee and hatred for General Sherman.[34]

   If Robert E. Lee is the most beloved figure in the American
Civil War, Union general William Tecumseh Sherman might be
the most despised. That is an educational challenge that Jim Opdenaker, an illustrator and painter from Lancaster County, Pennsylvania, has taken upon himself. At Manassas I stood with Jim
when a visitor, a self-identified member of the Sons of Confederate Veterans, came up to speak with him at the reenactment of
the first Battle of Bull Run.[35] This is how the first phase of this—
and I imagine many other interactions—sounded:

> "I'm Colonel Sherman, and I have my family here with me."
>
> "Oh. You're Colonel Sherman. The hero of the South."
>
> "That's right."
>
> "You done a good job."
>
> "Oh, thank you. I appreciate it."
>
> "I mean, you killed everybody that got in your way."
>
> "No, that's not true."
>
> "Most of them."
>
> "No, that's not true either."
>
> "You killed a bunch of them."
>
> "Nah. What do you consider a bunch?"
>
> "Everybody who was there."

   At this point Jim patiently began, "You know what? I'll tell you what . . . ," and
he told of the burning of Atlanta, of the famous March to the Sea, of Sherman's
admirers among Confederate generals. Jim began by speaking in the third person, then segued into the first person, speaking as General Sherman. (Although
Sherman was a colonel during the first battle of Bull Run, Jim spoke in the past

tense about the burning of Atlanta, and he carried Sherman into the future.) At the end of their five-minute interaction, both men were laughing. The visitor acknowledged, "You hear all kinds of stories," and if you live in Atlanta or Savannah or anywhere in Georgia, "you hear it differently." He said he got all his information from books, "written by people who are smarter than I am. So I can only go by what I read; the written word." Jim, a persistent teacher, warned him: "But even the written word. You don't know what side. Are they pushing an agenda? Do they want to add fuel to the fire? You know, there's a pun for you."

Holding to the facts was a consistent theme in my interview with Jim Opdenaker. He believes that the living historian should not use a historical persona to further his own political agenda. "I've always had an issue with this," he said. "Because I'm listening to you, not the general, and it's hard to separate the two, because you don't know one and you're trying to do it through another, and that's the problem I have. But to push any kind of agenda, I think, is wrong." The teacher at the Civil War site, Jim said, should not argue from twenty-first-century attitudes, because no matter how much you study, "You will never know how they *truly* felt. You'll never know deep inside." You can gather facts, but ultimately you are interpreting the actions of someone else.

Jim started as a reenactor, a private in the Bucktails unit of Pennsylvania. He was then approached by a man who impersonated General Ulysses S. Grant and asked Jim to portray Grant's chief of staff, John Rawlins, inspired by the strong physical resemblance between Jim and Rawlins. When the Federal Generals Corps needed a Sherman, because "everyone knows who he is," and asked Jim to portray General Sherman, he was reluctant. If Sherman was such a bad person, he told me, who would want to be him? But he read about Sherman's youth and upbringing, his family and war record, and he learned much: "Wait a minute, there's another side. This guy, he's not like everybody portrays. Some of the things are, but a lot of them aren't." Jim accepted the chance to counter conventional stereotypical history by talking to people directly, for, as he says, General Sherman is more hated now than he was during the Civil War:

> You say his name now, and the first thing you hear, is "Oh, he's the bad one."
>
> You have to listen to the stories. That's what we do in living history. It gives us a chance to explain, and answer questions, and to interact with the people, as opposed to the regular reenactments where they sit while the troops do what happened on the field, then it's over.
>
> But this gets you a chance to go one on one. We learn stuff from spectators. They learn stuff from us.
>
> But I want to tell them who Sherman was, why did he do this, why did he do that. You say, "This is what happened and this is what didn't happen. And you can judge for yourself." You can walk away and still hate the guy. And that's your prerogative. I don't mind.

Unbiased and informed education is Jim's goal as it is the goal of countless living historians who give their time and energy to relive the American Civil War so that the visitors can appreciate the human dimensions of the war that tore the country apart in the 1860s. Most of the men I spoke with who donned authentic-looking uniforms and taught themselves their persona's biography and combat strategies agree that the main goal of the living historian is public education. And efforts at authenticity of dress have a direct impact on the accomplishment of this pedagogical function. The accurately attired persona becomes a vehicle for instruction. As Jim Opdenaker taught me, "I'm not Sherman, but I portray him. Whatever I can do to help them, teach them something. They can teach me something. We all make out on it. So we learn from the spectators, and they learn from us. It's a win-win for everybody."

LIVING HISTORY

Colonial Williamsburg

F OR THREE-QUARTERS OF A CENTURY, MILLIONS HAVE TRAVELED to Colonial Williamsburg in Tidewater Virginia to behold and interact with men and women dressed in fine eighteenth-century clothing.[1] These costumed interpreters perform on the stage of a colonial town, their embroidered waistcoats, tricorn hats, and wide silk gowns harmonizing with the colors of the brick and clapboarded buildings of Colonial Williamsburg, "the world's largest living history museum." Colonial Williamsburg's personnel, in contrast to the reenactors of the Civil War, must authenticate and replicate a wide array of clothing, dress for soldiers and civilians, women and men, for people of different classes—the gentry, artisans, indentured servants, and enslaved African Americans. With few surviving garments and only a fraction of the documentation that is available for the four years of the Civil War, the reconstructed past at Williamsburg must be meticulously researched and precisely presented through the institution of the museum, where education and authenticity drive the choices of the costumes that are made, worn, and performed.

Williamsburg served as the capital of colonial Virginia for eighty-one years, from 1699 to 1780, when the capital was moved to Richmond. In 1926 philanthropist John D. Rockefeller Jr. founded Colonial Williamsburg, establishing the foundation that oversees among other components the 301-acre Historic Area, with its eighty-eight original buildings from the eighteenth and early nineteenth centuries and its many fastidiously replicated structures. The goal was to bring the town back to the "beauty and charm of 200 years ago."[2] Accuracy was an objective from the museum's inception. Rockefeller wanted more than the restoration and preservation of the past; he wanted the museum to "re-create and interpret colonial life," and "extensive research was undertaken to ensure historical

Duke of Gloucester Street. Colonial Williamsburg, Williamsburg, Virginia, 1978.

accuracy."[3] Scholarly precision was established early on as a goal for Rockefeller's architectural restoration: "As always, the password was authenticity."[4] Employing "a skilled research group," the Colonial Williamsburg Foundation relies on the knowledge of historians, architects, archaeologists, and curators to provide useful information for themselves and for others, including Revolutionary War reenactors. The foundation's official mission is "That the Future May Learn from the Past."[5] Public education is a principal objective and is accomplished through publications, exhibitions, seminars, and workshops at the museums and Historic Area, and through the Institute of Early American History and Culture in collaboration with the College of William and Mary.

The living history museum is based on its architectural assembly, yet clothing plays a vital role for employees and visitors. The mission statement on the foundation's website clearly states that it is the "costumed interpreters" who "tell the stories of the men and women of the 18th-century city."[6] The *Official Guide to Colonial Williamsburg* entices us to come and "see prominent colonial citizens wearing the fashions of the eighteenth century" and tells us, "The thriving Historic Area, with its knowledgeable costumed interpreters, offers an opportunity to step back in time and experience a taste of eighteenth-century life."[7]

The association of Colonial Williamsburg with eighteenth-century costume is so strong that "visitors were horrified" when the foundation outfitted the staff in "red, white, and blue polyester knit suits" during the bicentennial celebrations, for the historical "costumes had become a Williamsburg icon."[8] Orientation interpreter Karen Schlict told me that many visitors complained about the bicentennial uniform partly because modern clothes did not match the backdrop of the restored buildings and thus ruined their tourist photographs. Karen said, frankly, "We're a great photo opportunity."[9] Costuming has been a feature for the whole of Williamsburg's eighty-five-year history, and accurate costumes are now worn by all employees in the Historic Area; 834 people in 1,500 positions display the clothing of the period between 1769 and 1781, with 1774 as the base interpretive year. Unlike SCA players or Civil War reenactors, living historians at Colonial Williamsburg do not have to do their own research, nor do they buy and make their own clothes, since they have available to them a professional team whose job is to study, design, draft, sew, maintain, clean, and supervise the splendid eighteenth-century costumes that seduce the beholder and inspire the wearer.

COSTUME DESIGN AND RESEARCH

Brenda Rosseau, manager of Colonial Williamsburg's Costume Design Center, occupies the central position in the system of historic clothing at the foundation. She has worked there for fifteen years, nine of those as principal designer, a position now occupied by Tom Hammond. Before coming to Williamsburg, Brenda worked for eight years at the Jamestown Settlement, where she faced "totally different challenges" stemming from the lack of original seventeenth-century clothing. "Absolutely nothing survives from that period except archeologically; not even structures," she said. Colonial Williamsburg, with its small collection of extant, though mainly elite garments, poses other kinds of challenges.

The Costume Design Center is an impressive modern building where the fifty-nine thousand articles of clothing owned by the foundation are created, stored, cleaned, and tracked while in circulation at the homes and on the bodies of more than eight hundred employees. The center houses the following units: Accessories, where caps, shoes, scarves, stockings, and jewelry are issued and where shoes are repaired; Laundry Counter, where all garments, except stockings and undergarments, are cleaned or dry-cleaned; Operations, where garments are produced, fitted, altered, and maintained; and Research and Design, the unit responsible for costume design and development for the production and archiving of the clothing patterns used at the foundation.

Every item of clothing is owned by the foundation, and each employee is loaned the articles that comprise an "allotment"—the necessary pieces for his

Preston Jones, journeyman silversmith, in the uniform of the Virginia Regiment during the American Revolution. Colonial Williamsburg, Williamsburg, Virginia, 2011.

or her particular costumed position. The generous collection of clothing in the allotment includes all basic garment elements and accessories, including shoes, and multiple versions of some pieces to allow for style variation and cleanliness. Each item carries a bar code that connects it to the employee and tracks its current location at the employee's home, the cleaner's, or the repair shop. Along with their clothing, employees receive the *Colonial Williamsburg Costume Handbook* created by the Costume Design Center. The sixty-eight-page comprehensive guide informs users about costume policies as well as proper wear, care, and terminology; tips on how to adhere to extreme weather conditions (many costumed interpreters work outdoors); and illustrations giving directions about how to put on specific garments and offering options for wear. On page 45, for example, we find eight different styles of arranging a woman's neck scarf, each accompanied by a detailed line drawing. The handbook ends with a three-page bibliography of scholarly sources on eighteenth-century clothing, and employees are encouraged to engage in research about the clothing they wear. Whatever the interpreter's charge, visitors always ask questions about his or her clothing. The last page of the handbook shows a map of Williamsburg and warns interpreters to wear their costumes accurately whenever they are in the Historic Area: "All costumed employees should be wearing their costumes completely and correctly, with all anachronistic articles of clothing or paraphernalia out of sight when inside the bold-line boundaries indicated on the map below." As at Civil War reenactments, anachronisms of all kind are officially shunned, and visually decipherable authenticity is the goal.

For Brenda and her colleagues to outfit the employees of Colonial Williamsburg properly, they must know what was worn by the variety of people who occupied the town more than two centuries ago. Scholarly research is, of course, their primary concern and the main means for the achievement of authenticity.

What interests me is how the professional institutional research at Colonial Williamsburg compares with the amateur research of Civil War reenactors and

Inside the Costume Design Center. Colonial Williamsburg, Williamsburg, Virginia, 2011.

the hobbyists in the SCA. In a long and detailed springtime interview, Brenda Rosseau explained to me the process of adapting an antique garment for use in the Historic Area.[10] Her ideal process is what she calls a "three-pronged approach," in which the foundation owns an original article of clothing, plus a visual depiction of it being worn in an eighteenth-century drawing or painting, plus some written documentary evidence, a diary entry by the wearer or an observation by a beholder. But, Brenda said, this rarely happens: "Unfortunately, what survives is mainly the fine and the small. There is not a whole lot—in fact, there's very little Virginia- or Chesapeake-worn clothing that survives from the period that would be appropriate to the majority of the people that we're outfitting in the Historic Area." The collection of antique costumes held by the museum centers on thirty women's gowns and thirty men's suits, along with complementary secondary apparel and accessories, all dating between 1730 and 1800. Most of these garments are English and cannot be proved to have had any history of actual wear or ownership in colonial Virginia.[11] The natural tendency is to save and donate special and costly garments, so museums—the recipients of these clothes—usually feature the extraordinary clothing of the past, which is the case with most collections of historic dress, including Williamsburg's. Their solution is to "extrapolate downward" from the fine to the everyday. The final result, Brenda observed, is a costumed populace that is "gentry heavy." She elaborated, saying, "Only two to five percent of the population of Colonial Williamsburg would be dressed as we dress them now. And the other people are working—half of them are black and enslaved." Brenda's desire is to "dress everyone down just a little, with the exception of those who are character-interpreters in [the theatrical public program called] 'Revolutionary City.' . . . I would really, really like to push that, but right now we just don't have the time or the funding to do that."

It would be a vast financial undertaking for the foundation to replace thousands of lovely garments to achieve a finer level of historical accuracy. But as the costume historians admit, it is all an extrapolation anyway, since few extant garments remain from the era and the area. Today the museum's costumes not only suit the history of colonial Virginia, but they also reveal the history of Colonial Williamsburg. Brenda said they started dressing people in period clothing in 1934. The first six people to be costumed were female docents in the Raleigh Tavern, and then fine reproductions were made to be worn by the hostess-interpreters at the tavern and at the Governor's Palace.[12] As Brenda explained, "It was a colonial revival town, and there was this romantic idea of old Virginia." At the time of the nation's bicentennial in the 1970s, with the rise of the serious study of American material culture and the stress of the foundation's new curriculum on inclusiveness and social history, the costumes started becoming better researched and more accurate. Brenda also acknowledges the centennial of the American Civil War as an influence on costume studies, saying, "This huge bank of Civil War reenactors who were really, really committed to getting it right, I think that was an influence as well."

An important resource for scholars at Colonial Williamsburg is their collection of antique costumes and textiles held at the DeWitt Wallace Decorative Arts Museum and at the Abby Aldrich Rockefeller Folk Art Museum. The historic artifacts are useful for the staff, especially for the tailors and dressmakers, who examine, measure, and study garment construction, materials, and techniques. Information about eighteenth-century clothing is disseminated to the general public through symposia like "Costume Accessories: Head to Toe" and seminars like "A Reconstructed Visitable Past: Re-created Period Attire at Heritage Sites"; by mounting exhibitions such as "Fashion Accessories from Head to Toe" at the DeWitt Wallace Decorative Arts Museum;[13] and through publications such as Linda Baumgarten's excellent book *What Clothes Reveal: The Language of Clothing in Colonial and Federal America.* Linda Baumgarten is the textile and costume curator at Colonial Williamsburg and works closely with Brenda Rosseau on the costumes worn in the Historic Area. Responsible for the assembly of antiques as well as the study collection of costumes, Linda told me it is her professional responsibility to make available the garments in the collection, with its emphasis on Anglo-American, English, and American traditions—"the forces that shaped clothing here."[14] The study collection, begun in the 1940s,[15] is used by the Colonial Williamsburg staff and many others: scholars, theater directors, Revolutionary War reenactors, and reenactors of the French and Indian War.

Even with dedication to authenticity, concessions must be made at Colonial Williamsburg for practical, personal, and professional reasons. Departures from historical accuracy are permitted, but they must be carefully monitored and approved. Brenda Rosseau and Tom Hammond, the principal designer, along with curator Linda Baumgarten and two members of the Fashion Trades—tailor Mark Hutter and dressmaker Janea Whitacre—sit on the Costume Approval Board, whose aim is to "maintain costume standards."[16] The detailed process of submission to the Approval Board is outlined in the *Costume Handbook:* one must submit the garment or accessory for which one is seeking authorization with adequate documentation linking the item "to the appropriate decades(s) of Williamsburg or Virginia."[17] The handbook explains that the Costume Approval Board is "responsible for approving exceptions" to the dress trends of the various classes of people who inhabited Williamsburg. The board maintains "a low volume of exceptions within the costume program so that the overall costume plan is preserved." Although there is no "policing" of others in the SCA, and Civil War reenactors experience some monitoring at the battlefields and internal pressure not to be a "farb," at Colonial Williamsburg the participants are not hobbyists volunteering their time and efforts, but paid employees and professionals, and the *Costume Handbook* reminds employees, "It must also be acknowledged that in addition to the Colonial Williamsburg Foundation being an educational museum, it is a business that hosts thousands of visitors annually and must maintain acceptable and manageable standards of appearance to uphold the Foundation's mission and professionalism."[18] SCA events are closed to the general public; Civil War reenactments involve the public. But at Williamsburg, museum visitors— paying more than twenty dollars each for a one-day pass—expect a high degree of competency. As the *Costume Handbook* reminds the employees, "Therefore, these guidelines have been established to provide consistency and balance to what our visitors encounter."[19]

The historic costumes worn at Colonial Williamsburg—like all the costumes in this book—are not exact replicas of originals, but adapted versions suited for contemporary wear. The Costume Design Center explicitly states this in its handbook: "It is essential that the costumes balance historical authenticity with the needs of the modern wearer and the business demands of the Foundation."[20] Both Linda and Brenda emphasized that safety and comfort are the main factors that account for departures from historical accuracy. Unlike hobbyists, who wear their costumes occasionally, Colonial Williamsburg interpreters wear their costumes forty hours a week for years on end. These costumes are like an occupational uniform in that they are the required attire for a person's employment. The recreated historic clothes must be comfortable for modern people, allowing for differences in body type, body size, and posture (women are not, for example, trained to wear stays from childhood as they were back then). Brenda told me that these differences in body size and movement are taken into account from the moment an antique costume is adapted for use in the Historic Area: they make a muslin mockup of the antique garment and then modify it to fit the modern body. They also accommodate the wider array of sizes present today. The Costume Design Center, for example, currently has men's coats that range in size from 34 to 62. All the female interpreters are now fitted over stays that are based on an antique model but built on a modern body block to fit the contemporary person.

Safety, like comfort, leads to compromise with authenticity. The foundation must safeguard security not only for the visitor but for the employee as well, in accordance with federal governmental guidelines that ensure occupational safety and health (OSHA). Accessories like eyeglasses or shoes are necessary to secure the well-being of the interpreter (recall that glasses were allowed only if "absolutely necessary" at the Civil War reenactment at Antietam). Safety concessions can interfere with the historical accuracy of the costume. In hobby events where the participants sign waivers, it is not the responsibility of the organizer to ensure their safety. But at places of employment, such as a living history museum, employers are required to protect their employees, even at the cost of visual accuracy. Jamestown provides an example: costumed people reenacting Powhatan Indians skinning deer must wear latex gloves for self-protection, creating an anachronism that is often remarked upon and photographed by visitors.[21]

Safety and comfort are two of the reasons for modification and inaccuracy. The function of the costume is another. The Costume Design Center is in charge of outfitting everyone in the Historic Area but not the workers in the taverns, resorts, or hotels. The restaurant uniforms, according to Brenda, "give you the flavor of Colonial Williamsburg, but they are not necessarily historically accurate." The products division of the foundation provides children's rental costumes at the gift shops. Linda Baumgarten said that although a committee that includes a curator oversees the rental clothes, the historical "parameters are even looser," because the clothes need to be wash-and-wear; they need to be made of synthetic fabrics that do not demand the time, effort, and money that historic costumes do in washing, dry-cleaning, and ironing. Linda said these children's costumes are so compromised in authenticity that they are closer to Halloween costumes than to those worn in the Historic Area, "but there is nothing like that to really grab a kid." Something less than accurate can still arouse the historical imagination. Linda continued, "I see the little kids walking around with their little dresses. The little kid is not thinking, 'Is this machine-stitched?' 'Are the pleats half-inch or one inch for the period?' They are thinking of how they feel within this environment. So I think there are times when you can go further away from that range of authenticity and still really grab a little young scholar, a future scholar, hopefully."

The uniform of the tavern or resort employee is one version of eighteenth-century clothing. Another is the make-believe costume for the visiting child who wants to explore the museum in loosely defined period clothing. But the garments worn by the Historic Trades craftsmen, by the actor-interpreters in "Revolutionary City," and by all the other personnel in the Historic Area are not, according to Brenda, costumes in the Halloween sense. They are devices for interpretation: "Our problem, I think, lies primarily in convincing people that this

The English army during the "Revolutionary City" program. Colonial Williamsburg, Williamsburg, Virginia, 2010.

is an interpretive tool and it's not about them. What's important in this equation, it seems to me, is not their personal expression of self, but of this eighteenth-century prototype." Brenda explained that since clothing is so intimate, it inevitably becomes an extension of the wearer. But, she added, "It's not about them. It's about what they are trying to say about the past." Other examples of costume in this book—during Halloween or festivals, in the SCA or Civil War reenacting, can become vehicles for expressing the self in voluntary and celebratory scenes. But at Colonial Williamsburg the people in costume are professionals whose job is to adhere to the museum's mission. Brenda said, "We are, essentially, a museum and a business. And they have the responsibility to talk to the public and to interpret. It's not Halloween. It's not about their presentation of self; it's about the message." Yet, through interpretation one is able to present deeply held personal values. Colonial Williamsburg allows for the expression of multiple messages, messages that are embedded in its overarching educational mission. So, perhaps surprisingly, leeway of interpretation and personalization of message are achieved by the interpreters, particularly those in the trades and those representing the famous characters of "Revolutionary City."

COSTUMING THE AMERICAN REVOLUTION

In the street theater program "Revolutionary City," actor-interpreters portray people of America on the eve of the Revolution through scripted mini-plays.[22]

Colonial Williamsburg tells the story of the town through its important residents, called "nation builders," the highly identifiable personages of history: George and Martha Washington, Thomas Jefferson, Benedict Arnold, the Marquis de Lafayette, and Patrick Henry, among others. The founding of the nation is depicted by actor-interpreters who perform on the makeshift stages of "Revolutionary City" and who also appear in other venues, where they interact with the visitors, such as in the St. George Tucker House. The attire of these famous individuals is better documented than the clothing of the ordinary Virginians of the time. Paintings and well-preserved original garments exist at Colonial Williamsburg, Monticello, and the Smithsonian Institution, allowing for great accuracy when the costumes are designed. The meticulous costumes become tools of interpretation for the actors. Clothing helps them become historical characters while granting them the freedom to inflect history into their own educational agendas.[23]

During my first visit to Colonial Williamsburg, in the spring of 2010, I photographed a handsome, jaunty officer in a crisp uniform, wig, and plumed chapeau as he rode on the Palace Green in front of the Governor's Palace. The next day I

Mark Schneider as the Marquis de Lafayette at the Palace Green.
Colonial Williamsburg, Williamsburg, Virginia, 2010.

discovered that I had photographed the Marquis de Lafayette, and I got a chance to meet and interview the actor-interpreter Mark Schneider, who has been with Colonial Williamsburg since 1998.[24] Mark portrays several characters in "Revolutionary City," most prominently Mann Page and the Marquis de Lafayette. Beyond Williamsburg he also reenacts Napoleon Bonaparte, interpreting the French military general in the United States as well as Europe. I asked Mark how his costumes aided in his interpretation of historical personages. He said he appreciates the professional, accurate costume, since it helps him "to always be at my best." He is aware that "this is the Colonial Williamsburg Foundation, the largest living history museum in the world. People are coming from all over the world to see us perform. Professionalism is paramount because we are representing Colonial Williamsburg, representing the people from the past, representing the foundation." Actor-interpreters like Mark Schneider, unlike many others at Colonial Williamsburg, play real historical characters (as opposed to generalized characters defined by their occupation), so accuracy of the costume is necessary to achieving a truthful and artful depiction—as it is for the professional stage actors we will meet in the next chapter.

Mark said that since he spends so much of his time being other people (and different characters), the costume has to remind him, viscerally, of who he is portraying, helping him to pull the character from within himself. One venue where the nation builders perform is the Kimball Theatre on Merchants Square, "where you're in front of four hundred people when you do your performances." In acting for such a large audience, Mark said, "I need as much confidence as I can get." By wearing the custom-made garments constructed by the Costume Design Center, "I already have things in my favor that are working to assist me through that costume. 'Cause I know it's right. I know it looks good to the period. That will assist me." Having the Colonial Williamsburg team of professionals behind him—researchers, designers, curators, cutters, drapers, and tailors—gives Mark added assurance. "If it's not done correctly, and accurately," he said, "then that takes awareness from my interpretation, because I *know* it's not correct. So wearing that costume is like armor for me. If it's done correctly, it's going to assist me. I wouldn't have to worry about it. It speaks for itself." As we will see in the next chapter, on theater costume, an actor's clothing can be akin to another character, a "performing partner" who occupies the stage with the actor, filling gaps in the dialogue with meaningful communication about the time period and the specific person being portrayed.

Accurate costumes can help actor-interpreters like Mark Schneider by enhancing their work of historic interpretation. But the costume also aids the actor by taking him into the essence of the character he is portraying. Mark told me that the Marquis de Lafayette was said to be "a statue in search of a pedestal," a man who was "vain and very proud of himself." Mann Page, he said, was "a wealthy gentleman. He liked the best of things, which would include fashion as well. We have some surviving paintings of him, so we know, as a young man, he's looking good." Mark's costumes cannot be patched together by an untrained hand as some SCA garb is, for "these characters are themselves wanting to look good. And I, portraying that character, want to look good as well. Because that's how we need to portray them." Mann Page and the Marquis de Lafayette are real people, like the Civil War generals at battlefield reenactments. Interpretation must adhere to historical fact, especially when the facts demand attractive, refined, and well-made clothing. The period at the end of the eighteenth century and the beginning of the nineteenth, Mark told me, was known as the age of the military tailor, when "soldiers were feeling better, stronger, more confident in themselves because of their uniforms. The same holds true for the costuming I'm given." Portraying military officers and aristocratic gentlemen, Mark, like the historic soldiers, is buttressed by his commanding costume, which aids him in fulfilling his role within the Colonial Williamsburg mission of historical education.

Some "nation builders" are well-known characters such as George Washington or the Marquis de Lafayette. Others are lesser-known figures like Gowan Pamphlet, the "Baptist slave preacher," portrayed by the charismatic James Ingram. One of Mrs. Jane Vobe's slaves, Gowan Pamphlet, worked at her establishment, the King's Arms Tavern, in Williamsburg. James told me that the character he has been portraying for seventeen years was extraordinary because he was literate at a time when only about 20 percent of the population of Virginia could read and write. Baptists, James informed me, were known in the eighteenth century as "pamphleteers," so Gowan took the last name of Pamphlet for himself. He secretly ministered the new religion to his fellow slaves and eventually received his freedom, founding what was later known as the First Baptist Church in Williamsburg, which preceded a white Baptist church by thirty-five years.[25]

James, as Gowan, appears in several venues at Colonial Williamsburg, including the theatrical program "Revolutionary City." He looks dapper in a dove gray waistcoat, soft brown coat, white kerchief around his neck, and black felt hat. At his side he cradles a Bible. James explained, "Baptists only wore certain colors. And it's mainly because of being humbled, humility. The only colors you wore were brown, gray, black. That's it. And no loud colors—not the yellows, reds." The hat also signals his role: "You don't wear the cocked hat, as you can see; you

James Ingram as Baptist preacher Gowan Pamphlet. Colonial Williamsburg, Williamsburg, Virginia, 2010.

wore a rounded hat. And men wore their hats indoors; they didn't take their hats off indoors. Very proper for a dissenting new preacher—Presbyterian, or Baptist, Methodist—to be covered inside." As with Mark Schneider, James Ingram relies on his clothing to help him achieve character. "This costume makes you who you are," he said. "I can just walk down the street, and people will say, 'Oh, good day, preacher.' They don't know who I am. They can just tell by what I wear. The round hat, of course, dead giveaway, 'cause most people would wear a cocked hat. That's the norm, tricorn hat. And also they can see me with the Bible. This is part of my costume."

James's clothes suggest Gowan Pamphlet's identity to his visitors, but his garments can also help him tell the complicated history of slavery. "Costume is more than the material clothing that you wear," James said. He educates visitors by explaining that slaves reflected the status of their owners on their bodies. The governor's slaves would be in silks, the coachmen and footmen in plumed-feather hats, with the owner's colors on their livery and the family crest on their clothing. James said, "Two percent of the population of Virginia owned ninety percent of the wealth and ninety percent of the slaves. You would reflect your owner's wealth by your dress." A nuanced understanding of slavery can be gleaned from interacting with James in his role as Gowan Pamphlet, for he is an articulate, educated, well-dressed man, a sharp contrast to the stereotype of a slave in tattered clothes with ungrammatical speech. The historically appropriate costume aids the Colonial Williamsburg Foundation—through the body of James Ingram—to tell a local piece of African American history.

To assume the character of "nation builders," James Ingram and Mark Schneider are fitted in accurate costumes, but they must also be provided with detailed information about the character they put on with their waistcoats and breeches. James said, "Costume is not just the physical aspect of what you wear, but also the mental, the psychological. That's all part of how you present yourself in public." Every morning James puts on his clothing and his persona: "Once I have taken it on in the morning, I'm always in. I'm always in the eighteenth century." Once in, he can interact with the museum's visitors in the first person, though there are occasional moments when he steps out of character—for example, at special programs in the St. George Tucker House dedicated to "behind the scenes stuff."

SCA members portray fictional characters, so they can rummage through history and invent a persona. Civil War reenactors who portray historical characters, such as politicians or generals, must rely on their own learning. At Colonial Williamsburg the actor-interpreters have a professional team of scholars to direct their research and are encouraged to pursue their own studies as well. As a result, the "nation builders" can go off script during the interactive opportunities that outdoor museums afford the visitor. James told me of a time when Supreme Court justice Sandra Day O'Connor visited Colonial Williamsburg and his ongoing study on Gowan Pamphlet came into play. "I'd just happened to have seen her, out from my peripheral vision, and all of a sudden I started talking about the law," he said.

As in Civil War reenacting, interacting with the audience in an educational setting like Williamsburg is what keeps the costumed interpreters constantly learning and honest about the historical facts. The public educational mission of historic reenactments distinguishes them from many costumed events. The proponents of Swedish folk costume, for example, seek to educate the insiders, those who wear costumes to perform, but pay slight attention to the spectators. The institution of Colonial Williamsburg has established a pedagogical framework; the question is how much leeway the interpreters have in tweaking the foundation's agenda to reflect their own concerns.

In *The New History in an Old Museum,* anthropologists Richard Handler and Eric Gable claim that the higher administration mandates what the interpreters, "the front line," dutifully convey to the visitors. Colonial Williamsburg historian Cary Carson, on the other hand, asserts that the interpreters are free to be creative and imaginative, working within the guiding framework set by the foundation. Colonial Williamsburg, says Carson, is "a classroom"; the staff members are "team teachers"; and the interpreters, in turn, are "little professors."[26] My fieldwork at Colonial Williamsburg supports Carson. I found that interpreters, particularly those in the Historic Trades, connect with the visitors and teach history by utilizing their own knowledge and experience, delivering lessons that derive from a personally constructed curriculum.

The horrifying history of slavery presents a challenge that cannot be met in museums of living history—how does one reenact flogging and rape?—and critics of Williamsburg find it all too easy to locate gaps and flaws in the representation of African American life,[27] but by designating Gowan Pamphlet a "nation builder," the museum brings the topic of slavery to the forefront of its educational agenda.[28] James Ingram told me that as an African American man, he finds it important to portray Gowan Pamphlet in Williamsburg.[29]

> Telling the story of enslaved people allows me to not only tell the story of my own past, but a story of America. But it also is giving a voice to those that didn't have a voice.
>
> We have a real high mission here, this mission to tell this story, because it wasn't a story that they were able to tell. Many of these people did not have an opportunity to write their story down.
>
> And so it's my duty and my mission, every single day, to get up, to go out, to prove to people that this story was a part of the American story.

In the United States, museums take education beyond the classroom, especially for adults. But oftentimes adults have set opinions about the past. We have seen that adult visitors encountering Jim Opdenaker as General Sherman often carry preconceived notions about the general and his campaign in Georgia. Hollywood films like *Gone with the Wind* are among the sources of their preconceptions. Comparably, James Ingram feels that the history of slavery—a history filled with spatial and temporal complications—has been misunderstood, generalized, and homogenized, partly as a result of inaccurate popular renditions, including the film *Gone with the Wind*. James's educational mission is to teach about the complex, nuanced, and troubling institution of slavery by considering the environmental, social, emotional, and economic factors that varied by place and date—for example, the tobacco country of Virginia in the eighteenth century versus the cotton plantations of the Deep South in the nineteenth century.

During the bicentennial the educational mission of the Colonial Williamsburg Foundation expanded to include culture as well as politics, in order to foreground colonial life while following the road to revolution. The 1976 *Official Guide* tells us, "Colonial Williamsburg hopes that visitors will better understand and appreciate the life and some of the aspirations of the men and women of that earlier Williamsburg."[30] And this is where the important role of the interpreted trades—including the makers of clothing—comes in. The Historic Trades are one of the foundation's "Six Appeals," along with architecture, gardens, archaeology, decorative arts, and history.[31] The list of skilled reenactors is long: carpenters and cabinet makers, blacksmiths, silversmiths, gunsmiths, wheelwrights, printers and binders, coopers, shoemakers, basket makers, wig makers, apothecaries, farmers, gardeners, cooks, weavers, tailors, and dressmakers. There are eighty people in Williamsburg's Historic Trades, masters and apprentices, all of them talented, motivated, and dressed appropriately by class, gender, and occupation.

SOCIAL HISTORY THROUGH COSTUME

Williamsburg's current emphasis is on America at the eve of the Revolution, and the culture, lifestyles, and values of ordinary people are usually represented by what they made and wore. Through accurate historical costumes the educational mission of the museum has expanded to include people who are usually less celebrated, including poor folks and women. Terry Thon and Sarah Woodyard, two interpreters of the Historic Trades, offer alternative histories, as James Ingram does, by going beyond the story of the rich and famous characters of history books. Since the early 1980s the foundation has espoused a commitment to the "new social history," what Cary Carson called a "total history" and "everyman's history," a democratic view that all people's lives and cultures are important, an approach through which, Carson wrote, historians "elevate the lowborn to equal prominence with presidents."[32] During the first fifty years of Colonial Williamsburg's existence, the common people served as context for extraordinary citizens. As Carson said, "The 'lives and times' of ordinary people embroidered a variegated and richly detailed background that was needed to lend credibility to those few whom Rockefeller called 'the great patriots.'"[33]

The costumed focus at Colonial Williamsburg is on the beautiful gowns and fine military uniforms, as it is with the Society for Creative Anachronism, where the majority of the people dress as nobility. In *Time Machines* Jay Anderson observes that the SCA "prides itself on recreating the Middle Ages the way it ought to have been; that is, without peasants."[34] But in Civil War reenactment most of the participants represent the common solider, not the fancy generals. The story of underprivileged people is generally missing from history books, and it is usually missing from living history events as well.

Basket maker Terry Thon, among others, sees it as her mission to fill in the gap of historical knowledge by interpreting the life of the "lower-sort people" at Colonial Williamsburg. Terry has worked at Colonial Williamsburg for more than twenty-five years and was the first female coachman at the museum. She originally came for her love of animals and has held several positions at the foundation, ranging from ticket checker to agricultural worker. When I interviewed her in the spring of 2010, she was sitting on a stoop, weaving a white oak splint basket.[35] She wore soft cotton and linen clothing—shift, skirt, apron, cap—all in a soothing palette of ochre, mauve, light blue, and white. She told me she likes talking about baskets as a way to open the topic of social class: the kinds of baskets that poor people used are different from those of the rich. Terry sees her costume as providing an opportunity to discuss social class, as "a door to many things," but also as "a prop" for the visitor, because visitors are often at a loss for appropriate topics that can engage a costumed interpreter, and questions about what they are wearing seem an obvious and easy entry.

Orientation interpreter Karen Schlict told me that the staff "dress and undress in front of the public a lot, in small ways": untying an apron, explaining how the jacket fastens, or showing a corner of the stays. When Terry is making a basket, she keeps a piece of leather on her knee. People often ask her what its purpose is, assuming it is to protect her body from injury. When she tells them it is to protect the apron itself—made from valuable cloth—many visitors are surprised. Terry uses the apron—made by her from fabric vetted by the Costume Approval Board—to discuss the values, "the thrift and the integrity of the eighteenth century," when, unlike today, people "spent hours and hours making clothing."

> It's a great educational opportunity to be able to talk with people about why I'm wearing what I am. I prefer to talk about the lower-sort people, because I really think they get a short shrift here. Everyone likes the beautiful gowns, and I really enjoy the working clothes. They're extremely comfortable. And even in very hot weather, they're nice.

Terry Thon, who demonstrates the basket maker's art. Colonial Williamsburg, Williamsbu Virginia, 2010.

And people are very curious about them. It opens up an opportunity to talk to people about the costumes and about my place in society here. How many people actually wore these, as opposed to the silks and satins and the beautiful gowns.

I just think it's very important to let people know that many, many of our people are the poorest. Just like today—not everyone has a lot of money.

One reason the general public likes to go to historic sites, and even to art museums, is to admire splendor and opulence. George Vanderbilt's home in North Carolina, the Biltmore, or William Randolph Hearst's Southern California estate, Hearst Castle, are places where visitors can marvel at a level of extravagance that seems like a fantasy. At Colonial Williamsburg, a museum founded with Rockefeller wealth, the fine garments, homes, and decorative arts of the eighteenth century are a draw for most of the visitors.[36] So Terry's educational mission is admirable, for she has a personal interest in expanding the mainstream story. Once a male visitor asked her, "Don't you feel ridiculous wearing those clothes?" Recounting the incident to me, Terry said she told the man, "No, not at all. Because this is my history. I'm very proud to be able to wear part of my history. And I know my people were poor. I can tell you right now, I'm wearing exactly what they would be wearing." Terry is from Virginia, and her mother's family goes back to the eighteenth century; she is literally representing a part of her personal history. While identifying with the past, she remains clear about the fact that she is a contemporary person interpreting the past. When I asked Terry if she assumed a persona, she explained the reasons she does not:

> I try not to do that. Because I have a great respect for people of the eighteenth century. And I think it's important to tell their story. I try and remain as honest as I can be. I seldom say things that I don't know about.
>
> And I think if I took on a persona, I would perhaps be, I don't know, portraying a person as I think they were. And I really don't know how they are. And you can't help and do that. I mean, it's a path you have to take. But I try really hard *not* to be a person who lived in that time.

Terry explained that the Colonial Williamsburg policy is to speak in the present tense, but not necessarily in first person. She continued: "I never claim to be a person of the past. I don't say, 'I'm a farmer's wife.' I guess I would say that I would have been a farmer's wife, but I never say that that is who *I* am." When I asked her about the "magic moment," she said she has never had one nor sought one, for her goal is not to lose herself in the past, but to remain grounded in the present.

I do try and maintain myself in this century, though I actually kind of work at that. Because I think that it's important—the guests love to talk to characters. They do. I think to be able to do a character properly you have to be very talented to do that. And I don't think I'm talented enough to be a character. So I do try and stay in this century.

Avoiding the magic moment, as many at Colonial Williamsburg do, keeps Terry and the others focused on their educational mission, for their costumed activity is neither play nor leisure; it is a job, a vocation, a professional undertaking with strong pedagogical goals that are both foundation-driven and personally motivated.

Sarah Woodyard, the stylish apprentice dressmaker at the Margaret Hunter Shop on Duke of Gloucester Street, joins Terry Thon and James Ingram in a wish to expand the historical knowledge of the visitors to Colonial Williamsburg. Sarah's personal mission is to educate the museum guests about women's history,[37] adding another conceptual layer to the agenda of inclusiveness. Sarah describes the lives of eighteenth-century women, while Terry tells of the local poor and James discusses the plight of African Americans at the time. All of this enlarges the flashy story of the prominent men (and a few women) who shaped America on the eve of the Revolution.

At Colonial Williamsburg guests learn about history through the interpretation of the costumed staff, but the employees of the Historic Trades also learn through direct engagement with historic objects and replicas, using period and reproduced tools and techniques. Sarah Woodyard studied garment construction, women's studies, and economic history at Ohio State University. However, she has also learned much by wearing and making eighteenth-century women's clothing. Her work illustrates a basic premise of the study of material culture: that objects can tell about the people and their social and environmental circumstances as long as you learn how to listen to their nonverbal messages. Sarah is officially an apprentice milliner to Janea Whitacre, mistress of the millinery and mantua-making trades.

When I interviewed Sarah she was about halfway through a six-year formal apprenticeship that began in 2009.[38] In the few years that Sarah has been at the museum, she has widened her knowledge about the social activities of the time when the garments were made, bought, and used and about the people who stitched the clothes. She has also learned much about the thought processes of the maker in the act of creation, an embodied knowledge acquired only by creating period garments with period materials, tools, and techniques in the bodily posture of the period. Sarah said these are things that "you can only physically understand while you are sewing." By wearing accurate historical costume forty hours a day for five years, she has absorbed viscerally a feeling for eighteenth-century clothing and notions of hygiene. She told me that since she wears a cap regularly, her hair is cleaner at the end of the day and that wearing a shift as an undergarment keeps both the body and the outer garment clean, for the dirt accumulates on the shift and not on the beautiful dress.[39] Outer garments just need to be aired, not washed as often as the shift. This is the kind of mundane yet essential knowledge that Sarah likes to share with the seven hundred or so daily visitors who pass through Williamsburg's Millinery Shop.[40] "I think that's fascinating—when you talk about cleanliness in history," she said, "'cause that's something that a lot of visitors, you know, think that the eighteenth century was dirty, filthy—everyone was awfully stinky, smelled bad. But the clothing in some cases helps keep you cleaner, and that's something I've kind of noticed just through the wearing of them." Many visitors wonder about the stays—the corsets—that women of the period wore, and that undergarment provides a way for Sarah to discuss eighteenth-century women's bodies.

> A lot of people seem to see it as this constricting anti-feminist garment that was restricting women, but when you wear it, it becomes part of *you*. And you don't notice you're wearing them. I mean, you do to some degree, 'cause they keep you upright and they support you, but—I don't feel like someone is holding me down, I guess. I feel like it's a practical thing to be wearing. It's what you got.

Sarah came to Colonial Williamsburg with "an open mind" about wearing stays and petticoats. With an interest in recent approaches to material culture study, costume history, and women's history, she's "interested in history first, feminism second." Sarah believes that many visitors view eighteenth-century women through twenty-first-century lenses, projecting a contemporary understanding of gender politics onto the people of the past.

> Am I perpetuating some female role or myth? But at the same time, I really want to try to tell the story as honestly as possible. The eighteenth century was a patriarchal time. You can say that modern times are a patriarchal time.
>
> And I don't want to impose 1970s feminism on the eighteenth century. I also don't think that history is progressive, by any means. And that's something that is fascinating to me, because people think that women had no rights in the eighteenth century, and they certainly had rights in the eighteenth century.

Women had rights, and they enhanced their social and economic status by working as dressmakers and milliners (making accessories such as caps, cloaks, hats, muffs, and trims). Sarah explained that in the eighteenth-century pre-industrial era, "gown making was perhaps a higher skill because it was an apprentice trade," yet "sometimes history will degrade the work of women in the home. Whereas in the eighteenth century, women are working in the home, but they are getting paid for their work" and contributing to the household income while fulfilling domestic duties. The millinery and mantua-making trades were dominated by women such as Margaret Hunter, the owner of one of the six millinery shops in Williamsburg in the eighteenth century.[41] Today the Margaret Hunter Shop in the Historic Area, while also housing tailors Mark Hutter and Neal Hurst, celebrates in part the autonomy and skill of the entrepreneurial and enterprising women of the historic town.[42]

Our exploration of costume at Colonial Williamsburg began at the Costume Design Center, where the clothes are researched, drafted, made, stored, issued, and cleaned, and it ends at the Margaret Hunter Shop, where the art of making garments is interpreted for the general public. These are the two key nodes for the authenticity of the costumes in this living history museum. It is at the Margaret Hunter Shop that Sarah Woodyard works with fellow apprentice Neal Hurst, journeyman tailor Mark Hutter, and mistress milliner and mantua maker Janea Whitacre. Unlike the other 830 costumed interpreters at the museum, these individuals make the clothes they wear, sewn from fabrics they selected and purchased. Mark and Janea serve on the Costume Approval Board, so they are members of the team that confirms authenticity of construction, material, and style. All costumed employees at Colonial Williamsburg are regularly asked questions about what they are wearing, but the tailors and gown makers also interpret the tools and technologies of construction along with the style and comfort of the finished garments.

MARK HUTTER, JOURNEYMAN TAILOR

At Colonial Williamsburg costumed interpreters strive to broaden the historical understanding of their visitors by filling the gaps in conventional history—gaps of race, class, and gender. But there is another hole in standard historical analyses that does not result from a disregard for populations, but for entire sets of data. History as a discipline tends to be logocentric, stressing written documents and undervaluing the documentary power of material objects. In text-based study, when written sources are favored, the evidence from material culture is ignored, but learning from artifacts has been a goal of outdoor muse-

Journeyman tailor Mark Hutter. Colonial Williamsburg, Williamsburg, Virginia, 2010.

ums from the time of Artur Hazelius, at Skansen in Sweden, to the living history museums of America today.[43] At Skansen and at Colonial Williamsburg, historic crafts and trades are featured and preserved because the tools and the processes of creation, as well as the finished products, provide insights into the social, economic, and political histories of the people represented by the museum.

Mark Hutter, the journeyman tailor at the Margaret Hunter Shop, has always appreciated the role of objects as primary documents for historical understanding. Growing up in New York state, he served as a "junior curator" and later worked at the museums of historical societies in New York and Rhode Island, understanding extant items of clothing as texts, not as mere illustrations for written accounts. He started a tailoring firm for reenactors, which prompted him to seek out and study original pieces in order to reproduce them. Mark told me that reenactors who dress in military uniform are usually knowledgeable about the specifics of the unit they portray, but they rely on the tailor's research for the accuracy of civilian clothes. Mark learned to appreciate the tailor's trade and its changing technology as well as the garments the tailor produced. With a triple degree in history, art history, and theater from Randolph Macon College, and a drive for researching the trade and creations of the tailor, Mark Hutter arrived at Colonial Williamsburg, where he has worked full-time since 1996.

Mark said that the "ultimate goal" of the historic trades is to "research and, in some cases, resurrect the skills of the trades, the technologies of the trades." Mark's shop produces some fabrics in-house, and they also make trim, buttons, hooks and eyes—items that were not part of the tailor's, milliner's, or mantua maker's trade in the eighteenth century. The interpreters at the Margaret Hunter Shop have had to learn to produce the auxiliary pieces they need, because, as Mark said, "These details tell us so much; they mean so much if you understand them as reflections of larger systems. Each becomes a learning tool and a teaching tool. They teach us so that we can then teach the visitor." Many garments are constructed for an in-house study collection that other museums and university programs use as a resource. Mark and his colleagues also make replicas of old clothing to be used by interpreters or to be put on exhibit at Colonial Williamsburg when the original is too fragile to be displayed.

A crucial detail here is that the occupants of the Margaret Hunter Shop—Mark Hutter, Sarah Woodyard, Janea Whitacre, and Neal Hurst—are all actually makers of clothing. At the events of the Society for Creative Anachronism, the participants are not, in fact, medieval kings and queens. Civil War reenactors, while well-researched, are not really privates or officers in the Union or Confederate armies of the nineteenth century. At Colonial Williamsburg, James Ingram portrays Gowan Pamphlet with flair and knowledge; though an African American and sympathetic with the character he enacts, he is not a Baptist minister. But Mark Hutter *is* actually a tailor; he does not simply play a tailor in the manner of an actor on the stage. Interpreting a trade from the angle of a practitioner is basic to Mark's work. He said, "I think the visitor can detect the difference between somebody who's just saying it, and somebody who can say it and do it. And, of course, it's better yet if you're actually doing it as you're saying it. And that's what we try to do as much as possible here." When the crowd thins, Mark sews, sitting crossed-legged on the work board at the window, but during busy times he tends the counter so that he can interact with large groups of visitors. Janea Whitacre, mistress of the millinery and mantua-making trades, has been at Colonial Williamsburg since 1982. She told me that when she first started working there, employees were issued machine-made costumes. Knowledgeable visitors would grab the edge of her sleeve, turn it over, and see that it was not handmade, which "compromised the validity" of what she was saying. They started making their own clothes, Janea said, to prove "that we knew our trade, we wanted to be in handmade products."

The craftsmen of the Historic Trades, including the Fashion Trades, are engaged in the maintenance of the tools and techniques. They understand that the accuracy of the garment depends on the use of authentic means of production. As Mark said to me, "I could not make eighteenth-century garments—successful eighteenth-century garments—by twenty-first-century means. I feel the only way to truly reproduce the object is to also reproduce the technology. And so that leads me to the work of studying and practicing and preserving the technology here." To that end, Mark has put together "The Taylor's Apprenticeship: A Curriculum in Seven Years" for his apprentice, in which the "processes and products"—the garments, technology, and tools—are specified in each year's stated "Goals," "Skills," and "Knowledge" categories. Mark demonstrates eighteenth-century garments not only by using the appropriate period tools and techniques but also by wearing the proper period clothing.

Wearing the clothing that a tailor of the eighteenth century would have worn gives Mark a direct, bodily understanding of the historical craftsman he portrays. It is like "experimental archaeology," Mark said; it gives him a sense of the materiality of the eighteenth century, and he commented that he is able to "understand the physicality of another time and place when it literally swathes you." Mark explained that the garments he wears while at work "become facts worn on the body. And in order to learn from them, they have to be—hopefully they are—correct, but they should always be reexamined." Our knowledge of historic clothing should not be static, Mark argues, but "we have to continue to reexamine the physical past—and find new understanding, new relevance, new meaning in it." One lesson he has learned from wearing the costume is that his bodily movements and postures are affected: "I couldn't understand the work of an eighteenth-century tailor if I wasn't wearing an eighteenth-century waistcoat and coat. Because the very cut of the coat affects the way that I sit when I'm doing my sewing." When Mark works at home, or out of the public eye, wearing modern clothes but sewing eighteenth-century garments, his posture is different, his position is different, and the work "does not flow." He said, "From my own experience I can say that I know I work more efficiently doing period work in period clothing than I do when I'm wearing jeans and a T-shirt." Wearing twenty-first-century clothes is a hindrance. "The system is broken when that cog is out of place," he said. "You don't have the whole eighteenth-century system to speed the work along, and so it adds a depth of knowledge, depth of understanding, but it also, actually, helps us in our work." The garment the tailor wears is not decorative, but crucial for his work. Mark said, "It helps us when working in an eighteenth-century environment, doing eighteenth-century work, to wear eighteenth-century clothing." Mark is so comfortable in historical clothing, which he has worn every workday since 1981, that he sees it as daily dress and not as a costume; his clothing is less performative and more natural.

> And so for me, I really don't consider it *costume* any longer, in the sense that it is my primary means of assuming or understanding the eighteenth century in this case.
>
> I have variety in the wardrobe to choose appropriate clothing for the work that I am going to be doing. And the company that I'm going to meet. And the weather. The same considerations that everybody faces when they get up every morning.

Wondering about the impact of his acquired historical knowledge and experience, I asked Mark Hutter if he has ever had a "magic moment" of the sort that SCA and Civil War reenactors cherish.

> Have I ever experienced a lapse in the time continuum, and thought, "Wow, it's 1774"? No. But I definitely have had moments of revelation that are sort of—that I think are the closest to that sort of experience.
>
> And some of them can come at odd times, and in unusual ways, and they're not always particularly about clothing.
>
> But they all help us to understand the past better. It's making connections. One bit of information finds another and it leads to another understanding.

The deep, accidental connection that a "magic moment" can provide is valued because it enhances the education of the interpreter, Colonial Williamsburg's "little professor," who can then pass this comprehension on to the visitor. And that is the fundamental goal of the costumed interpreter, particularly those in the Historic Trades, who are not famous personages but are there to teach visitors about the culture, values, and history of the past.

We end our exploration of Colonial Williamsburg with a focus on interpretation, arguably the primary activity at the living history museum. The mission is to deliver meaningful information to the visitors, to reward the guests with something that aids their understanding of American history and culture. Mark Hutter told me that when he discusses the tools, techniques, and products of his trade, he puts them in "broader socioeconomic, political, religious, cultural,

Mark Hutter demonstrates
the tailor's art at the
Margaret Hunter Shop.
Colonial Williamsburg,
Williamsburg, Virginia, 2010.

global-trade aspects that set those things in a more meaningful realm." Talking about stitches per inch, he said, while of interest to connoisseurs of dress, has "no real educational value," because it is not interpretive but a mere delivery of facts. If the facts are not situated in cultural contexts, "the visitors have not walked away with anything that has significance to themselves in the twenty-first century."

On March 18, 2010, I watched Mark in the act of interpreting—keeping the counter at the shop while families and school groups passed through. Many customers, especially children, were impressed with the fact that Mark was actually a tailor, more than an actor, as this rapid-fire exchange between a ten-year-old boy and Mark illustrates:

> "Can you make hats?"
>
> "Yes."
>
> "Coats?"
>
> "Yes."
>
> "Leather coats?"
>
> "Yes."
>
> "Any color?"
>
> "Yes."
>
> "Awesome!"

Shortly after this exchange, a female visitor asked about sewing machines. Not dodging a question that was beyond his historical scope—as many first-person interpreters do—Mark patiently explained that the sewing machine was not a threat to his profession until about the 1840s: "I have three-quarters of a century before I have to worry about machines taking over my work." But he said that while the housewife readily accepted the sewing machine, many professionals in the textile trades were put out of work by technological progress. Mark's objective is to communicate a nuanced history, with its diversity of reactions to comparable stimuli. As he explained:

> The majority of visitors to historical settings have this assumption that in the past you could tell somebody from the exterior. You could walk the street and judge somebody wholly by external attributes.
>
> And we tend to believe that, for some reason, they were—individuals as well as society—were simpler.

And so we combat that—instead of combatting, we try to help explain that constantly here. And recognize that people are always diverse. Societies are always complex. And you can really only understand them from the inside.

It is Mark's personal agenda to convince visitors that the people of the past were as interesting, as complex, and as multidimensional as we are today. He is able to offer his vision within the framework provided by the Colonial Williamsburg Foundation, interpreting the trades in relation to the themes of America on the eve of the Revolution: the creation of the new republic, the effect of wartime on the colonies, the story of the English empire and colonization, and the racial and religious stories of early America. To this list he adds his personal mandate to explain that material culture matters in understanding history. Mark is a scholar of material culture, as I am; we are both members of the Costume Society of America. Mark and the others in the Margaret Hunter Shop use clothing as items of material culture that carry deep meanings and messages. "Most visitors are *surprised* to find that garments—even things so seemingly personal and insignificant as underwear—can lead to larger stories," he said. "Or that those larger stories can be found in understandable objects. Things that we can all relate to—like underwear, or shoes, or stockings."

The actor-interpreters of "Revolutionary City" must remain within a tight historical frame, in the period from 1769 to 1781, when the actions of the street theater take place. But someone like Mark, who is not impersonating a particular individual, but telling a broader story, can and does move beyond sharp cutoff dates, as we saw with the example of the sewing machine. In the tailor shop Mark makes garments that range from the 1760s to the 1780s, but he has also produced items that range from 1607 into the 1840s—items that are kept behind the counter and used during discussions with visitors to illustrate changes and continuities before and after the base interpretative year of 1774. Mark Hutter wears the authentic clothes he makes, teaching the visitor that the garments, the creation process, and the tools of the trade are all useful in untangling the multifaceted social history of a diverse population in the colony of Virginia. He told me that his job is "a lot more than putting a needle through a piece of fabric."

The interpretative style has changed over the last few decades at Colonial Williamsburg. Janea Whitacre said that twenty-eight years ago, when she first started working, they were given a script from which they delivered a ten-minute prepared speech. Now all the members of the staff have more freedom to emphasize certain aspects of their trade and its relevant history, and to meet the moment and the perceived interests of the audience. Mark Hutter believes many first-person interpreters use their character's ignorance of the future as an excuse to dismiss topics they do not understand themselves, but the visitor is there to learn, and if interpreters don't answer the question, they will have wasted a teachable moment. Mark, like the others I spoke with at Colonial Williamsburg, understands the responsibility to "the past and to your present visitor." One way the costume historians, actor-interpreters, and Historic Trades interpreters at Colonial Williamsburg fulfill their responsibility to historical accuracy is by wearing accurate costumes, keeping one foot in the present, the other firmly in the eighteenth century.

HISTORY AND HERITAGE: RELIVING THE PAST IN COSTUME

One of the intentions of this book is to show how costumes are used to express heritage during public events. In Salvador da Bahia the men of Filhos de Gandhy connect to Africa in order to situate themselves in contemporary Brazil. But most Afro-Brazilians have never been to Africa. Their heritage is uncertain; their connection to the continent is separated by time and space. But although their costumes are imaginary and fantastical, their commitment to cultural retention and race consciousness is real, and it is realized, in part, through the costumes on their bodies. In Sweden the costumes remain in situ. There was no violent separation of people from their homeland as there was during the slave trade. The Leksand folk costume is a medium for the maintenance of heritage, allowing adjustments to fashion and occasions of use. The garments are historically accurate, culturally authentic.

In the United States costumes are also used to express heritage—shared history and identity. One function of the costumes in the Society for Creative Anachronism is to express pride in a generalized European heritage. Accuracy of costume is not a requirement. Anachronism is assumed. But the way to stand out is to wear garb that is well-researched and well-made, adhering as much as possible to historical antecedents.

Reenactments of the American Civil War usually take place near national historic sites, places designated by the government for their historical magnitude, which are sites of heritage for the nation. Civil War reenactors and living historians consider authenticity and role-playing to be serious pursuits. But the participants are self-directed, investing their own money and research skills to authenticate the uniforms they wear; their internal drive for authenticity yields a polished, earnest approximation of what was worn during war. In accurate uniforms the living historians look the part so that they can play the part, engaging in a personally defined educational mission to impart historical knowledge to the general public.

History, heritage, and education combine in the living history museum. Recall that what inspired Artur Hazelius to found Skansen, the world's first outdoor museum, was the church boats filled with costumed parishioners in 1872. Hazelius collected traditional costumes, buildings, and artifacts for his ethnographic and open-air museums in Stockholm, believing that the farmsteads, crafts, and examples of regional dress should be preserved for future visitors in an interactive setting where culture and its relevant material objects were properly contextualized.

Likewise, at Colonial Williamsburg history is self-consciously reconstituted and interpreted by a team of trained professionals within an institutional pedagogical agenda, where both authenticity and public education drive the costume choices. But unlike Skansen, where national regional diversity more than a particular historical period guided selection and presentation, Williamsburg was founded long after the period it depicts, so a scarcity of extant material culture, not of buildings, but especially of clothing, provides a challenge to the staff. Most of the original garments in the Williamsburg collection are extraordinary examples, and most come from England, not Virginia. In Williamsburg accuracy lies in more than appearance; it is also a matter of the techniques employed by the milliners, mantua makers, and tailors.

Interpreters at Colonial Williamsburg participate in an educational celebration of the nation's political heritage. Within that frame they are free to follow personal agendas of race, class, and gender, and the workers in the trades can enact—and so preserve—their traditions of creation, expressing a heritage of production. All of them are living historians. This book's living historians engage seriously in the study and presentation of a chosen culture or era. Folklorist Jay Anderson ends his volume *A Living History Reader* by noting that living historians "are increasingly borrowing the tools and techniques of academic historians," leading them to "realize that the academic has much to offer in historical theory, methodology, and knowledge of relevant primary sources."[44] But as we noticed with tailor Mark Hutter, craftsmen and practitioners of material arts— those who make and use the things that are studied by academics—can, in turn, offer deep knowledge to scholars of material culture. Some of that experiential understanding comes from designing, drafting, draping, sewing, and wearing period clothing.

One definition of costume is that it is a style of dress peculiar to another time or place; costumes can function as vehicles of space and time travel. Some living historians achieve time travel in a "magic moment" when they are carried back-ward by some visual or physical stimulus, often accurate costuming. Costumes are—to use Jay Anderson's metaphor—time machines. Although SCA player P. J. Schultz and Civil War reenactor Mark LaPointe both felt they had experienced a flash of the past they were portraying in costume, none of the interpreters I spoke with at Colonial Williamsburg yearned for a "magic moment." The *spectators* at Colonial Williamsburg are the ones who want a ride in the time machine. Visitors who were canvassed by the Guest Research Unit said they "wanted experiences that helped them 'feel like I am [transported] back in time.'"[45] Whether you are transporting yourself or your beholders back to the past, historical knowledge, proper behavior, and authentic-looking costumes are vehicles for the journey. (In fact, Jane Malcolm-Davies's studies of historic sites tell us that the more professional the costumes of the interpreters, the greater the reported educational value to the visitors.[46])

Accurate costumes play a vital role in enhancing the experience of visitors and participants at many kinds of historical sites, and the differences among heritage sites hold implications for costuming decisions. Examples from the SCA, Civil War reenactments, and Colonial Williamsburg reveal the different levels of research and historical accuracy that are expected and acceptable along with how accuracy of costume is achieved, judged, and monitored. Locations vary, as do the authenticity and motivations grounded by heritage, but the sincerity of the participants make for meaningful experiences in costume.

In Sweden old family pieces and an unbroken connection to one's past lead to a robust costume tradition, one relying on self-motivation as well as on oral history and the advice and guidance of local experts. In Civil War reenacting there is a richness of historical sources and a narrow time frame in which self-education and communal pressure ensure the creation of an accurate uniform. Colonial Williamsburg presents a complex assembly of information, not much of which comes directly from the place and the date. The informational range is wide, geographically and temporally, in comparison with that of the Civil War reenactor—three days at Gettysburg, four years of war—and it must stretch to encompass many kinds of people: rich and poor, black and white, men, women, and children. These challenges, combined with the organizational demands of the Colonial Williamsburg Foundation and the expectations of a paying audience, drive the museum to rely on a team of experts, professionals whose job is to research the wearing and making of the costumes and their relevant technological, political, and historical contexts.

In Sweden the strength of the local tradition leads to authenticity. In Civil War reenacting the abundance of data leads to authenticity. At Colonial Williamsburg dedicated and specialized scholarship ultimately makes authentic costumes possible. By considering costumes in a variety of situations, linked by concerns for heritage and accuracy, we find that a satisfying level of authenticity can be achieved by different means, the goal being to envision and reconstruct a piece of the wearable past.

The next move is to shift from historical authenticity to an authenticity of artistic performance. The last three case studies focused on history; in each of them costumes offered entries to the past—to a dreamy Middle Ages, to a bloody Civil War, and to the nationally mythic moment of the American Revolution. But costumes can also draw their wearers and beholders into a deep place of emotion, of philosophical reference and aesthetic fulfillment. In the theater actors and their audiences—whether they participate actively or passively—journey together to other times and places, experiencing other cultures and personalities. In the theater social collaboration and artistic achievement flourish, and costume provides the channel for that grand pursuit.

ART

Costume and Collaboration on the Theater Stage

T HE EXAMPLES OF HALLOWEEN, CARNIVAL, FOLK DRESS, AND historic reenactment offer a clear correlation: as costumes become more elaborate and professional, so do the events and the performances of the people wearing them. We end our exploration of costume use with a consideration of performances in which costumes are made to convey specific stories to an audience while moving the spectators emotionally and transforming the actors psychologically.

The case studies in this book teach us about the roles of creation, of individual satisfaction in the midst of collaboration, of personal pleasure in a socially cooperative endeavor. As in organized sports, collaborating in costumed events allows people to become part of a team of specialists, to relax into their own roles knowing that all the other aspects of creation lie in the domains of other competent players. The division of labor does not necessarily hinder individuality, or inhibit freedom of expression. The collaborative nature of theater grants the stage director, the costume designer, and the actor great leeway in the execution of his or her creative work within a web of excellence. All instances of costume use entail a performative dimension, but the presentation of personal identity through collaboration is most obvious on the theater stage.

PATTERNS IN DRAMATIC COOPERATION

A survey of the genres of theatrical performance—masquerade, folk drama, the professional stage, and the Hollywood movie—demonstrates that as the number of people involved in the collaboration increases, the production becomes more professional, plans are more elaborate, and meanings become more complicated. Before we move to the topic of contemporary American theater, it will be helpful to take a look at a brief schematic sketch of the range of patterns in cooperation in costumed theatrical performances. We begin with masquerades.

In the small town of Ogidi in the Yorubaland of southern Nigeria, in 2006, we witnessed the sudden appearance of a being named Agbo, a mound of green and brown leaves that sped over the ground, gliding without hands or feet to mingle with the crowd, then to disappear before appearing again.[1] The actor was completely lost in the costume; his behavior was erratic, unpredictable, and disruptive, as is the case with many African masquerades.[2] At Ogidi a small group of men gather in the bush, out of sight, to make the costume, dress the player, and prepare him to receive the spirit. There are no scripts, no choreographed moves, no stage director or costume designer, and no stage—Agbo can go anywhere he wants. The frame for the drama is not a physical space, but an emotional frame of mind that enables the ritual.

At the other end of the spectrum of collaboration is the production of a professional film, with its enormous budget and its vast assembly of individuals who are tasked with the creation of the film and its costumes. The increase in specialization shapes the nature of the collaboration; the stream of final credits of a typical Hollywood movie lists hundreds of people, including a large staff devoted solely to the costumes. The final credits for the film *The Last Emperor*,[3] for example, name its costume designer, James Acheson (who won an Oscar for his beautiful Chinese garments), and thirty others in the makeup department and costume and wardrobe department, including a hair designer, hair stylist, makeup artist, costume property maker, wardrobe coordinator, wardrobe assistant, cutter, costume appliqué worker, military costume designer, costumer, and dozens of assistants to these people. Add to this list a costume department supervisor, costume department foreperson, costume key person, aging person, dyer, stitcher, milliner, sketch artist, feather dyer, shoemaker, jewelry maker, lace maker, leather worker, laundry person, and location alteration tailor.

As budgets and specialization increase, distance opens between the actors and their audience. Agbo's player knew everyone in the crowd through which he dashed, and everyone knew him; his masking needed to be complete to sustain his mystery. But the Hollywood film rolls before an unknown audience composed of nameless representatives of a targeted demographic while the screen fills with the gigantic faces of celebrities immediately recognizable to their fans. From Agbo to Hollywood: the interactive community of friends and relatives gives way to a vast, dark, anonymous mass and a few glitzy stars.

Between these extremes lie a variety of dramatic performances. Our quest is to understand the actor on the stage and the identities she enacts in costume, but

Irish mummers. Drawing by Henry Glassie from *All Silver and No Brass,* 1976.

we begin by considering theatrical collaboration in order to appreciate the roles of the playwright, the director, and the costume designer.

FOLK DRAMA

In the past in Ireland, "strawboys" would appear without invitation at social moments, on Halloween and at weddings and wakes. Their arrival was sudden, like Agbo's, and their disguise was complete. Their faces were hidden, and around their necks they each wore a ring from which straw hung. Unlike Agbo, they did not personify spirits; they were mischievous young men motivated by pent-up hostilities.[4] Acting impulsively, with no script and no stage, they were masquerades. But when the strawboy became Jack Straw, one in a mumming troupe, he was part of a play, a performance with a plot, a script, and a cast of characters. From Agbo to mumming, we take a step toward theater and enter the realm of folk drama.

Mumming seems to have come to Ireland from the British Isles in the seventeenth century, and in Ireland it assimilated the older Irish folk customs of the strawboys and the wrenboys.[5] To exemplify the tradition I focus here on mumming from the County Fermanagh, in Northern Ireland, relying on the data collected by Henry Glassie and presented in his influential book *All Silver and No Brass.*[6] The mumming play, as it was performed into the 1930s, involved house visits during Christmastime. A troupe of about ten men marched through the

The Druid Theatre production of Vincent Woods's *At the Black Pig's Dyke,* 1992. *Photo by Amelia Stein.*

cold to every house, knocking on doors and asking for admittance. In the houses where they were welcomed, they performed their comical play of death and resurrection, in which Prince George kills Saint Patrick, and then Patrick, revived by a doctor, rises, ready to fight again. The troupe was composed of young Catholic men, farming lads from the community, and depending on the number of actors who showed up to go out on a particular night, the plot of the play could expand or contract.[7] The Fermanagh mummers normally included these roles: Captain Mummer, Beelzebub, Oliver Cromwell, Prince George, Saint Patrick, the Doctor, Little Devil Doubt, Jack Straw, Miss Funny, and Big Head, a musician who played a reel at the conclusion of the drama.[8]

The troupe's leader played Captain Mummer. Functionally, he was also the artistic director and stage director: he gathered the men, was responsible for the troupe's behavior, and was the one to ask for admittance at every house. Each character recited a specific rhyme. The rhymes were traditional, but one man, in the Fermanagh case James Owens, recalled the rhymes from his youth and wrote down each character's part, so the drama had a script and lines to memorize, as in the theater today. The troupe's members gathered in a house to rehearse their lines and to make their own costumes. Most of them dressed alike, in wide trousers; belted monochrome tunics; old boots; and tall, conical straw hats, festooned with ribbons, that rested on their shoulders, covered their faces, and hid their identities. The individual characters were differentiated by rhyme and role, but only minimally by costume: Saint Patrick's shirt was a bit longer in order to look like a bishop's robe; Prince George had a lighter-colored tunic to look like armor; Beelzebub carried a club and a pan. Two characters, however, dressed differently. The Doctor wore a black suit, a top hat with a veil to hide his face, and he carried a doctor's bag. Miss Funny, a man in drag, wore a dress and carried a purse to gather donations from the audience. All the members of the squad were disguised, so guessing their identities became part of the event. With a successful guess they would take off their hats and join the residents for refreshments.

Each man in the acting troupe was his own costume designer. In the December before the play, they made their straw hoods, and in March they burned them together, around Saint Patrick's Day. The stage was the kitchen floor of a country house. At the beginning of the drama Captain Mummer acknowledged that his play was different: "Act of young, and act of age, the like of this was never acted on a stage."[9] Unlike masquerades or strawboys, the mummers performed in a confined space, and when the drama was over, they joined the audience for food, drinks, and dance, converting their temporary stage back into a place for socializing, eliminating the distance between performer and spectator. To bring unity to a divided community was the goal, said Peter Flanagan, who played Miss Funny in the Fermanagh mumming troupe.[10]

Mumming disappeared in the 1930s and 1940s, but it has now been revived in many places in Ireland and England. Today's mumming plays are not performed in private homes but in public places like schools, festivals, and bars.[11] And mummers have been resurrected on the theater stage.

FOLK DRAMA ON THE THEATER STAGE

When a strawboy becomes Jack Straw in a mummer's play, he acquires a script and a performance frame. When the mummers move from the kitchens of their neighbors to the venue of a folk festival, their performance becomes more tightly controlled, their acting more naturalistic, and their costumes vary to signal small differences of character. Then the complexities implicit in folk drama spread and clarify on the professional stage.

Irish playwright Vincent Woods took the idea of the mummers—anonymous men in disguise—and put them into his powerful play about the Irish Troubles. In *At the Black Pig's Dyke,* a band of mummers, led by Captain Mummer, act on the subversive and metaphoric violence of the mummer's play to commit murder in an Irish community laced with suspicion and jealousy within a country rocked by religious strife. The play premiered in 1992 at the Druid Theatre in Galway, and Monica Frawley designed both the costumes and the set. Vincent Woods gathered ideas for his drama by reading studies by Alan Gailey and Henry Glassie. When I asked Vincent about the costumes, he replied, "I could really imagine how these straw costumes would be hugely effective in theater, but I didn't even write with that as a primary instinct. In a way, all that came in behind the words, at least for me."[12] As a poet and playwright Vincent focuses on the words spoken by the characters: "I may have a faint idea of how somebody looks. But that's almost more physically manifested in the way they speak. For me, the dress, the costume, what they wear as an actor in performance is really given to somebody else. It is given to a designer who can envision much more than I ever could."

Monica Frawley used Henry Glassie's drawings in *All Silver and No Brass* and her research in the archives of the Irish Folklore Commission to create costumes that were, according to Vincent, "highly theatrical and grounded, absolutely grounded, in what I knew of this tradition." Monica was "taking the tradition, and making something profoundly theatrical from it." The costumes had to be modified for the stage. Since the actors had to see and be heard, Monica altered the tradition, giving the tall straw hoods slits for the eyes and mouth.

The result was a triumph. Vincent Woods recalled, "That transformation from the drawn page—drawn and painted page of Monica's design—to the stage was as profound as the words moving from the page to the stage. And one of these rare times when all those energies seem to match each other and make for something as good as it can possibly be." The success of *At the Black Pig's Dyke,* which has been staged frequently over the past twenty years, issued from an effective collaboration of scholar, ethnographer, playwright, designer, actor, and audience. An amalgamation of separate talents yielded a profoundly significant work of art—for the author, something as good as it can possibly be.

PROFESSIONAL THEATER

The move from folk drama to professional theater involves a greater number of roles for specialists in the creation of the final artistic product. In Irish mumming the amateur players, farming men by day, made their own costumes; a troupe member, another young farmer, acted as the stage director; and the action took place in the kitchens of rural houses. However, theater productions require trained actors; other professionals in the roles of author, director, and designer; and the action occurs on a stage built for drama. The shift from folk drama to theater involves a move from the domestic into the institutional and commercial, replacing community members with trained professionals, neighbors with a paying audience, the kitchen with a proscenium stage.

A professional theater production usually includes an artistic director, a director, an assistant director, a scenic designer, a lighting designer, a costume designer, a stage manager, an assistant stage manager, and the actors. With the addition of each of these roles, there is greater division between the audience and the players. What separated a spectator from a mummer was his costume, and then he revealed his identity and joined his neighbors for a feast. The separation of audience and actors on the performance stage has focused the objections of modern critics, who have called for more proximity between the audience and the spectacle onstage, for more interactions with the spectators and more improvisation on the part of the actors—all of which are characteristics of folk drama. Theater critic Harold Clurman laments that the deep pleasure of watching a show has become "increasingly robbed by the cash-register or race-track climate which pervades our playhouses"; we are present merely to pass judgment on the production placed before us.[13] In *The Theater and Its Double* Antonin Artaud argues for a return to a more ritualistic form of theater, one in which the audience becomes part of the drama instead of passively listening to the words of the text.[14]

A playwright dreams up a story. His text is subsequently interpreted and realized first by an artistic director, then a director, and last by the actors. To begin to understand this process I spoke with Charles Morey. At the time of our interview he was the artistic director of the Pioneer Theatre Company in Salt Lake City,

Utah. He is also a playwright, a director, and an actor.[15] In January 2009 his play *The Yellow Leaf* premiered in Salt Lake City. The play is set in 1816 and centers on the relations between Lord Byron, Mary Shelley, and Percy Bysshe Shelley. In reading the script before attending the performance, I noticed an absence of explicit descriptions of the set and costumes. When I asked Charles about this, he explained the creative process of a playwright and articulated the central theme of this chapter: the freedom each artist has in collaborating within a team of professionals. Charles said that, unlike George Bernard Shaw, who "writes a novel in his stage directions," he does not provide much description of the visual world of the play. When I asked why, he said that as a director he does not need to be told these things: a director can intuit what the sets, the furniture, the clothes should look like. He continued: "The script as it exists now is intended for those, for professionals, who read enough plays that they visualize automatically. And I don't feel I need to burden—*overburden* them with stage directions." As a playwright Charles can relax into his art, knowing that other trained professionals will do right by the direction, the lighting, the set, and the costumes for his play. (For the world premiere of *The Yellow Leaf,* Charles, though an accomplished director, chose not to serve as the play's director.) Like William Shakespeare—who was a dramatist and also a producer and an actor—Charles has a sympathetic understanding of the other roles in the collaborative process. He described Shakespeare's texts as "an example of scripts that were put together for one purpose, which is to hand to other professionals to do the play with. So he didn't feel any need to describe the production at all, because the production was to be made out of that." It does not matter that Shakespeare's texts lack stage directions. What is important to understand is that dramatists—William Shakespeare in his day, or Vincent Woods and Charles Morey in our day—are free to write, trusting that directors and designers will do their part well.

A successful collaborative process begins with the playwright and works along the chain of command from the artistic director through the director to the designers and actors. In 2007 I saw an excellent production of George Bernard Shaw's *Arms and the Man* at the Lyric Stage Company theater in Boston.[16] In the script Shaw describes the dress of Raina, a pretty young woman living in Bulgaria in the late nineteenth century: "She wears an underdress of pale green silk, draped with an overdress of thin ecru canvas embroidered with gold. She is crowned with a dainty eastern cap of gold tinsel."[17]

I interviewed the costume designer for the production, Molly Trainer, who described what she does as "painting in 3-D," "manipulating" what the audience sees onstage.[18] Molly told me how much she enjoyed the collaborative process of

Ellen Adair as Raina Petkoff and Barlow Adamson as Captain Bluntschli in George Bernard Shaw's *Arms and the Man*, 2007. *Photo courtesy of the Lyric Stage Company of Boston.*

theater, working with the director—"the captain of the ship"—but also working with the actors. She said she actually enjoys it when actors "utilize and expand on" her costume ideas. Molly takes the vision of the director and "massages it" to fit her own understanding of the costumes. In this production of *Arms and the Man,* for example, the director, Spiro Veloudos, wanted an art nouveau look reminiscent of the paintings of Gustav Klimt. Working together with the scenic designer, Molly decided on a shimmering gold palette for the clothes, evoking the colors and mood of Klimt's *The Kiss* or his famous portrait of Adele Bloch-Bauer. In her mind, and in her "show bible" binder of research, Molly joined Klimt's paintings with the prints of Czech artist Alphonse Mucha for inspiration. She shopped in New York and Boston for the silk fabric in a "pale sage" hue that Shaw originally envisioned for Raina's dress. To the three-quarter-length sleeves of Raina's empire-waist dress Molly added sleeves with fluted bottoms in a silk crepe fabric that reminded her of *shibori,* a Japanese dyeing technique, adding a touch of ethnic splendor to the art nouveau dress. Molly wanted the actor playing Raina, Ellen Adair, to wear a gold pendant necklace and provided her with one. But Ellen had a better option at home, one that hit the dress at a better point, so Ellen's own necklace was used during the run of the show. In this case the actor contributed the final piece, completing the collaborative arc that began with the playwright 113 years earlier.

THE COSTUME DESIGNER

The objective of a costume designer is to travel to the place, time, and emotional landscape of the characters she will dress. Designer Susan Hifferty, chair of design at the New York University Tisch School of the Arts, uses the word "journey" to describe her work with stage directors. She goes on a journey, and her clothes help the actors on their own journey to the place where their characters reside.[19] Once again, costume is seen to function as a vehicle for travel in time and space. The journey for Hifferty climaxes in her own version of "the magic moment," when all the elements of design have come together in the visual universe of the play.[20]

Magic is a recurrent theme in the theater. The designer experiences a "magic moment" in the creative process, and the audience is often seduced by the "magic of the theater." The actor is given a gift by the costume designer, a "magic garment," so she, like Prospero in Shakespeare's *The Tempest,* can put on a fantastical item of clothing that will help her "concentrate the powers of imagination, expression, emotion, and movement into the creation and projection of a character to an audience."[21] Such garments serve both the actors and the spectators. The costume must function to define the character visually by setting it in time and space; by establishing its age, gender, social class, and personality; and by reflecting the changes the character undergoes as the plot progresses. This communication is achieved through a purposeful selection of garment type and cut, fit, fabric, and accessories. The character's identity is revealed through the style, color, scale, texture, and silhouette of what the actor wears onstage.[22] In its artistic communication the theater costume is often stylized and abstracted, speaking symbolically through its exaggerated profile, color, shape, or size. Even if not exaggerated in look, the costume is unlike everyday clothing; it is used for effect and must move and act in a way that regular dress does not. Fabric materials, construction, and color are chosen to work under the stage lights and within the action mandated by the plot of the play.[23] All kinds of "tricks" are employed to make these magical garments look like ordinary clothes but function as extraordinary stage costumes.

Costume designers have four main options for the acquisition of garments: (1) they can "pull" clothes from their costume stock; (2) they can rent costumes from other theater or professional costume houses; (3) they can buy pieces in stores, including vintage and secondhand venues; or (4) they can "build" a costume from scratch, employing the skills of a pattern maker, cutter, draper, tailor, stitcher, finisher, and milliner to realize the garment. The other personnel involved might include a costume shop manager, a costume supervisor, a costumer, a project manager, a wardrobe crew, a wardrobe supervisor, and dressers, who literally dress and undress the actors, helping them with quick changes or difficult costume pieces such as corsets.[24]

Whether the costumes are pulled, rented, bought, or built, my interest in this book is the collaborative process involved in the realization of the costume. In reading costume design manuals, I was surprised by the slight consideration given to the body type, comfort level, and vision of the actor. It seems that costume designers are mostly taught to work closely with the director and the other designers, letting the actors adjust to their design only when they come into the show instead of seeking their input at the outset.[25] In an ideal collaboration all the participants would work together in the production. That is why I have chosen to feature Boston-based costume designer Rafael Jaen, for he is exceptional in consulting with the actors at an early point in the process of creation.

Rafael Jaen is a strikingly handsome, well-dressed man. In meeting him for the first time, it's easy to trust him on matters of style and fashion; if he presents himself so well, he must do the same for the actors he dresses for the stage. (New York–based actor Lena Hurt told me that she, like many actors, scrutinizes the clothing of a costume designer; if the designer is wearing clothes that fit well— both physically and aesthetically—then the actor can relax in the knowledge that her costume will also be flattering and appropriate.[26])

Rafael was born in Venezuela but received his costume design education in the United States. At the time of our interviews, he was a professor of costume design at Emerson College in Boston; he is now assistant professor of performing arts, in the College of Liberal Arts at the University of Massachusetts Boston. A well-respected designer and teacher, Rafael was particularly clear in teaching me about his principles and philosophy of design.[27] In his youth he acted a little, but he trained as an architect in Venezuela. He is also an accomplished tailor, having owned a custom couture studio in the 1980s that specialized in resort and workout clothes, and he also tailored suits and bridal gowns. As we will see, his personal experiences directly influence his designs. His sympathies with the actors and his sense of volume, color, and garment construction distinguish him among costume designers.

To understand his take on the art of costume design, I asked him to tell me what a "costume" is. He laughed and declared this to be a "great question." Rafael's students had been urging him to see the television show *Project Runway* because of the recurrent jokes in which items of apparel are ridiculed for looking too much like a "costume."[28] He thought the show conveyed a "limited idea of costume as disguise you wear for Halloween." This is one definition of costume, perhaps the most popular one, and it suggested the example I used to begin this book. He elaborated:

> And I thought to myself, now, costuming—if you think of it as a dress code—costuming—I could wear a costume. Maybe I have my costume that I wear when I dress as a costume designer because I want people to look at me and trust me: "Okay, if he dresses nice, or a certain way, has a style, then, that is the costume designer."
>
> I think that what costuming is for me in the theater, specifically, and what makes it different from fashion, or what we wear as everyday people, is that in serving the story and not being realistic, it will do things that regular clothes will not do.

Rafael explained that the stage costume must be realistic but not actually real. He gave me a hypothetical example: a 1940s frock designed for the opera, for the musical theater, or for "straight" theater. Each of these three dresses would have the characteristic Christian Dior silhouette of the era, yet each garment would behave differently. For the opera version the dress would have a hidden girdle that would work with the diaphragm of the singer so that she could sing comfortably. The musical theater dress would have gussets and inserts so that the gown would secretly stretch, allowing the actor to dance without hindrance. The dress for drama could also require special gussets so that the actor could move or gesture in a way that ordinary people usually do not do in daily life (people with big gestures are often accused of being too "dramatic"). Rafael explained that while all three of these dresses might look the same from a distance, up close, after scrutinizing the construction, one would find what he called "the tricks that we use in the theater." Further, theater costumes are built differently from ordinary clothes, for they must last night after night, enduring the rough use of each performance and repetitive laundering and dry-cleaning. The "tricks" Rafael describes also apply to choices of clothing color and makeup. He said that actors can look good wearing certain colors in the theater that they could never wear in real life. Onstage, the right makeup and especially the right lighting can create an overall, steady tone that the natural contexts we usually inhabit could never supply.

Costume design manuals, such as Rebecca Cunningham's excellent book *The Magic Garment: Principles of Costume Design,* provide detailed descriptions of the aesthetic principles that costume designers employ. To see the theory in practice, I asked Rafael to describe his own philosophy of costume design. In response he stressed his appreciation of the roles of the playwright and director in shaping the character as well as his comfort with the collaborative nature of theater. More than most costume designers, Rafael pays close attention to the actor, a practice that greatly affects his designs. This is how Rafael articulates his task for costume design:

> I need to give voice to the history of the character, history that may have happened before the play or after the play.
> I need to give voice to the storytelling that is taking place in the narrative of the play.
> I need to give voice to the vision of the director, because he may have a certain point of view that he wishes to communicate.
> And then, more importantly, I need to work with the actor, to find out what this actor in particular is finding as the emotional root of this character, or the actions that they find in certain words of the musical that they are singing or what they are talking about.

Returning to the dress code of daily life and how it informs his costumes, Rafael said that he tries to "contextualize" a particular character through his or her clothes. He needs to "arrive at a place that I feel confident that this character will wear that. Why would they get up that morning and wear that?" To answer this question Rafael must get into the psychology of the character—a practice also utilized by actors—and apply his understanding of the clothes we wear as "everyday people." He must then project it into the "unrealistic" world of the theater, where clothes look like they do in real life, although they differ in construction, fabric, and color choice, and although they are heightened to effect communication.

Rafael is often asked if there is a formula for costume design. He believes that there is and that one must answer these three questions to create a successful design: What is the underlying emotion? What are the qualities of this particular character? Where are the actions? Through careful script analysis the costume designer must engage with the actions of the play: "What am I seeing? What am I hearing in my head, costume-wise?" Loud shoes punctuate an entrance; a movement can be enhanced by the swish of taffeta; a hat or a cape being removed can be a symbolic way to reinforce a revelation in the plot. However, the answer

Costume designer Rafael Jaen in his office at Emerson College. Boston, Massachusetts, 2007.

to such questions is based on cultural interpretation, which might or might not translate for the audience. This is particularly true of the coded symbolism of colors. For example, if a character is sad, Rafael said, you could dress him in grays or blues, but does that necessarily connote sadness for each member of the audience? Rafael continued, saying that in theory a young, virginal woman is usually dressed in white or off-white, or the lightest hue in the color palette. If the costumes of a production are black, the virgin wears gray. A pale tone for the young woman's dress seems to be a cultural assumption in the United States, but Rafael, who grew up in South America, said that in Latin culture, in the initial ball scene in the Capulet home in *Romeo and Juliet,* for example, Juliet is dressed in red, the fashionable Italian color of the period. American audiences would be surprised to see a fourteen-year-old virgin dressed in red, a color we associate with seduction, not innocence.

Rafael describes the dilemma of the designer. After meticulous research on the fabric and color choices of the period in which the drama is set, a good designer must compromise, making adjustments to fit the contemporary expectations of the audience. If he were to design for an American production of *Romeo and Juliet,* instead of going with the period color—red—he might have to dress Juliet in white for the scene in which Romeo first sees her at her parents' dance.

And so we further hone the definition of the stage costume. In Rafael's words: "And that is what makes it a *costume:* it's not realistic. It's—I hope it's firmly based in reality—but when it translates to the stage and it's telling a story, it has to adapt to be able to tell that story. I count on the projections of the audience." The costume should communicate without necessarily calling attention to itself. For when it does, it can distract the audience from the play. Rafael said, "If the audience begins to think, 'Why is Prospero in *The Tempest* wearing a cape with feathers?,' then we didn't tell the story."

A good costume designer is one who selects the clothing that tells the story, underscoring the acting, the directing, and the meaning of the plot. Rafael, like other designers, finds it "bittersweet" when his costumes enhance the production but are not mentioned in reviews by theater critics, who seem to focus on the actors and the direction. When costumes are inappropriate or ugly, they are certainly mentioned in reviews, but adequate or even excellent clothes often pass without remark. In any collaborative endeavor it is difficult to remain embedded within the team of participants. In theater the great challenge is to work holistically, to blend into the production yet gain recognition as an individual. This mixture of social obligation and individualistic desire is best met by the actor who realizes a character through her body, her psychology, her ability to become someone else while remaining herself. Rafael generalizes on the egos of those in the theater:

> And that is the danger, you know. I think, for us designers, we want our work to be recognized, and sometimes, when we are really into it, we may make choices to, like, "Notice my work. I don't care about anybody else. I want to get an award and be noticed." And you know, that's part of theater, we all want that, but I think the true collaboration is to know what to tone down and think, honestly, "Is that telling the story, or is that telling another story? Is there another story being told that I am not aware of?"

A fashion designer's goal is to create clothes that will undeniably signify him by the cut, silhouette, fabric, and details, as Christian Dior did with his signature "New Look" in the 1940s.[29] A costume designer, on the other hand, must also make clothes beautifully, with much creativity and flair, yet the garments must speak not of him but of the period and place of the drama, the mood of the scene, the temperament of the character. There is another fundamental difference between fashion designers and costume designers. Rafael, like many designers, pulls about half of his clothes and builds the other half; many pieces fall somewhere in between. Pulled pieces are often altered, dyed, retailored, and embellished. Some of these alternations can be reversed, and the garment can return to the theater's stock in its original state. Pulling is a way to save time and money and, for Rafael, an added creative challenge: "Can I make this look like that?"

For Michael LaChiusa's contemporary drama *See What I Wanna See,*[30] Rafael designed a wide variety of costumes, including a pair of Japanese kimonos as well as men's and women's evening dress from the 1950s. He built the kimonos from scratch, taking inspiration from Japanese *manga* comic books. For the 1950s vignette he bought the men's suits and was thrilled to find an authentic Dior gown in a donation box that had come into the costume stock of Emerson College's theater department. The gown was in terrible shape, not ready to be worn onstage, so Rafael "steamed it to death," changed the hem, added some panels so the actor could dance in it, and painted the fabric to look like origami paper. By altering a found piece, Rafael achieved the characteristic period silhouette and made the dress conform to the actions required of the actor, and by painting it he was able to connect this vignette visually to the earlier Japanese one. (The *Boston Globe* review of the show did give a nod to Rafael's designs.[31])

When a designer makes or remakes a garment it belongs to the theater company that paid for its labor and materials, or, if the contract stipulates, it returns to the designer and enters the costume stock of his place of employment. The costume designer does not own the piece, nor does he keep it in his private collection. I asked Rafael if he ever tagged his name on the pieces that he made from scratch; he said no. When he owned his own couture line, every piece had his company name and his logo, but with costumes a certain level of anonymity is preferable, since it allows the next designer to alter a piece and claim someone else's design. Some theater companies, when renting costumes, allow for modifications as long as the garment is not dyed or cut. Many alterations are easily reversible, so they signal the unique vision of the costume designer only during the run of the play. While the garments are not the intellectual property of the costume designer, his sketches are, and they are copyrighted. Designers who belong to the union—as Rafael does, both to the USITT (United States Institute for Theater Technology) and the USA (United Scenic Artists) 829—receive royalty payments for their original designs when a production goes on tour.

A more sensitive topic is altering the original costume concept by the actors once the designer has left the show. Many years ago, in an "off-off-off-off Broadway" production that Rafael worked on, the actors decided to wear their clothes differently and even made changes to his original costumes. He was hurt by the results: "Wow, all my work and they just felt like they can change it." Now belonging to the union ensures that his costumes will not be changed, but, more important, Rafael starts to work with the actors immediately, bringing them into the process early on. He chooses to attend the rehearsals and said, "I want it to be a collaboration. I want it to work, and I want it to make sense. I really want to make sure that I have communicated and collaborated with the actors, so they understand what they are doing. They may not—as a person—they may not agree with the clothing that I am giving them, but as a character, I want it to make sense." When Rafael takes the time to explain to the actors why he has made specific costume choices, he intends to aid their performance on the stage, enhancing the entire production. Rafael's creativity and artistic pleasure depend on the actors—for they are the ones who will literally showcase his art on the stage night after night. So he works to help them find their characters. Like everything in the theater, his effort is mutually beneficial. The sooner the actors are brought in, the more they internalize Rafael's vision of the characters and their clothing choices, the closer the entire production will come to a unified and harmonious realization of the drama.

Meeting the cast, and especially *seeing* the actors, is important for Rafael; it allows him to gauge the appropriateness of his costumes for the particular body types of the actors as well as for the characters they portray. Rafael recounted an incident from many years ago. The director cast a lead actor, and Rafael was told that she resembled a famous Hollywood actor, beautiful, toned, and fit. Visualizing a sexy physique, Rafael made preliminary sketches, but once he met the actor, he realized that she did not actually resemble the celebrity and that the costume he had sketched would be wholly wrong for her. But by this stage in the process the director of the play had become attached to Rafael's original design. Rafael noticed that the actor herself was uncomfortable with being asked to wear such a revealing costume. Unsuitable for her, it would flatter only someone with a toned body (someone like the celebrity Rafael was incorrectly led to believe she resembled). He learned much from this experience:

> I don't assume that my director knows how to design. I don't assume that my director is really observant of body types. They may be. But maybe they are not.
>
> Because I know when I see the actors—I can look at an actor at this stage of my career, I can say, "What's their height? What's their weight?

What's their size?" I can spec them in a second. I learned to do that, because you need to, on the spot sometimes, pull costumes. And put things together, because, you know, clock's ticking. But I don't assume that my director knows.

And even, for some reason, I may do rough sketches, research, arrange things like the color palette, put all that together, and then I won't commit to the final sketches until I meet the cast.

I don't want any surprises.

If the actors have been cast but they are not in town yet, I get their emails and ask for basic sizes and their headshots. Sometimes actors don't have their current measurements, or they choose to forget.

But I do as much as I can to get a sense of who is this person physically, because that is what I am working with. And it's part of the design. You know the costume is not going to work in telling lies.

Rafael does not assume that actors know their correct sizes or that directors know how to read body types. But he trusts his own skills, which are his unique contribution to the theatrical collaboration. He is able to combine his experiences as draper, tailor, and architect to give him a wide perspective on the whole process of costume design.

If I draw something, I know that it can be built, because *I* can build it. If I spec something—money-wise, design-to-cost—I know what it is, because I have managed costume shops for a long time. If I am talking about clothing as environment, I know what it means, because I understand the visual language of architecture. Or set design, for that matter. Or lighting. So that is what I bring to the equation.

To play well in collaboration, one must know one's own part and understand the parts of the others. By understanding the physical space—the architecture, set design, and lighting variables—Rafael can choose clothes that work within that environment. His skills as a draper help him inform the cutter when a costume is being redesigned to suit the body of a particular actor—an undertaking that often involves altering the design enough to hide the wearer's flaws. This brings us to two additional, albeit unofficial, mandates of costume design—to make the actor physically comfortable, and to make the actor attractive. Many actors I spoke with told me that when they are onstage, there are so many things they must remember—the blocking of their movements, the entrances and exits, their lines—that they do not also want to be aware of their costumes. Heels too high or pants too tight distract the actor from performance. It is easy to sympathize, for after the designers and the director have moved on to the next play, the actors are left there, alone onstage, realizing a collective dream for the run of the production.

Many years ago when Rafael was working in a costume shop, the foreman told everyone they had to wear corsets all day as they went about their usual jobs. After a few hours Rafael became aware of the physical hardship that the undergarment entailed and how hard it was to concentrate on work when one was so conscious of one's body. As a result of this experience, his design process involves asking actors if they have problems with their bodies—feet, knees, or lower back. His designs hide flaws in the physique and compensate for weak points in the actor's body. This was a revelation to him: "So you start to think, 'Wow, this is a human being,' and no matter how much training they have, I need to be aware of this." One of Rafael's costume design teachers taught him that designers must make actors look good onstage; they must avoid making them look "wrong or intentionally ugly." The actors are the only ones in this collaborative project who appear onstage; everyone else is behind the scenes (only their work is seen). Like Hollywood actors, theater actors are often recognized by their fan base, and their attractiveness, when appropriate to the play, becomes a variable in judging good costume design.

Rafael understands that if the actor is not pleased with the costume, her performance will be affected, and that the performance of the actors is a key factor in the play's success. He says his goal is to "facilitate" the work of the actor by designing a garment that not only allows her to breathe, sing, dance, and gesture but makes her feel comfortable and look beautiful as well. The costume designer's hope is to bridge the gap between the director and the actor by helping her—through her clothes—to arrive at a mutual understanding about the character. He gave me two examples of this process, both involving designs he made for Ellen Adair in Boston.

The first example came from a production of Shakespeare's *The Comedy of Errors,*[32] which was designed to suggest the films of Federico Fellini. Rafael evoked the contours and types found in Fellini films, including the voluptuous bodies of actors like Sophia Loren. He explained that in costume design the theory is to focus on the dress of the principal characters, since they carry the weight of the story and have the most stage time. In designing for the ensemble, one has the freedom to design purely for affect, allowing for outrageous costumes, since these are seen for only a short time—not long enough to distract the audience, but enough to serve as catalyst for the main action. The kitchen maid in *The Comedy* of *Errors* was played by Ellen Adair. Shakespeare describes this "kitchen-wench" as a "beastly creature," "spherical like a globe," a "fat friend," and even a "mountain of mad flesh."[33] During our interview, two years after the production, Rafael remembered that the maid was "atrocious" yet had some "sass" about her; she is determined to get a stranger, Dromio of Syracuse (whom she mistakes for her husband), to sleep with her. So Rafael did not simply design a typical costume for the kitchen maid; instead he provided Ellen, who is slim, with an enormous padded bra and padded buttocks that when placed underneath a black maid's dress with white apron, gave her the exaggerated voluptuous silhouette of the women in Fellini films. Rafael's extravagant costume furthered the comic thrust of this hilarious play, but it also helped the actor find the "character's spine." The bra was weighted down, heavy with seeds, affecting Ellen's center of gravity, changing her gait, and adding a jiggly, sassy feature to her every step.

In my interview with Ellen Adair, she mentioned this costume as an instance in which the costume designer helped her find the character.[34] Seeing the costume led her to understand "Oh, *this* is who I am." Although the "gigantic breasts and the gigantic butt" were, according to Ellen, "kind of cartoonish" and unrealistic, they "completely created the physique" of her character. She said that when actors work with Rafael, they go to his studio before rehearsals have begun and receive detailed descriptions of the costumes, along with his sources of inspiration, and are shown sketches and photographs. Ellen said Rafael is rare among designers in taking the time to explain his costume choices. Most designers show the actors the costumes without a detailed rationale for the decisions behind them. But Rafael walks the actors through the process, Ellen said, telling them, "'This is why I did this.' And that is part of the reason I love his costume design—because it's so much richer for me as an actor to be able to add his insight to my own." Seeing the costumes before Ellen has even started rehearsing helps with her initial conceptualization of the character: "We are immediately on the same page. I sort of start in line with his vision, and I know that I will have this gigantic butt for the show. All of my attention, through the motion of my character, was centered in my hips. So it was really low, and kind of wiggly."

That was not the only time that a costume created by Rafael guided Ellen toward her character. Ellen refers to his costumes as "gifts," presents the designer gives to the actor during her quest to embody the character she will portray. In Amy Freed's *The Beard of Avon,* Ellen played both the boy actor Geoffrey Dunderbread and Lady Lettice.[35] The play takes place in London during Shakespeare's time and includes what Rafael calls a "Shakespearean twist"—a woman (the actor, Ellen) playing a boy (Geoffrey) who plays women in the play. The first task

Actor Ellen Adair, 2004. *Photo by Paul Sirochman, courtesy of Ellen Adair.*

for Rafael was to make Ellen look like a boy, which was particularly challenging since he found her to be so tall and so beautiful, "like a fashion model." He had to make her boyish yet still attractive and somewhat feminine, because men in the play fall in love with Geoffrey, mistaking him for a real woman. Rafael chose to make her look androgynous: "First, I had to tell myself to believe that she could look like a boy. What do we need to do to get rid of the stuff that I thought were her female traits?" He started at the head, hiding Ellen's long hair under a blue cap, a coif, and deemphasizing her face by the addition of pale makeup. (Ellen remembers that the shade was called "alabaster" and that it was like wearing a mask, since it "neutralized" her face.) Rafael also needed to hide her feminine silhouette. This he accomplished by wrapping her chest with a bandage to flatten it, then covering her with a chemise of coarse muslin, the choice of fabric signaling a man's garment. Added challenges were the quick costume changes required for Ellen to transition from a boy to an aristocratic woman and then back. For this reason Rafael made her a pair of balloon breeches that doubled as a crinoline slip beneath the dress she wore as Lady Lettice. He also gave Ellen heavy men's shoes to help her walk like a man. Her pants created a new silhouette and, being so puffy, helped her to affect a male gait by forcing her legs apart. While this costume, with its coif, wide breeches, and coarse muslin chemise evoked a boy, Rafael felt it also needed to be beautiful and poetic; "there has to be something lyrical," he said, for Geoffrey sings songs about love in the play and has many admirers. To achieve this effect, Rafael added decorative gold stars to the pants in order to evoke the imagery of the songs the boy sings and to add a soft touch to the costume.

In my first interview with Ellen, she mentioned these balloon pants as an example of a favorite costume piece that enhanced her performance. The pants helped her walk like a man, and, being worn under all the dresses Geoffrey wears when he plays female characters in the plays-within-the-play, Ellen was constantly reminded that she was not a woman playing women, but a woman playing a boy playing female characters, since she felt the pants beneath her dress. The pants that doubled as crinoline kept her legs apart and "proved, then, a difficulty that I had to work with when I was playing a woman. So I had to work on other ways to make that physicality of the woman that I was actually playing to be very different, without actually being able to put my legs together." Those pants were a bit too big around Ellen's waist, providing another, but unintended, gift to the physical work she had to do for the role. Ellen as Geoffrey would pull up the pants, and that "became the primary gesture of my character." During the run of the show, Ellen was asked if she wanted the pants taken in, but by that time she did not want to abandon that characteristic, boyish gesture. Whenever Geoffrey finished a scene in which he was playing a female role, Ellen would hike up the pants underneath whatever female costume he was wearing. "It made me, as the actor, really feel like I was getting back into the reality of those pants." Ellen and Geoffrey transitioned back into maleness, while still in female dress, by pulling up the pants. Ellen was pleased that it is a "contemporary male gesture" among young men who wear "gigantic big pants that are precariously belted around their thighs—you always see them hiking their pants up." This contemporary gesture by an Elizabethan youth helped Ellen feel like a "fourteen-year-old boy," a good actor who is good at portraying women, but who is happy to remind himself that he is male. The costume helped Ellen achieve a nuanced psychological reading of her character.

IN ARCADIA

The theater is the center of a spiral of artful collaboration: The playwright creates a world; the director interprets it for the production; the set designer creates the physical environment within which the actors develop the blocking of their movements; and the set offers the background, the physical context for the costume designer's clothes. For Rafael the set is the "paper" on which he is "painting." Working together, this crew generates "the magic of the theater."

One moment of magic for Rafael comes when he shows the actors his costume sketches. "They are engaged and there is something wonderful that happens when they see the sketch at the time," he said. "And some of them will look at the sketch, and they start standing like the sketch." Actors are being shown the clothes, and through these garments they are learning about the character, whose socioeconomic status, morals, and psychology Rafael helps to refine: "If you tap into the character, the actor, intuitively, will go there." Since the sketches are finalized only after Rafael has met the actors—or at least seen their headshots—he waits to connect the actor to the character, as he explained in an email: "I want to make sure that my research and sketches resemble the actor playing the part. I believe that it helps him/her in identifying with the design idea when they see themselves."[36] After that, his job is done and he retreats behind the scenes.

When all the members of the collaborative team have done their parts, a successful product becomes possible. Let us consider the case of Tom Stoppard's *Arcadia,* a production that involved Rafael Jaen working once again as the costume designer with the artistic director Diego Arciniegas and the actors Ellen Adair and Lewis Wheeler.[37] The play is set in Sidley Park, an English country estate, and the actions alternate between the early nineteenth century (1809–1812) and

Female costume sketches for Tom Stoppard's *Arcadia*, 2005. Publick Theatre, Boston, Massachusetts. *Photo courtesy of Rafael Jaen.*

Male costume sketches for Tom Stoppard's *Arcadia*, 2005. Publick Theatre, Boston, Massachusetts. *Photo courtesy of Rafael Jaen.*

the present (1989). Ellen and Lewis played the nineteenth-century characters Thomasina Coverly and her tutor, Septimus Hodge. In 2006 this production of *Arcadia* won Boston's Elliot Norton Award for best production, and Arciniegas's artistic guidance won him the Norton Award for best director.[38] The play also received four IRNE (Independent Reviewers of New England) nominations: Ellen Adair for best actress; Lewis Wheeler for best actor; Diego Arciniegas for best director; and best production for a drama/comedy.[39]

Rafael explained his design concept for the costumes in a long email message to me. His first goal was to highlight the themes of the play. He was particularly inspired by the idea of algorithms:

> An algorithm is a specific set of instructions for accomplishing a task that will terminate in a defined end-state. I thought that the play was structured (programmed) in a way that reflected this process. As the scenes play out, a character from the past and one from the present set out to complete a mathematical equation. The characters from both periods get closer together till scenes from both times are played simultaneously. . . . When we arrive at the play's climax, the events from the past terminate in a defined end-state.
>
> I explored the idea of designing each costume as an algorithm, each character would have a complete set of combined pieces that would get added or removed in a methodical way; their colors would get stronger or subtler depending on the actions of the play. I used the same "formula" for all the actors. It included a base costume, outerwear, millinery, footwear, and specific accessories. These were combined in a way that reflected the time period, the character's age, the time of day and the contrast between indoors and outdoors. The socio-economic status was equitable amongst all the characters—higher middle class academics by today's standards.[40]

An added challenge to the design is that Boston's Publick Theatre is an outdoor space, and the costume designer cannot rely on steady light, temperature, and humidity as he can in an indoor venue. Rafael had to take the natural environment into account when deciding on the particular hues of each nineteenth-century costume within a "romantic palette": Thomasina in "youthful pastoral pink"; Septimus in "light new gold"; Thomasina's mother, Lady Croom, in "bright old gold silks." The background against which these colors would be seen had to be considered, for, as Rafael said, "My costumes had to compete with the gorgeous trees and lush surroundings of the outdoors venue" of Boston in the summer. Ellen told me that when she was introduced to the costume concept by Rafael, he showed her a picture of a young girl wearing a bonnet, an English painting from the beginning of the nineteenth century. Everything in the scene was moving in Ellen's memory of it—the garments were fluttering in the breeze—and she realized that

> Rafael had constructed the costumes for that show almost knowing that the wind is going to pick up and it's going to blow, and capitalizing on this. So he talked about specifically adding layers to things, or sort of light, more gauzy, diaphanous material in order that if the wind picked it up, it would blow the veil, or I remember the ribbons in the bonnet, when I was sixteen-year-old Thomasina.

An excellent costume designer takes into account the intention of the playwright, reinforces the themes of the story, and accounts for the physical environment. The result is a gift from the designer to the actor, who uses the costume to lose herself into the character, into the world of the play. The designer's work is done; he exits and the actors enter.

THE ACTORS

Ellen Adair was in her mid-twenties at the time of my initial interviews with her. Her education at Boston University centered on the study of English literature; as an artist, she has worked professionally in the theater and on television. At the beginning of my interviews with her, in 2006, she was based in Boston; later she toured nationally with the American Shakespeare Center in 2007–2008; and she is now based, as theater professionals must be, in New York City. In 2014 she and her husband, Eric Gilde, formed the Happy Few Theatre Company. Ellen is tall and attractive with pale skin and dark hair. When she played Thomasina in *Arcadia,* her hair fell in tight ringlets around her shoulders. With her flawless skin and small features, she is reminiscent of the beauties of the nineteenth century. In an early interview she told me how much she loved the costume for Thomasina, knowing

Lewis Wheeler as Septimus Hodge and Ellen Adair as Thomasina Coverly in Tom Stoppard's *Arcadia,* 2005. Publick Theatre, Boston, Massachusetts. *Photo courtesy of Rafael Jaen.*

that Rafael wanted to "make costumes that these people live in. Instead of, you know, feeling like they were maybe kind of fantastical. I think that may be part of the reason that, to date, my costume for Thomasina was my favorite costume that I have ever had."[41]

According to Rafael, Ellen wore "a pink shift made out of two-layered batiste, silk organza pinafore with embroidered flowers, ankle length." What Ellen appreciated about the garment is that it did not feel or look like a costume, a "fantastical" creation for the stage, but rather that "it felt real. It felt absolutely real." "I remember, when the first time that I put it on, in the costume shop, I had this feeling of elation. Like, finally my skin fit in the way I had always wanted it to, now that I was wearing this dress," she said. The dress helped Ellen realize the character of Thomasina Coverly, aiming for a feeling of truth: "To see it on yourself and to not feel like that it looks like a costume, that it just looks like my clothing. It feels more real, and that's at least what we're striving for."

Lewis Wheeler, another Boston-area actor, comes from a theatrical family: his father is a director and his mother an actor. He studied theater and film at Cornell University and has an MFA from the American Film Institute. He acts onstage as well as in television and film. With his charming smile and "Byronic" curly hair, Lewis was appropriately cast as the charismatic tutor Septimus Hodge in *Arcadia*. For Lewis, Rafael chose, in his own description, "a romantic and masculine poet's shirt out of Egyptian cotton, fitted knickers made out of spring wool, and high leather boots." This outfit not only accentuated Lewis's physique but also helped the actor time-travel. Lewis said this about his costume:

> That was a show where the particularly period costumes did help me plug into that character. Long cuffs. A long jacket. Shirt with frilliness, you know, things going on up here.
>
> It's one thing if it's a modern play, and you are wearing blue jeans and sneakers. But when you are doing something that is in another time and place, those costumes help you to get there, and feel different.

I asked Lewis if seeing himself in that costume, in the mirror, is what helped transport him to another place.[42] He replied by explaining that it is not just the visual effect of the clothes but the sensory one as well.

> Yes, a little bit. But just the way you *feel*. The way it *feels* on you. Having all of this physical weight, and flowing material, makes you carry your body differently. It helps you to feel not like yourself, in a good way. Even though you are still using yourself, it helps you kind of *shift* who you are, into being that person.

His Septimus costumes transformed Lewis into a "romantic, hero-y kind of person," making him feel "dashing, a little elaborate in a kind of poetically, romantic way."

The art of the actor is to inhabit the character through his body. An actor aims for a notion of truth, and costume is one venue for the achievement of realism in art. Costumes affect actors through how they make them feel—both how the costume feels physically against the skin and how the actors feel psychologically while wearing those garments. It is the task of costume designers, as Lewis explained to me, to help an actor achieve that feeling: "They say, 'Look this isn't a costume. This is not wardrobe. This is your clothes.' And so you have to feel as comfortable in it as you do in your own clothes of your own life." The actor, for his part, must accept this gift of garments. As Lewis said, "For a lot of plays, you are given your costume. You have to live with it or work your way into it. And that can be sometimes hard, because it is not a skin that you are used to using."

We have already seen that some of Rafael's costumes have helped define the character for Ellen, whose objective onstage is "to be interesting, and be truthful, and be appropriate. Everything I do as an actor is about trying to get to the greatest truth. I am looking for ways for things to feel natural." Ellen told me there are many ways of coming to truth in acting. Costume—along with research, voice, and gesture—can be utilized to prepare the actor for the attainment of a truth that should be present in every single performance. A feeling of achieved realism, of truth in art, is a variable that cannot be controlled or guaranteed beforehand as the costumes, props, and other external devices can be. Ellen said, "Truth is the ultimate goal. And, like truth in anything, it is always fleeting, and always a goal that can still, every second, be lost, be attained, be lost, be attained, and that is why acting is so much fun, because your work is never finished."

As soon as the actor is cast, she starts working on her character, picking up clues from the playwright, inspiration from historical research, and working within the artistic mandates of the director and the various designers. She works on the voice, the stance, the gestures, the beats of the scene, but the costume is an offering. Ellen described it like this: "In many ways gesture does the same things for an actor that costume does. But costume is like a gift. Gestures are something that I have to work on. And I have to get from myself. My body and gesture can come very organically out of costume." The gift of the costume can help the actor on this journey, whether her approach is internal to external or vice versa.

One modern style of acting was defined by Russian director Konstantin Stanislavski in the late nineteenth century. His famous "method" urged actors to internalize the character, using their own experiences, imagination, and feelings to bring the character to life on the stage. Stanislavski trained actors to achieve a sense of "stage truth." If the actors did not believe in the reality of the moment, they could not reach the audience, enabling the spectators to suspend their disbelief in the ambit of the theater. In what is called "internal to external work," actors use their own thought processes and experiences, ingesting the mood, objectives, and psychology from close script analysis and drawing the character out from within. In "external to internal work," actors begin with outward behavior instead of inward feeling, using gestures, postures, the center of gravity, movement, voice, dialect, and speech, and they reach the core of the characters through the outward features that define them. The two tracks are interrelated, obviously. As Ellen said, "Through external cues, I will come to an internal truth that will then feed back to the external." On both of these paths to theatrical truth, costume is important; it either helps you externalize through the clothing the emotion of the character, or it helps you get to the character by what he wears and how these clothes condition his movements. Celebrated Shakespearean actor Sir John Gielgud understood how inappropriate external cues hinder the actor's search for truth:

> I do not like Shakespeare being acted in any period later than Jacobean, because it seems to me that if you are playing in Restoration costume with big wigs, in eighteenth-century costume with white wigs and high heels, or in Victorian clothes with full skirts, strapped trousers and frock coats, you cannot sit or stand or move except in the way these clothes demand. The furniture makes different demands too—the way you sit on chairs or sofas. If you are trying to speak Shakespeare's English it complicates matters to set the play in any period later that that of Charles I.[43]

The Stanislavski method of attaining the greatest amount of stage truth can be contrasted with German director Bertolt Brecht's concept of the "epic theater," in which both the actors and the audience empathize with the characters but retain a sense of distance in order to achieve a better understanding of the art form. Brecht's theory breaks the imaginary "fourth wall," the wall separating the fictional setting of the play from the audience members. As Ellen explained to me, Brecht "was interested in reminding the audience at all times that they were watching a play. 'We are watching a play; this is not real.'"

Costumes can support the Brechtian effect. When the 2007–2008 touring troupe of the American Shakespeare Center, the "Piercing Eloquence Tour," worked its way from Staunton, Virginia, to Indianapolis, Indiana, I watched Ellen and the other members of the cast in *Henry V*. The actors came onstage in their street clothes and gradually added more costume pieces until all were transformed by appropriate costumes. As the play wound down the actors slowly changed again into their everyday dress. As an audience member I found it effective to watch the actors become the characters and then transform back into themselves for the curtain call. They took me, steadily, away from my world, into the world of Shakespeare's history; then they delivered me back into the theater space of Indiana in the twenty-first century. Ellen told me that the actors were asked to wear their "rehearsal clothes" onstage until they would be replaced by their costumes. I noticed that Indiana native Evan Hoffmann, the actor who played King Henry, first appeared wearing an Indianapolis Colts T-shirt, referencing the local football team and confirming his regional affiliation. Ellen, who played several scenes in *Henry V* as the Boy, wore a skirt to begin. "I took delight in really presenting myself as a girl, and knowing that the next time that the audience was going to see me, that I'd be a boy," she said. "I didn't want to appear sort of gender-neutral. Most actors delight in the opportunity to show how different they can become." Ellen used this Brechtian device to showcase herself as an actor, for when she played the Boy, she indeed seemed to become him, successfully bridging the various obstacles between the actor and the character—time, geography, social circumstance, age, and gender—for she was thoroughly feminine when later in the play she was the French princess opposite the English king.

The American Shakespeare Center's "Piercing Eloquence Tour" also included a production of *The Merchant of Venice,* for which all the actors sat on benches at the edge of the set onstage. What was highlighted was the ability of the actors to sit and watch the play, laughing and reacting as audience members, then suddenly to stand up and instantly inhabit their characters. The virtuosity of the actor was on display, as was the role of the costume. In *The Merchant of Venice,* two women, Portia and her maid, Nerissa, play male barristers: Portia becomes a "doctor of laws" and Nerissa becomes a "lawyer's clerk." The audience watched the two female actors, Ellen Adair and Ginna Hoben, become lawyers before our eyes, since their costume changes happened onstage. We saw how a robe and a wig could help an actor get into a role. In this case part of the external work of the actor—that of donning a costume—was externalized, literally, by taking place onstage instead of backstage.

The actor's command, according to Stanislavski, is to "continue to live" onstage, not to "begin to live." For the actor to achieve this truth, the "active combination of fact and fiction," she needs to respond to two kinds of stimulus, one external, one internal. Acting coach Walt Witcover describes these basic "ingredients" as the "inherent conditions and demands of the stage" and the actor's own experiences.[44] The play's demands and the physical environment of the set and costumes are external components to which the actor must add the internal element of her own history, will, and psychology. Costumes not only help the audience visualize the "transformation" that the character has undergone; they also help the actor internalize this same transformation. Costumes function for both wearer and viewer. In Moira Buffini's play *Silence,* for example, Lewis Wheeler played Ethelred Rex.[45] The costume changes in this show established the "character arc," helping Lewis change in front of our eyes from what he called a "wimpy, bratty, whiny king" into "this terrible, Adolph Hitler/George W. Bush character." He laughed, and then elaborated:

> When you get to change costumes like that, that helps. Because you can come onstage, you don't have to do anything, you just stand there. And people know, "Oh, look, he's cleaned up; he's different; he's got a sword like a warrior."
>
> And so, so much of what you communicate is, or can be, without words and without particularly big action. You can just let your costume do the talking, really.

COSTUME: THE EXTERNAL FACTOR

Until recently theaters did not routinely provide costumes for their actors. It was not the responsibility of the theater company to engage in the time-consuming and expensive endeavor of designing and making or buying an appropriate costume for each character. The theater either had a stock of costumes that the actors rummaged through, or actors provided garments from their own private wardrobes. Smaller community and regional companies still do not have the budget to hire a costume designer or purchase costumes for the actors. In the late nineteenth century the young Konstantin Stanislavski famously bought Eastern fabrics and props for a production of *Othello* that he was directing. He wanted the costumes to fit the play instead of using clothes pulled from the theater's costume stock. The costume can be so vital that costume designer Jac Lewis refers to the costume as a "performing partner"—the garment is a collaborator in the actor's pursuit of stage truth.[46] The costume idea can be provided by several people—the director, the costume designer, and even the playwright, if he, like George Bernard Shaw, describes in detail what the characters wear.

From the time the actor has successfully auditioned for the play, the character is taking shape in the mind—and the body—of the actor. As Ellen Adair said, "Anywhere from the last fifty to the last ten percent of the character as a fully dimensional human being, I think, comes from the costume." She described the feeling of exhilaration when in the last few weeks, the set, the costume, and the lighting all come together: "I am inhabiting the world of this play as if it were real."

The costume is her partner. In the American Shakespeare Center's production of *The Taming of the Shrew,*[47] Ellen played Bianca, wearing an extravagant 1950s frock, brightly patterned and made extra puffy with the help of a substantial turquoise crinoline. Ellen recalled, "That dress just did a whole lot of acting for me. The dress was always going to make a statement for me, no matter what I did."[48]

In our earlier discussion of *Arcadia* we saw how fittings can be thrilling for the actor. Trying on the pink dress that Rafael had made for Thomasina made Ellen feel as though a version of herself had consolidated; her skin finally fit. Fittings can also be disarming. Lewis Wheeler said that a fitting can be an uncomfortable experience precisely because the actor will be physically confronted with the costume designer's version of his or her character: "And that is always scary because it is adding this part of your character that you are still working on. You are rehearsing, and you have just been wearing blue jeans or whatever, and suddenly you go to try on this stuff in some workshop. It's a nerve-wracking thing."

Actors are often given rehearsal shoes, corsets, or props so that they can become accustomed to wearing restrictive and unusual garment pieces. These are often provided during the first two weeks of rehearsal and greatly affect the actor's realization of the character. Many actors, like Ellen, want to be attired in something appropriate during rehearsals to help them embody the motions and feelings of their characters through the clothes. That does not always happen though. In Janet Kenney's play, *More Than What,* Ellen had a scene in which she wore a wedding gown. The fluffy white dress was not issued during the rehearsal period; it came later on and she found adapting to it difficult.[49] In *Marie Antoinette: The Color of Flesh,* which debuted in 2012 at the Portland Stage in Maine, Ellen played the French queen.[50] In preparation for the role, she read Antonia Fraser's biography of Marie Antoinette, from which she learned that the queen's walk was soft, light, almost like gliding. When the play went into rehearsal, Ellen was issued the wide side hoops for the dress—the panniers—but not the actual dress, which was very heavy. When the dress arrived, it worked against the affected glide that Ellen had incorporated into her impression of the queen. Playing the part in wrong or different clothes often disrupts Ellen's constant desire to achieve stage truth.

> It feels like something is not right. It feels like, you know, your clothes are on inside out. Or somebody put itching powder down your back.
>
> It's not that bad. But for me, rehearsing in something that is very inappropriate, even just in feel, I feel less professional, somehow.
>
> And I feel like I'm less likely to take the work that I do seriously, because it's less possible for me to get completely into the world of the play.

Actor Lewis Wheeler, 2004. *Photo by Peter Urban, courtesy of Lewis Wheeler.*

The world of the play—the magic of the theater—most often comes to life during "tech week," the week leading to the opening night, when the actors finally move into the actual theater, onto the set and among the furniture, where they experience the effects of the lighting and sound and wear their costumes. As Lewis described it, when the dialogue, the actions, the physical setting, and the costumes are placed in relation to one another, the arc of transformation begins to reach completion:

> It does make a big difference. It's hard to say, because it all contributes. Where, you know, you're in a rehearsal room. It's a generic room. You're wearing blue jeans. There's just flat, boring lighting. Everyone else looks the same.
>
> And then you get into the theater, and it's this *combination* of, you know, the set suddenly around you. The lights. The theater is dark. It's easier to put yourself in a place. Then your costumes. Sound. And each one of these little elements kind of adds to that world. The atmosphere. The mise-en-scène.
>
> The more of that that is there, the more real it becomes.

To Lewis's statement Ellen added that costume was for her the most important of these little elements, since "it affects the biggest change for me, because it is the most personal." Lewis agreed: "Costume is the one thing that belongs to you. The set—it might be your house, your room, so that is sort of yours." But costume is the element that literally drapes your body in performance; "it's right there by your body." *Mise-en scène*—"placing on stage"—is the moment when all the elements of the theater come into a coherent whole: the action, the physical setting, the lights, sound, and costumes.

Many actors have told me that another important component needs to be present for the world of the play to come alive: the audience. While it might not be seen, its presence is imperative for the actor's successful performance.

Actors generally do not react or interact with the audience during the play. There are exceptions—actors on the stage of the reconstructed Globe Theatre in London recover the mood of Shakespeare's era by interacting with the audience, and some modern theatrical events retrieve the dynamic of folk drama by drawing the spectators into the spectacle. One time when actors do engage with the audience is during a "talkback with the actors," an event that happens right after a performance and often includes the director and the actors, who return to the set in their street clothes. The sight of the actors wearing their own clothes—as opposed to their costumes—signals to the audience that these people are representing themselves, not the characters you just saw in the play. Questions about the plot are addressed to the actors in the third person, and they in turn answer appropriately, using third-person pronouns. In living history museums that utilize first-person interpretation, such as Conner Prairie in Indiana, the costumed individual answers in the first person, professing ignorance about the modern age. During talkbacks the uncostumed actor answers in the third person, free to range widely through time and space in her response. In the museum as on the stage, the presence of a costume signifies an assumed persona and sets limits on a character's worldview.

The talkback can be disorienting, undoing much of the enchantment that the actor worked so hard to achieve, that was consolidated during tech week and accomplished in performance. In an email message, Lewis articulated this feeling:

> Talkbacks always take place after a show with the actors, and you are definitely there *as actor.* You are *out* of costume, in your street clothes, and it is a strangely analytical moment—*just* having finished the play, jumped out of costume, now sitting on a folding chair on your *set,* looking out at the audience with the *house lights on* [emphasis in original]. Very bizarre!
>
> Breaks the illusion and suspension of disbelief with a big bang! One actor in my last show didn't want to go to talkbacks—he didn't want to shatter that illusion—and didn't want to hear audiences and other actors "deconstructing" the artwork that he was a part of.
>
> I completely understand that point of view. But I do enjoy the talkbacks—you are kind of "representing" your character.[51]

The actors take the audience on a miraculous journey by experiencing the enchantment themselves on the stage. The actor's aim, according to theater critic Harold Clurman, is to "tell lies like truth."[52] We have seen how actors—during rehearsals and on the stage—use little lies in dress to work toward truth. To comprehend theatrical costume fully, I found it helpful to consider the actor's view of costumes in some of this book's other settings, returning to the most conspicuous American context in which costumes are worn: Halloween.

I asked Ellen Adair to describe some of her favorite Halloween costumes. She recalled dressing as Ozma of Oz and, more abstractly, as a bag of jellybeans and as a strawberry. Ellen agreed with me that the main criterion for the selection of a Halloween costume is to make the wearer attractive. "I never wanted to be ugly for Halloween," she said. "There's no real delight in that. It's about being, maybe prettier than you really are—being a princess or being a Swedish girl, or Ozma of Oz, being sort of more glamorous than yourself." I asked Ellen to compare wearing costumes for Halloween and wearing costumes on the theater stage. In her answer she alluded to the capacity of clothing to make the wearer more beautiful because the garments are beautiful in themselves:

> It's not just about putting on pretty clothes; it's about putting on new bodies. The clothes simply inform those new bodies—it doesn't feel to me anymore to be about the exact same thing that it was when I was six years old.
>
> It doesn't mean that I don't take delight in wearing pretty clothes. But that I take delight in the costume being appropriate.
>
> And so if the appropriate costume is a sack cloth—that's what I want to wear. Whereas as a child, I wouldn't necessarily have enjoyed that: "You get to go as a beggar for Halloween. Won't that be fun?" No, it's about it being pretty.
>
> Whereas, now, what's fun about putting on a different body is about it being different.

Ellen describes two distinct things—one is the act of dressing up in pretty clothes for the purpose of play or going out on Halloween; the other is the professional act of costuming for the goal of becoming another character. In dress-up clothes you are not playing somebody else; you are a version of yourself in different clothes. In dressing up you do not lose yourself as you do when costumed on the theater stage. What Ellen dislikes about Halloween is that the costume is not worn in a character-based context: you are in costume, but you are playing the role of yourself without the aid of a playwright, director, or fellow actors. To illustrate this point, Ellen told me about a time in 2002 when she dressed up as Hermione Granger, a character from J. K. Rowling's *Harry Potter* books. She made herself a costume—a little tie, a vest, a long black skirt, and a black dress cut up to look like a robe. She went around all evening asking questions and writing things down in a notebook she carried with her. In our interview in 2008, Ellen recalled the night many years ago:

> Last time I really dressed up for Halloween it was in college. And I hadn't dressed up for a while. But I was going to this kind of a costume ball with my then boyfriend, who was a theater major. And this college ball was in the School of the Arts. There were a lot of theater majors there.

The only people I really remember from that party were actors. Maybe it's because actors are that way.

And it wasn't just me, but it was a lot—a number of people went there—and because they were actors, and they're so deep in it, and also you're now twenty, so you don't know anymore how to play fifty percent make-believe; you only know anymore one hundred percent or zero percent. There were a few people—myself included—who weren't just dressed as that character, they *were* that character.

It was the most fun Halloween I ever had in my life.

For years whenever someone from that party ran into Ellen, they called her "Hermione," attesting to the fact that she had successfully assumed the persona of the fictional schoolgirl for the party. Having read the *Harry Potter* books, Ellen had used the costume to become Hermione for the night, putting the character's clothes into a loose script that provided her with a frame in which to improvise and create. As our conversation progressed, I expanded the contexts in which costumes are used to include Renaissance Faires and living history museums, asking for her thoughts on these comparisons. Ellen emphasized that what separates them from the theater is the presence of a script, a created world within which the costumed person operates. She conceded that both of these venues can include short plays, but those plays are not *Hamlet*. The improvised or scripted texts of the Renaissance Faire or "Revolutionary City" at Colonial Williamsburg are hardly as magnificent as scripts by Shakespeare, Beckett, or Stoppard. But it is precisely the theater frame—the result of a collaboration among the playwright, director, designers, and actors—that provides the greatest opportunity for engagement in the process of art. As Ellen so beautifully stated:

> So we know we have these lines that we have to say. And so, therefore, we're more free to believe them because we don't have to worry about making up what we're going to say next.
>
> Sometimes I joke and I say I make believe for my job. And that's kind of true. But it's a little different from kids' play. And it's a little different even from adults playing a role and improvising, because we have this play and this is where it begins and this is where it ends. And it only can take place with these people, and only takes place in this space, with these people watching, with these costumes, and the necessity of all those different things blend together to create what is a truthful and compact whole world.

It's sort of like two seconds before the play none of this is real. Then it's completely real within this. And then it's not real again as soon as we are bowing.

The playwright creates a world that is like ours, but abstracted, exaggerated, refined. Costume is not utterly unlike daily dress, and the onstage world bears a resemblance to our own, but in the theater's art, our values, emotions, and realities are easier to read. The lies on the stage lead ultimately not to stage truth, but to a truth beyond the confines of the theater space.

Collaboration is essential to the achievement of truth on the stage and for the actor in quest of honesty. In addition to the external factors of costume and script, there are also internal factors carried by the human being whose body, psychology, and creativity will inhabit and animate the play's world.

THE INTERNAL FACTOR OF THE SELF

A theater production begins with a text, moves through the selection of a director and designers, the creation of sets and costumes, the crafting of sound and lighting. But it will rest finally on the actors who perform the same play, with energy and commitment, night after night. Before every show the actors prepare by limbering their bodies and stretching their voices, by applying their makeup and dressing themselves in the clothing and mind-set of a character. Ellen put it this way: "Psychologically what I'm putting on mirrors physically what I'm putting on." To complete our exploration of theatrical costume, it is necessary to locate the point where the actor ends and the character begins along with the role costume serves in this transformation, this powerful blend of fact and fiction.

The character we see onstage cannot be the character as it is written on the page. Rather, it combines the person that a playwright invented and the actor who lends a body and mind to the character. A character exists by living in a human body. The actor must take the character from the playwright's text, incorporate mandates from the director and the costume designer, and internalize these through the filter of the actor's own philosophy, psychology, and experience. Lewis Wheeler explained:

For me, as an actor, I—a lot of people see it as playing this role. This character, something external to yourself, which in a sense it is. But for me it's really taking that character or role and using my own personality and history and experience and mixing the two.

In my attempt to learn when this mixing takes place, I asked Ellen to describe her general routine before each performance. She begins with vocal and physical exercises for about ten minutes, and then she changes clothes. "Putting on my costume, and getting my hair, and putting on my makeup is possibly the most important part of the ritual of getting into character," she said. At that moment, Ellen told me, she is starting to mix herself with her character: "When that life ends, and this life begins, and I am now two people in one person." The character has begun to emerge but it has not arrived yet. The character does not sit in the dressing room; it needs a stage and a script to live. The person in the dressing room is the actor midway in metamorphosis. "This is Ellen putting on the voice and the body of the character, but this is not the character yet." The point when the actor ends and the character begins varies from actor to actor. Sir Ian McKellen, the British Shakespearean actor, describes this moment in an interview for the *New Yorker*: "'I get myself into a little routine, which involves getting the hair right and putting on a little makeup,' he said. 'That will be the moment when I step over the line into the play.'" At the time of the interview as he prepared to go onstage, transformed by costume, McKellen looked at himself in the dressing room mirror, saw himself as the character, and exclaimed: "There he is!"[53]

The mingling of actor and character can prove to be difficult at times. Ellen talked to me about the difficulty of separating the character from herself.

> It is a problem. You want to assign a pronoun to your character, and which one do you pick? I often say "I." However, when I am thinking about the relationship between myself and my character, I have to use "I" and "she," but really all of it feels more like "I" than it does like "she."

I commented that her actor's art was to turn "she" into "I," and for the audience watching her it should all be "you." Ellen agreed. The separation between the actor and the character is fluid. In Lewis Wheeler's opinion, "It's not a hard line between your real life and the part you are playing. It's a porous thing going back and forth." Actors might incorporate into their daily lives some traits of the characters they have devised for the stage. Ellen told me she had picked up gestures from her characters, embodying and incorporating their ways of communicating. The actor's own self expands every time she plays a new role, and the experience of playing different characters accumulates, adding layers to the actor's laminated personality.

This identification of the actor with the character extends beyond the body to clothing as well. One way to manage this is to lend the character not only your body and your voice, but some of your own clothes, which then become part of the character's costume. Lewis often adds a personal item to the costume he wears onstage, providing his own "finishing touches." He does so in order to retain a bit of himself when he claims the character: "I guess I get somewhat proprietary about some of my characters. I really want to bring something of my own into the wardrobe." In 2007, during the time of my interview with Lewis, he was playing Briggs in a production of Harold Pinter's *No Man's Land*.[54] For that role he was allowed to go to a sizeable vintage store in Cambridge called the Garment District to pick out the leather jacket his character would wear. He came to a rack of about a 120 leather jackets.

> I went down the line, trying each one on. And finally found just the right, perfect one. That was sort of worn in, looked kind of—made me a bit seedy-looking. Wasn't too fancy. Was kind of long and baggy and all that.
> And when you find it, you just sort of know, you know it's the right one.

Such input from the actor is possible only when the costumes are being pulled or bought, not when they are being built in the costume shop. In this particular production the character Briggs also wears a pinky ring. The costume designer gave Lewis a couple of choices, but none of them felt right. They made him feel "uncomfortable," preventing him from fully realizing the character. So Lewis went to Harvard Square and tried on several rings until he found the perfect one, one that's "a little bit classy, little bit seedy." The ring helped him make the transformation: "It just makes me feel like that is mine, meaning the character is *mine*." The last finishing touch for this character was a tattoo on the forearm. This was Lewis's idea, though, of course, it had to be approved by the costume designer. Every day of the show's run, Lewis would draw a tattooed cobra on his arm. That bit of body art would be seen only for a few seconds, in a scene when Briggs rolls up his sleeve, but Lewis knew it was there and it made his work feel more truthful for him. These examples show that while the designer's costumes might be perfect, as Rafael's were for Ellen in *Arcadia*, actors can do more than accommodate to their costume designer's vision; sometimes they help refine the character through their own choices about costuming.

The character who wears something from someone's personal wardrobe has been influenced by that person's own style. But an actor may also want to appropriate something from the character's costume, as she has appropriated some of her mannerisms. As Ellen said to me, "If I could really lift the pieces of costumes—'lift' in, I guess, the sense of steal—from shows that I have been in, I certainly would if I could." While falling in love with several pieces of clothing

Lewis Wheeler as Briggs in Harold Pinter's *No Man's Land*, 2007. Photo © T. Charles Erickson, courtesy of American Repertory Theater.

(including the dresses worn by Thomasina in *Arcadia* and Mary Shelley in *The Yellow Leaf*), Ellen has occasionally been able to purchase a costume piece or shoes. I asked Rafael Jaen if it is possible to acquire part of the costume. He said that in theory actors could buy a piece from the producer, since costumes are the property of the production company, not the designer or the shop personnel. And on some occasions the actor may receive the costume as a gift, but this is rare. However, actors are not usually given the privilege of possessing clothing that was "theirs" during the run of the show.

Although clothes cannot be lifted from the stage nor removed from the theater, other aspects of the character's appearance may leave with the actor—hairstyle, for example, or facial hair and body weight. In Pinter's *No Man's Land,* Briggs is, in Lewis Wheeler's description, "a thug in London in 1975, a gay/bisexual, rough-tough, rough-trade kind of guy." For the play Lewis wanted to look "tough and un-handsome" by shaving his soft curly hair, putting on some weight, and growing a Fu Manchu mustache. During the time of our interview, Lewis was sporting this tough look and was made aware of it as he moved through Boston.

> I've noticed now, just walking down the streets, how people respond to me differently. Usually—because I am kind of a friendly person—people are warm and engaging and all that.
>
> But now, just whenever—on the subway, or buying something—people are much more, kind of, wary of me. Just because I look kind of frightening.

As Lewis walked, people moved away from him and a mother even pulled her baby stroller away from him on the subway. Experiencing the effects of that tough style outside the theater helped him get in touch with that character, to feel what it must be like to be such a person. The transformation was successful; strangers on the street thought he was "sinister." The result made Lewis lonely, feeling detached and alienated, in sharp contrast to the way people normally gravitate toward his big smile and friendly demeanor.

With the help of costume, actors gather a wide variety of experiences—both onstage and off. Unlike Ellen, who is always beautifully dressed, Lewis does not dress to be interesting in daily life. He is "sloppy and lazy" in his everyday dress, he told me, because he "dresses up" for his job. And through his job as an actor, he said, he realizes a fuller version of himself, bringing all the varieties of his personality into one complete being. As the sinister Briggs, he found it "fun" to play a bad guy, experiencing the world—whether London in 1975 or Boston in 2007—from that vantage point:

Acting is the transformation of yourself into this character. Even though you are using yourself, you want to be seen as this other person. With a new name, maybe a new accent. A new look, hairdo, whatever. Wigs.

And that costume is part of that transformation. It really helps you solidify. It's like a lever. It helps you, like a tool, to make that transformation more complete.

It's like Halloween, where people will only do it once a year. And they will wear some costume for a party, or if a man dresses up as a woman. And that same kind of fun, of just being playful, is acting.

It's playing dress-up that you do as a kid. To be able to do that on a regular basis, I think, it is, it's a treat. It is fun.

People usually get stuck in a slightly narrow, pigeon hole of who they are. It just seems that way—in their job, how they look. It's the rare person who is able to have different looks or be able to be free about how they appear.

And if you are acting, you get to have that transformation all the time.

It's Halloween every month.

PLAYING SOMEONE ELSE

Professional actors, like the other people we have encountered in this book, seek transformations and experiences through costumes and the contexts in which costumes are worn. Having access to social outlets in which hidden or suppressed versions of the self are released and exposed can foster the psychological growth and emotional maturity of the human being. In a long and moving interview, Ellen Adair and I talked about the psychology of acting. Echoing Lewis's statement, Ellen also believes that acting allows you to tap into aspects of a person's personality that aren't usually exposed. "Because just playing myself is not really any fun," she said. "I believe that it is all myself, but I really act because I am homesick for the parts of myself that I don't normally get to be. So it's all about being able to stretch into those parts of myself that just my daily life does not include."

Ellen plays a character that is not entirely unlike her. Something in her physical or mental makeup made her audition for the part and get it. Playing that character onstage allows her to work on herself while internalizing the character and then externalizing it for the audience. During the period of rehearsal, and sometimes during the run of the show, the character lives within the actor, giving a name and a fictional biography to something that has probably always been there. Ellen put it this way:

My character is the thing that I carry around with me all the time, and I am thinking about all the time in my life, at that point.

And that's why it's such a sad, sad—for me—sad thing to not be working on something all the time. It's like empty nest syndrome or something. Because I am so used to there being a little part of my heart where no matter what I'm doing—whether I am showering, or reading, or eating dinner, or going to another play—there is some part of me that is just trying to collect thoughts, and collect experience, and collect emotion around this character.

The actor goes about her life gathering the emotions that will be used in the character to provide background for the plot and to make sense on the stage. Ellen returned to the difficulty of separating the character from the actor, describing this unique bond as "unlike any human relationship, because you are the same person even as you are two people." She describes this relationship in a poem she wrote called "Flesh and Blood."[55]

> A character is like a child,
> in her constant need for love,
> in the way she will not tire
> of drinking up your love,
> unlike adults, who sicken.
>
> A character is like a parent
> in her patience,
> in the way she scoops you up,
> and that whole life she lived
> before you came.

Far from being someone else, the character is really a part of the actor, a relative, part child, part parent. It will use the actor's body to live, and it will borrow her creative energy. As Ellen described:

My character is like a child, but more literally my flesh and my blood, and my bones, my eyes, my brain, and my tongue, and my teeth, and my soul—every energy that I have is going towards creating this person.

And I want to dedicate all my body, and all my mind, and all my heart, to being this person.

The usual dichotomy—oversimplified and inaccurate—between dress and costume is that dress represents who you really are, and costume is worn when you are pretending to be someone else: dressing up for Halloween, reenacting the Civil War, or portraying a character onstage. All the case studies in this book trouble and falsify the conventional dichotomy. In this chapter professional actors have taught us that the costumed character onstage is not someone else, but a distinct visible version of the self. While ostensibly representing another character, the costume permits the exposure of an actor's truer self by highlighting a facet of his or her personality that cannot be fully realized in daily dress, a facet that emerges in the rendition of a complete human being with a biography, experiences, and aspirations. The stage allows for this revelation of the self within the confines of a script and a collaborative performance.

At the end of a play's run, the sets are taken down, the costumes are returned, but bits of the character remain in the actor's body. Ellen said she missed Thomasina, the character she played for the three-month run of *Arcadia:* "I will never look down and see her. I will never be her again." For while Ellen might play the character in another production of the play, Thomasina, as Ellen lived her, was possible only on that particular stage in Boston, with those particular actors, with that particular pink dress designed by Rafael. The character has gone, and the last night of the play can be devastating for the actor. Ellen said this about saying farewell to a show:

> It feels like such an absolute loss.
>   It's a different loss to cope with, because I know it's just me, always, at the end. I want to be able to hug the souls of my characters, and there is nothing there to kiss good-bye. There's nothing to lay down to sleep.

All the people we have met in this book use costume to reach beyond the tight limits of what they are allowed or expected to wear, of who they are expected to be. The professional actor takes this expansive impulse as far as it can go, employing it as a tool, an impetus for art. We end this chapter, and our exploration of costume, by considering the theater as an abstracted, heightened version of daily life in which art enhances our understanding of the mundane. Ellen does professionally what many of us do in the costumed events that lie within our reach:

> I track my life by the characters that I have been fortunate enough to be. And I mean *be,* not play. But really become.
>   My theory of acting is that every human being has this huge amount of capabilities of what they can do, but that no single human experience

can actually allow you to be everything, because certain choices will be cut off, or certain circumstances will cut off some of the possibilities of what you can be.

And I really act because I want to use the whole of myself. But because it *is* the whole of myself, I don't really think of the characters that I get to be as any less myself than the character I play every single day, as the sort of closest approximation of what this circumstance allows, of what these choices have brought me to.

CONCLUSION

Costume as Elective Identity

MY APPROACH TO DRESS, EXEMPLIFIED IN THIS BOOK'S CASE studies of costume, is folkloristic, an approach that uses ethnographic methods to situate actions in the contexts of creation, communication, and consumption.[1] If material culture is defined as "culture made material,"[2] and dress is a form of material culture, then dress (or costume) can be read as material manifestations of culture. Costume requires creators, so study must recognize individuals and individual interpretations of the costume traditions, standards, and goals. In focusing on the individual in the creative act, material culture studies combine attention to the object—its form, technology, and aesthetics—with attention to contexts of production and performance, where influences, processes, and procedures of evaluation come together. In acknowledging the centrality of contexts, we note those that are visible and tangible and those that are hidden in the mind yet fill the acts and products with meaning.

Costume—special dress chosen for extraordinary contexts—enables the expression of personal and social desires. All dress signals the wearer's identity, but costume enhances, elaborates, and exemplifies certain dimensions of the self. Sometimes costume is the sole outlet for deep emotions, becoming a means for social connection, artistic creativity, and psychological release. Folkloristic study stresses performances in which creative communications are shaped in accord with traditional genres that remove acts from the quotidian flow of things and bring attention to their merit and message.[3] Deep meanings emerge in the telling of a myth, the enactment of a ritual, the weaving of a carpet, the preparation of an elaborate meal, or the making and wearing of costumes.

Communication normally involves at least two people: one to give, one to receive. That exchange enables the expression of identity—by one to another, in conjunction with others, in opposition to others. The personal exists through the social.

The size of the social unit conditions the nature of the message. When one person tells a joke to another, face-to-face, the message can be shaped for the listener and sent easily. But when an author writes a book the social unit expands vastly. The author needs a wide range of people in support: makers of paper and ink and glue, mechanics who make and run the presses, the staff of the publisher—director, editor, compositor, designer, publicist, and smart people in the warehouse. Through an intricate network the author can compose a complex argument, then have it made permanent and distributed to great numbers of unknown readers. In performance a costume is more like a book than a joke. It relies on a social network that enables the costumed individual to operate. There is usually collaboration; there is always an interactive context, even when the aim is a private expression of identity.

Through the act of costuming, individuals interlock into a larger unit ranging in size from a few to tens of thousands. The challenge is for the individual to attain a sense of fulfillment, becoming able to create art and express personal identity while participating in the social give-and-take of a group. For the group to form and maintain itself, it is often necessary to suspend personal history and personality, temporarily suppressing aspects of the self that might interfere with collaboration. In the diverse examples I have offered in this book, individuals choose to express certain identities while repressing others.

In every context of costume wear we find a variety of personal motivations. Some Civil War reenactors see themselves as living historians with an educational aim. Some are in it for political reasons, to seize the forum for an expression of their own critical agendas. Others reenact as a way of honoring their heritage, forging a connection to ancestors who fought and died. Still others engage in the hobby for the pleasure of fine uniforms and weapons, or for a chance to do some amateur acting by impersonating a nineteenth-century person, or because they want to hang out with their buddies. The same costume in the same event can carry different identities, self-consciously selected to portray some aspects of the individual's personality and values.

Identities are not fixed and permanent. They shift and shape in context. While the ascribed identities constructed by others run beyond control, elective identities—that is, those brought to the fore by costumes—are intended, the result of personal motivations. In this concluding chapter, let us now consider the categories of motivation, the kinds of desire that lead to the costumes that express elective identities.

SOCIABILITY

One way a cohesive social unit is formed is through a shared clothing code. Uniforms are meant to replace personal identity with a collective one. Members of a sports team wear matching uniforms as a way of signaling to themselves and others that they are part of one united group. (Something about a difference in professional sports is revealed by the fact that baseball coaches and managers wear the same uniform as the players, as though they were comrades in a common cause, but basketball coaches wear suits and ties, unlike the jerseys and shorts of the players, implying a distance between management and labor.) Forming a collective identity through a shared costume code is a goal for many of the people we have met in this book. In every case performed costumes led to social identities and offered opportunities for social interaction. Many people began wearing costumes in order to be with their friends, to participate in the momentary engagement with others that wearing a costume permits. Costume conventions, known as "cons," bring large groups of people together, usually over a weekend in a hotel or convention center. Examples include Star Trek conventions that gather costumed fans of the television series; DragonCon, an assembly of fantasy, popular culture, and science fiction fans, many of them followers of the "steam punk" movement; and "Cosplay," an assembly of people who engage in role playing and dress up as their favorite Japanese manga or anime characters. In all of these instances individuals form a network centered on shared interests, values, and taste, forming an alliance that is mainly expressed through elaborate costumes.

Every year during carnival in Salvador, ten thousand men create an allegiance with one another through a costume evocative of race, religion, history, politics, and gender. Wearing the costume of Filhos de Gandhy communicates to the individual, the group, and spectators this shared communal bond; it is what brings strangers together in the first place, and it consolidates occupational and familial associations. Jom Silva parades as a Filhos de Gandhy with his buddies from the police force; it is a way to reinforce the occupational bond they share. For Ildo Sousa carnival is a time to dress up and parade with his brothers, son, and nephew, along with members of his family's Candomblé *terreiro*. Filhos de Gandhy is a form of "confraternity" for Ildo and for thousands of others in Salvador.

For many of the fifty thousand men who reenact the American Civil War,[4] becoming part of a group is the objective. It is emotionally gratifying to find a common identity among other "history buffs" as people form into the social units of regiments and armies that carry regional and ideological identities and offer opportunities for performance to living historians and dedicated reenactors.

Confederate soldiers at rest at the reenactment of the first Battle of Bull Run. Manassas, Virginia, 2011.

Most of the reenactors I interviewed valued the "camaraderie" of traveling, drilling, and camping together in a way that paralleled an actual military experience. Participants usually form a group based on age and gender, seeking friendship among other like-minded people. John Schlotter, who impersonates Union general John Hartranft, was not deeply interested in history: he became a reenactor to be with his friends. Dwight Hensley chose to impersonate Confederate general Richard Garnett so that he could be with his friend Niles Clark, who played General George Pickett. Dwight and Niles chose Dwight's persona together, because General Garnett commanded a brigade in Pickett's division. Reenactors often pass through certain stages of life. Many men reenact as privates when they are young, leave the hobby when they are newly married with young children (the recipients of their free time and money), and then return, usually as living historians, with their wives and kids in tow. That was the case with Jay Vogel, Frank Orlando, and Jim Opdenaker, all of whom reenact Civil War generals. The social unit has shifted over time, but sociability is still the goal.

There are thirty thousand members in the Society for Creative Anachronism. Many of them self-identify as "socially awkward," and many "SCA participants are involved in high tech fields—computers, aerospace, high energy physics," spending their time "with highly complex, modern technology," yearning for a venue to unwind by devoting "their leisure time using simpler technologies in a less modern setting."[5] The society divides into smaller units: kingdoms, principalities, baronies, shires, guilds, and households. SCA participants join some small unit to engage with others in the joys of "the game," literally wearing on their bodies the colors, favors, and emblems of the subgroup they belong to. All SCA activities are communal, members gather for the wars and pageants, but they also do other things together: attend seminars and workshops, camp, cook, sing, engage in craft circles, and even gather to make their costumes together in events called "stitch and bitch." I met Thomas Harmon at an SCA event in 2009.[6] He told me he wears blue jeans to work during the week, then dresses up in his garb over the weekend during SCA events. The garb is the vehicle for his transformation into his sixteenth-century French persona, Philippe de Lyon. The clothing is uncomfortable and "hot as hell," Thomas said, but it "covers all of my mundane-ness." His costume expresses his social allegiances, as he explained to me in a follow-up email:

> The medallion that I am wearing is for the Order of the Laurel. It is a Peerage for mastery of the Arts and Sciences. My field is the Courtly Arts (dancing, tennis, music, service, flattery) and Historical Rapier studies. The bronze scarf that I wear is for the Order of the Bronze Ring. It is our highest Fencing award. The green garter is my Lady's favor and I wear it on my left arm above my awards so that it is the closest thing to my heart.[7]

Every time Thomas looks in the mirror, he sees in his costume the social identities that have been bestowed on him as a result of his belonging to the SCA.

HERITAGE

In a list of motivations for costuming, socializing comes first—the desire for social connection, for the creation of a circle of friends. A second motivation lies in the wish to express a sense of heritage. Traditions are declared "heritage" in order to ensure historical continuity, and costumes frequently become bodily signs of a commitment to heritage, a willingness to assume responsibility for a continuity that simultaneously connects one to the dead and the living. There are many ways that heritage shapes connections to others through shared costuming practices.

In Sweden, Kersti Jobs-Björklöf connects physically to her ancestors by wearing the costumes of deceased family members. She served her community by re-

Sven Roos and his daughter, Kersti, lead the fiddlers to Tibble. Midsummer, Dalarna, Sweden, 2007.

searching and publishing the costume code for Leksand with her mother, Karin, and by directing the local ethnographic museum established by her uncle Knis Karl Aronsson. And Kersti seeks a connection to the future by passing her accumulated knowledge and costumes to her granddaughter, Anna. For Kersti, and for many in Sweden, wearing the folk costume is a clear manifestation of a personal commitment to heritage, a material statement of her determination to preserve a local art despite massive historical change.

The aim of several of the Civil War reenactors I spoke with—Mark LaPointe, Mike Sipes, Niles Clark, and Wayne Brunson—was to honor their ancestors who served in the Confederate or Union armies. For these men, and thousands of others, wearing the uniforms of the American Civil War is a sign of familial

and regional pride, an emblem of a patriotic desire to associate with the soldiers who fought when the nation was bitterly divided. Many reenactors are veterans of military service, and through their quest for accuracy they express a proud occupational heritage. Mike and Linda Fowler portray married medics who work together in the medical treatment tent of a living history encampment. Linda depicts a nurse and Mike an infantry captain who wears a doctor's apron over his Union uniform. In their daily lives both of them work as paramedics and emergency medical technicians, and Mike once served as a police officer. For the Fowlers, reenacting and teaching about the medical practices of the Civil War provides a way to connect to their own medical tradition. For them, heritage is not about family, but about profession, another strong marker of personal identity.

Heritage involves self-conscious efforts at preservation. Artists on the stage work deliberately within the tradition of the theater. Playwright Charles Morey intends a connection to Shakespeare in the deliberate lack of stage directions and costume descriptions in his own play *The Yellow Leaf.* In the creation of strikingly modern dramatic works, Vincent Woods drew directly from Irish folk drama in *At the Black Pig's Dyke* and positioned himself in the great lineage of Irish theatrical art by following W. B. Yeats and J. M. Synge in staging for a new age the ancient Irish story of Deirdre in *A Cry from Heaven.*[8] Collaboration in the theater permits Vincent to express his connection to his country, its folklore, and its acclaimed literary tradition.

Actors on the stage draw into their identities the occupational heritage of the theater. Ellen Adair, who works predominantly in classical theater, acknowledges the debt all actors and authors owe to William Shakespeare for the "banquet of our language."[9] In two of her poems Ellen pays homage to Shakespeare. In "Song of the Young Poet" she sees acting as "a religion of tradition, embodying the history, / the wine and bread of poetry, / Shakespeare descending from the universal passion, / to make my body into the worded incarnation."[10] In a second poem, "Stratford," Ellen says that as an actor her "mouth resounds around your disintegrated pen, / wherever an entire mind is made of lines."[11] Responding to the playwright's gift of enhancing the actor's identity through his creation of character, she writes: "My self is only a character I play / for want of any other." Costumed performances on the stage permit the actor to participate in the long history of dramatic tradition. The poem ends with a call to "acknowledge God / in the theatre is the playwright, / blowing around the globe / as fast as speech." Ellen knowingly upholds the tradition of stage performance. This is how she explained her craft in an email she sent to me in the summer of 2012:

> I thrill in acting because I am participating in the tradition of what it means to respond, of what it means to be human, of that which separates us and that which binds us. It is larger than the tradition of the craft: it is the tradition of humanity.
>
> There is this wonderful line in Julius Caesar that I can't remember at the moment, about (I paraphrase) "how many ages hence shall this our scene be acted in accents now unknown," that always gives me chills to hear it, because it is still alive and still being performed: the words have been exhumed and walk again.

PROTEST AND SPECTACLE

One intended function of costume is to create community. Another goal is to express heritage, satisfying the self, serving the community, and informing an audience of unknown others. Another motive for public costume lies in protest, an activist's desire to assert contrary opinions.

The Society for Creative Anachronism—a gathering that requires historical garb for participation—was founded with the purpose of "protesting the 20th century." Likewise, Kersti Jobs-Björklöf protests globalizing homogenization and critiques a lack of local awareness by wearing her folk costume to every church service and every ceremonial occasion in Dalarna. Wearing a costume can allow people to separate the message from themselves while using historical characters as vehicles for their own commentary on current affairs. This is the case with some Civil War reenactors, Northern men in Confederate uniforms who adopt historical personae in an effort to critique the actions and ideologies of the government today. Costumed interpreters at Colonial Williamsburg adhere to the museum's mission while protesting inequalities of race, class, and gender in the historical record and in contemporary society.

Costuming in public creates a spectacle that displays a group's solidarity and entices others to join in. The members of Filhos de Gandhy gather for the celebration of carnival, parading on specific days along specific routes. In Sweden costumed fiddlers lead a parade to the festival grounds, where people sing and dance around the maypole. In Pennsylvania members of the Society for Creative Anachronism engage in annual summertime pageants and fights at the Pennsic Wars for an internal audience of other SCA participants. At Gettysburg, to commemorate the anniversary of the July 1863 battle, thousands of people watch skirmishes from the grandstand, and at Manassas, during the sesquicentennial of the Civil War, thousands watched the grand parade of uniformed men when the armies marched through town. At Colonial Williamsburg the spectacle of the American Revolution is put on display during the "Revolutionary City" performances and their accompanying fife-and-drum parades. And finally, on the theater stage, the result of artistic devotion is a magical sight for an attentive audience.

The spectacle comes out of collaboration, signals unity, and offers an invitation to participation. Members of the Society for Creative Anachronism use their costumes in public to proselytize, enticing the curious to join the group. During the Midsummer celebrations in Dalarna, people are inspired to take pride in their regional heritage, to keep the past alive and relevant. On Civil War battlefields, spectators are tempted to become reenactors. At Colonial Williamsburg visitors are encouraged to continue their self-education about the Revolution and about American history.

Spectacles attract people, preparing them to receive a message, a message that might carry profound political and social opinion. When Filhos de Gandhy was formed more than fifty years ago, the stevedores and laborers used their fantastical costumes—long tunics and towel turbans—to protest the fact that Afro-Brazilian people and their religion were not allowed in the streets of Salvador during carnival time. Today Filhos de Gandhy continues to protest the inequalities of Brazilian society by bringing attention to the richness of their African culture, religion, and music, persuading the residents of Salvador to learn about Candomblé and the black consciousness movement.

Similarly, in the United States African American men oppose social injustice by dressing up during carnival time. The Mardi Gras Indians of New Orleans wear flamboyant beaded and feathered "suits" to raise awareness about the discrimination they have suffered in the city. Herreast Harrison is the widow of Donald Harrison Sr., the chief of the group called Guardians of the Flame.[12] Mrs. Harrison told me that the Mardi Gras Indians have always "masked" as Indians: "Okay, we can mask as native people, but we're expressing our true identity, which is African." The purpose of the disguise, of the beautiful costumes, was "masking to express your true self. To unmask yourself and be who you really are. It is masking to unmask your identity." Mrs. Harrison explained that the making of the suits also serves as an outlet for social action. "For men of African descent, who were here in America, and particularly here in New Orleans," she said, "the construction of the suits themselves also expressed freedom in their form and in how they were constructed and made." Suits are taken apart at the end of Mardi Gras to be made anew each year. When the next suit is made, Mrs. Harrison said, the creator thinks of what he wants to voice: "What theme will my suit express this year? What am I trying to say to people? What am I trying to express about how society is advancing? How is it relating to people? What is my community's needs? How will I express that through my masking?"

Mrs. Harrison said that the early Mardi Gras Indians were "the first civil rights activists." They paraded down the streets of New Orleans despite the violence and physical harm they endured. The late chief Donald Harrison Sr. used the beautiful costumes of "masking Indian" as a means of social activism. His widow continues his mission by running the Guardian Institute to teach elementary school children about the "heritage and legacy" of New Orleans. Social action naturally leads to education.

EDUCATION

Social activism is a form of education. The men of Filhos de Gandhy and the Mardi Gras Indians both attract large crowds during their carnival parades, and their beautiful costumes draw people to them. Both groups are "playing Indian" to reveal their African heritage. Through their songs and costumes they protest discrimination and educate the people around them. Many of the people we have met in this book hold public education as their primary goal, which they achieve by donning a costume every day. The living historians at Colonial Williamsburg—James Ingram, Terry Thon, Sarah Woodyard, and Mark Hutter— are trained and paid professionals working within an institutional agenda that they inflect to meet their personal pedagogical objectives. These educators serve as "little professors" in their various eighteenth-century classrooms, teaching about early American values, politics, social life, and technologies.

One aim of wearing a costume is to assume the persona of another. When this is managed successfully, the costumed performer creates a third person, an amalgamation of the wearer and the character in one body. This is a goal on the theater stage, as actor Ellen Adair has told us. During "talkbacks" the audience interacts with the actors, who speak about their characters. The event's aim is education; the spectators often ask about the personal motivations of the characters and the social and historical context of the play. Living historians engage in a version of the talkback, but they remain in first person as actors do on the

Jim Gossert as nineteenth-century
Indiana governor O. P. Morton.
Monroe County History Center,
Bloomington, Indiana, 2007.

stage (though not in the talkback). One can speak with General Washington or Thomas Jefferson at Colonial Williamsburg after watching the "Revolutionary City" play, and the actor-interpreters will answer as if they were the historical personages they portray in the drama. James Deetz is credited with developing first-person interpretation when he was assistant director at Plimoth Plantation.[13] He believed the living historian was not the interpreter; rather, the visitor was the interpreter. Going to a living history museum is akin to doing fieldwork in an unfamiliar place, according to Deetz, an archaeologist and anthropologist with a PhD from Harvard. In Deetz's view the visitors interpret while the museum personnel serve as informants, explaining the life, values, and worldviews of those who inhabited the past.[14] For this kind of education to work, the costumed person must channel himself into the character whose clothing he wears, merging his identity with that of the person he is enacting. So one reason to wear a costume is to become another person for the purposes of education.

At a Civil War encampment in Indiana I met the governor of the state at the time of the Civil War, O. P. Morton, who was played by Jim Gossert.[15] Jim is from Toledo, Ohio, where he attended a high school that was "ninety-five percent black." He has lived in Indiana since he graduated from college and got a job with the Eli Lilly pharmaceutical company in Indianapolis. He studied chemistry, theater, and history in college. Jim has also been "studying the Civil War" since he was ten years old and describes himself as "a historian by nature." Jim impersonates the Hoosier governor at schools and Civil War events. At some African American schools, kids have angrily told him, "You are a racist." And Jim answers, "I am not, but Governor Morton might have been." He feels it is his responsibility to teach people about the past, in both first and third person. When I saw Jim's performance, he addressed the crowd as the governor, speaking about the war, consistently situating his remarks in the context of 1864. Governor Morton asked for questions, and no one had one, but they gave him a round of applause. Then Jim exited his character, remained onstage in costume, and asked us, "As my own self, Jim Gossert, do you have any questions?" The audience questioned him for forty-five minutes, bringing up the Civil War and then the recent war in Iraq. Wearing the costume of the nineteenth-century governor—long black coat, fitted vest, silk cravat, top hat, pocket watch—Jim was able to command a contemporary audience, first by impersonating a historical character, then by answering questions from the points of view of the governor as well as himself. Jim uses costumed performances to educate and to share his passion for history with those gathered around him.

Costumes are chosen to reveal certain aspects of identity and to fulfill certain desires—desires for social connection, for the preservation of heritage, for the right to protest or educate—and costumes are made and worn to answer the inner need to create.

Placed on view, as an artistic communication, the costume comes to judgment. Beauty is one criterion of judgment and one desire of the costumed performer. One reason why men in Salvador choose to parade with Filhos de Gandhy is that the costume flatters them; it exposes the arms, elongates the body, and highlights the face beneath the jeweled turban. Some men work toward a personal magnificence of ensemble, carefully putting together bead necklaces and other accessories, embellishing their standard garments with sequins, cowry shells, and feathers. Excellence of creation distinguishes members of the Society for Creative Anachronism who are awarded formal laurels for their artistic effort. In a society where a do-it-yourself philosophy dominates, the well-crafted costume is unusual and deserving of the honors bestowed upon its creator. In Sweden handwoven and embroidered aprons, bodices, and skirts are widely admired in the community; the textile creations of the sisters Karin Gärdsback, Britta Matsson, and Anna Halvares are praised throughout the parish.

Beauty—of an item of costume, an entire ensemble, or a costumed performer—is one criterion for judgment. Accuracy is another, the beautiful crafting of an impeccable ensemble, and this is the artistic pleasure that motivates Brenda Rosseau, Mark Hutter, and Janea Whitacre, the designer, tailor, and dressmaker at Colonial Williamsburg, respectively. They recreate garments with consummate artistry, using materials, tools, and techniques like those of eighteenth-century Virginia. Janea Whitacre, the mistress of the millinery and mantua-making trades at the Margaret Hunter Shop, told me she once wore a nineteenth-century gown that she had made to a gathering of professional costume historians. Someone at the event was upset with her for wearing what she believed to be an original heirloom dress to a social function. To Janea, this was an instance of artistic excellence: to reproduce a garment so perfectly that even an expert was fooled.

The aesthetics of accuracy shape into a command among reenactors of war, and the beauty and perfection of the costume provide fulfilling experiences for the wearer and beholder in the context of the theater, where magic and illusion also prevail. Susan Claassen is an actor, director, playwright, and the artistic director of the Invisible Theater in Tucson, Arizona. Once she realized that she resembles Edith Head—famed Hollywood costume designer and winner of eight Oscars—Susan decided to impersonate Edith onstage. Much research went into her creation of the persona.[16] With help from biographer Paddy Calistro and the Academy of Motion Picture Arts and Sciences, Susan studied hours of taped interviews to learn Edith's speech patterns, and she acquired official rights of likeness and publicity. To perfect her impersonation, Susan needed to get the look right: she consulted with fashion designer Bob Mackie, who served as Edith's sketch artist; commissioned a wig from Renate Leuschner; and painstakingly reproduced Edith's "signature necklace." Before every show, Susan puts on her makeup "the wrong way, because she was older than I am. Rather than try to conceal every wrinkle, I put makeup into every wrinkle." Relying on a social network of experts; benefitting from the collaborative tradition of the theater; and with her picture-perfect clothes, hair, and makeup, Susan becomes the Hollywood designer in her play *A Conversation with Edith Head*. In the manner of a living historian, Susan as Edith interacts with the audience after the show, taking questions while remaining in first person and within the period that ended with the designer's death in 1981.

Susan told me that in 2009 she played at the North Coast Repertory Theater in Solana Beach, California. In the audience was a woman named Gladys, who had served as a model for Edith Head in the 1930s. Susan addressed Gladys from the stage, in the first person, engaging the former model, still beautiful despite her age and now confined to a wheelchair. The result was electrifying. Susan recalled: "Now, I know I'm not Edith Head. And she knows I'm not Edith Head. But there was that moment of shared illusion. And the audience was just weeping, because this woman was so happy." After the show, Gladys's son approached Susan to say, "If she were—God forbid—to die tomorrow, this would have been one of the happiest days of her life." It was a testament to Susan's skill, and when I remarked that she had given a great gift, Susan replied, "And to get it; for someone to say that to you." It is the actor's art to become someone else onstage. When that effort is validated, a deep personal wish has come true. The actor becomes someone else onstage, and most of us yearn to become more realized versions of ourselves. Costume can serve both of these aspirations.

INDIVIDUALITY

Our survey of costume's intended functions, of how motives are realized in costuming, ends with a consideration of the roles extraordinary garments play in opening paths for the exploration and communication of the personality, providing expressive outlets for aspects of the identity that are hidden during daily life. We start with P. J. Schultz. When he joined the SCA in Arizona, he was working as a general manager for one of the Marriott hotels, a position in which he had

Sarah Woodyard of Colonial Williamsburg at the Costume Society of America meeting. Las Vegas, Nevada, 2013.

Sarah Woodyard in costume. Colonial Williamsburg, Williamsburg, Virginia, 2010.

to be polite, "follow etiquette, and have people yell at me all day long." The SCA was for P. J. a "one hundred percent opposite" experience, giving him an arena to use some of his frustrated, pent-up energy in the physical activity of combat. In addition to physical release, occasions for costuming often afford psychological liberation. This was generally the case with the professional actors we met in this book; they exercised unused aspects of their personalities by becoming different characters, employing the Stanislavski method to draw their characters' minds and emotions from deep within themselves. The actor's embodiment of another is confined by script, set, and a stage, but reenactors must represent their characters in unpredictable contexts and speak without the benefit of a script. The aim is to take on the persona so completely that the character meshes with the reenactor's own self. That is the goal of the living historians on the battlefields of the Civil War and on the streets of Williamsburg, who amplify themselves when they are in character.

Living historians take pleasure in losing themselves into their characters. Frank Orlando, for example, signed an email message to me, "Your obedient servant, RE Lee." Richard Cicero, a member of Lee's Lieutenants, signed his email, "I am, My Lady, Your Obedient Servant, Major Johann August Heinrich Heros von Borcke, A.N.V.—C.S.A." Sarah Woodyard, the apprentice dressmaker at Colonial Williamsburg, knows the appropriate eighteenth-century fashions "like the back of my hand" and can break them down into aesthetic principles and apply them to the garments she makes and wears. Yet what she wears reflects her own sense of style within the historical confines. The dressmakers and tailors select their own fabrics and choose what they want to make at the Margaret Hunter Shop, and Sarah wears pink and red, her favorite colors, in fabrics of her choosing, while portraying a historical character. She observed that the staff at Colonial Williamsburg must wear eighteenth-century clothing issued to them by the Costume Design Center, but far from being uniforms, there is so much personal leeway that "everyone has his own look here." After Sarah leaves work and goes home, her costume remains part of her body, for she said that wearing a corset at work has improved her posture dramatically. The costume reflects her personal identity and affects her everyday look and identity as a stylish young woman.

The most conspicuous occasion for costumed performance in the United States comes at Halloween, the one day of the year when many adults dress up for work and parties. I gave the example of Halloween at the beginning of this book, and in all of the chapters that followed I showed how all dress, daily or special, carries the wearer's identity. Halloween is not an exception, as it gives people a chance to try out and try on different versions of themselves, just as the theater gives to its professional actors.

Michael Kent (Mickey) Woods was a stylish Midwestern college student at the time of our interview.[17] In 2007 he dressed up in a costume of his own invention he referred to as a "slutty sailor": navy polo shirt, cutoff jean shorts, white belt, white suspenders, knotted kerchief, sailor's cap, white knee-high tube socks, white slip-on Vans shoes, and a silver hip chain. He wore shorts to pun on the saying that sailors use their "sea legs" while on board a ship. Mickey wanted to "challenge" the idea of the sailor as a strong man of honor, in service to his country on a ship: "The traditional sailor suit costume, it's actually quite conservative: white shirt, white long pants," he said. "I wanted to do something that was just a little different, a little edgy." In ordinary life Mickey feels confined by a gendered norm of attire: "For a guy, there're certain standards that people think you should fit in as far as what you should wear, what you look like, how you present yourself." His "slutty sailor" costume "went against all of those things," and it was "probably one of the boldest things that I've done." All day—at school and at several different parties—Mickey got both negative and positive reactions. "I thought I looked damn sexy," he said, "I carried myself throughout the whole day as if I were never dressed up." In costume Mickey tried to behave as though he were wearing everyday clothing.

Halloween gave Mickey—as it does for millions of people—the excuse to dress outrageously: "A day like Halloween, it's all about dressing up and being spirited. And just sort of being in the mood to do something that you probably wouldn't do on any other day. Why not dress up?" In Chicago, where Mickey grew up, his father would buy the costumes his two sons wore for trick-or-treating. Mickey recalls dressing as a Teenage Mutant Ninja Turtle, a costume—and a cartoon—he despised. He wanted to dress as a bunny, but "girls were bunnies." Now an adult, he amplifies his identity—as a fashionable, creative young man— by the way he dresses on a daily basis and by the costumes he chooses. In 2007 he returned to wearing a costume for Halloween. "Technically this is the first year that I dressed up probably since I was maybe eleven," he said. "Technically it's my first, liberated, like, true Halloween."[18]

Halloween costumes can exaggerate and clarify tendencies in daily dress, though more often, it seems, they allow for the exposure of something suppressed. Joseph Burnette II, the young man with whom we began this book, the one who celebrates his admiration for the band Mudvayne in his costume, said of Halloween:

It's a chance to be theatrical. It's one day of the year where it's not seen as so much of a social taboo to masquerade a little. I say I'm cashing in on that chance. I love being able to be something I can't be in the everyday life—just show the theatrical nature of who I am.

Recall that Boston-based actor Lewis Wheeler said he does not dress up for Halloween. For him Halloween comes frequently. Lewis's profession lets him refine and develop his personality by playing a wide variety of characters on the stage. He is satisfied. Most people don't get that chance, so they must capitalize on any opportunity to masquerade—on Halloween, during carnival, on the recreated battlefield. Costuming seems especially important for men. Military uniforms are one of the few acceptable fancy garment options for males, and many of the costumes worn by men who were interviewed for this book—in the SCA, during Civil War reenacting, at Colonial Williamsburg—are military uniforms; even the folk dress for men in Europe is usually derived from military attire. Cumberland Clark, in his book *Shakespeare and Costume,* writes that during Elizabethan times, men "indulged" in the "richness, colour, and originality" of "the new fashions" with the same enthusiasm that women did, and in fact "the men were probably on the whole the more magnificent."[19] Today male dress is generally drab, and for many men, costumes provide the only occasion to dress in rich clothes and fine ensembles.[20]

British actor Ian McKellen said it is easy to mask your identity and play somebody else; what is hard is to come out as yourself: to not disguise, but to actually be yourself.[21] Millions of people use costumes to be able to perform another version of themselves in the demarcated social contexts of costume use. The two types of garments—costume and dress—are interrelated, and to understand one we must see it in relation to the other, for forms and motivations shape the meanings and functions of all clothing.

ELECTIVE EXPRESSIONS

We all hold within us many identities—trial lawyer, mother, seamstress, history buff, tango dancer. The clothes we wear on a daily basis usually favor one of our identities, and for many people their daily dress conforms to some standard of the workspace. Versions of ourselves appear in different contexts, under different conditions, and some remain coiled in invisibility.[22] The people in this book stand for the many thousands who find release for key aspects of their identities only in costume on special occasions.

Ellen Adair as Marie Antoinette in Joel Gross's *Marie Antoinette: The Color of Flesh*, 2012. Photo courtesy of Portland Stage, Portland, Maine. Photo by Mark Rockwood.

Actor Ellen Adair, 2013. *Photo by Xanthe Elbrick, courtesy of Ellen Adair.*

All clothing is significant, a matter of assembling outfits for contexts in which they become personally and socially meaningful. But daily dress is a solo act whereas costume comes of collaboration. Daily dress derives from a sequence of acts and exchanges as it moves from maker to merchant to consumer, but the producers of costume work as a team, interacting to create garments for a spectacle.[23] A parade in Salvador, a skirmish at Gettysburg, a play on the stage: the spectacle carries its participants into union and away from the mundane.

All clothing embodies motives and hopes, but costume stretches toward magic. Halloween costumes are "make-believe." In Brazil costumes are called "fantasy," and carnival is called "opera" and "mystery." The Society of Creative Anachronism calls the world it shapes a "dream." Living historians yearn for "magic moments." Actors on the stage combine to create "the magic of the theater."

Many people told me they felt "transformed" when they put on their costumes for Mardi Gras or historical reenactments or the stage of a regional theater. The transformative quality of costumes suits them for ritual. The Yoruba boy dons his leafy costume to become Agbo, a spirit from the other world. Swedish people wear folk costumes for transformative rites of passage, for confirmation, marriage, and burial. Costume is to daily dress as ritual is to daily life—heightened in beauty, power, and meaning.

All clothing is real. Daily dress is real as labor is real; costume is real as art is real. When an outsider asked Kersti Jobs-Björklöf if the Leksand costume was real, she replied it was real enough for the dead to wear it for burial. The Irish playwright Vincent Woods believes that "theater isn't about presenting a slice of reality. It's much more than that." Ellen Adair, who knows the reality of performance before an audience, said that life on the stage is more real than real life.

Art is real, an exaggerated, elaborated, embellished, refined, perfected reality. Through the apparent artifice of a painting, a novel, a play, a costume, we come to a deeper perception of reality, of authenticity, of truth—words used consistently by this book's people in costume. The dislocation of disguise leads to a new awareness. Costume complements daily dress to fulfill the reality of the self.

Folklore is "artistic communication" in Dan Ben-Amos's famous definition.[24] Folkloristic study focuses on communications that break the quotidian flow by means of artistic formulations and intensification of meaning.[25] Stories rise out of dull conversations to carry their tellers and listeners away.[26] Festivals interrupt time's relentless motion with music and a release from labor. Holiday meals contrast through rich elaboration with the ordinary food of ordinary days. Costume, comparably, divides from daily dress in form, materials, expense, and intensity of message.

In their difference, costumes provide options for the expression of cultural opposition. Afro-Brazilian costumes contrast with those of the popular white *blocos* to symbolize pride in African heritage. Swedish folk costumes and the costumes of historical reenactors differ from today's drab dress that implies a mindless compliance with the current status quo. The actor in a splendid Elizabethan costume who recites Shakespeare's grand lines stands in opposition to a popular culture slipping ever lower in artistic merit.

All clothing is chosen to meet the personal and social needs of the self, and a study of costume helps refine our understanding of the function of all dress in life. In the second act of Shakespeare's *As You Like It* the character Jacques says:

> All the world's a stage,
> And all the men and women merely players;
> They have their exits and their entrances,
> And one man in his time plays many parts.

The first two lines are often quoted, but the last two lines hold particular importance for this book; throughout our lives we play many parts.

Daily dress is the clothing for some of those parts, but costumes enable other parts to be played on the various stages that life slides beneath our feet. We are always acting some part for which we must dress. Every morning, in our most common creative activity, we get dressed, and in getting dressed we answer the question of who we plan to be for that day; we choose an identity. Some identities seem to be thrust upon us. The workaday dress for the office or for the service job behind the counter might not reveal who we really are. But our identities in costume are always elective, motivated by will, true to the self.

The people we have met in this book have taken their exits. One remains on the stage to speak their collective sentiments, the actor Ellen Adair. She, too, will exit after delivering the final two lines that summarize the book's message, that costume enables the election and enactment of identity in all its dimensions. Ellen said:

> There is a part of me that knows that I would be always discontent with one version of myself.
> I am the most myself when I am playing someone else.

NOTES

INTRODUCTION

1. I am describing the 147th Anniversary Gettysburg Civil War Battle Reenactment, which I attended on Saturday, July 3, 2010. The annual event is organized by the Gettysburg Anniversary Committee, a private organization not affiliated with the National Park Service, and takes place on a farm just north of the battlefield. Admission was thirty dollars per person, with an extra ten-dollar charge for an opportunity to sit on the bleachers of the grandstand.

2. This is Dan Ben-Amos's classic definition of folklore from his "Toward a Definition of Folklore in Context," 14.

3. See Glassie, chapter 2, "Material Culture," in his book *Material Culture*; quotes from 41 and 67. See chapter 16, "The Study of Body Art," in my *Grace of Four Moons* for how dress can be studied as material culture.

4. The basis for the folkloristic theory of performance was set by Dell Hymes in *Foundations in Sociolinguistics*; it was shaped for narrative analysis by Richard Bauman in *Story, Performance, and Event* and *World of Others' Words*; it was applied in the field by Henry Glassie in *Passing the Time in Ballymenone*, and used in analysis by Lee Haring in *Verbal Arts in Madagascar*; and it was the frame for the dominant definition of folklore by Dan Ben-Amos in "Toward a Definition of Folklore."

5. Inspirational models of material culture study by folklorists include: Jones, *Craftsman of the Cumberlands*; Vlach, *Charleston Blacksmith*; Rinzler and Sayers, *Meaders Family*; Burrison, *Brothers in Clay* and *From Mud to Jug*; Zug, *Turners and Burners*; Pocius, *Place to Belong*; Ferris, *Local Color*; Fry, *Stitched from the Soul*; Bronner, *Carver's Art*; Evans, *King of the Western Saddle*; Holtzberg, *Keepers of Tradition*; Eff, *Painted Screens of Baltimore*; Patterson, *True Image*; Glassie, *Folk Housing in Middle Virginia, Turkish Traditional Art Today, Art and Life in Bangladesh,* and *Prince Twins Seven-Seven*. I found a useful model of an assembly of case studies in Glassie, *Potter's Art*.

6. Roach-Higgins and Eicher, "Dress and Identity," 7.

7. Ibid, 10.

8. Eicher, "Clothing, Costume, and Dress," 152.

9. Many of the articles in Joanne Eicher's *Berg Encyclopedia of World Dress and Fashion* address the difference between dress and costume and mention identity as a central concept in this distinction between categories of clothing.

10. Keech, "Powerful Secrets," 34; emphasis in the original.

11. Two books that deal in particular with Frida Kahlo's style are Rosenzweig and Rosenzweig, *Self Portrait in a Velvet Dress,* and Garduño and Rodríguez, *Pasion por Frida.* Iris Apfel's style was celebrated in the exhibition *Rara Avis* at the Metropolitan Museum of Art and the accompanying catalog by Eric Boman, *Rare Bird of Fashion.* Valerie Steele's *Daphne Guinness* discusses the clothing philosophy and ensembles of the heiress and fashion icon.

12. *Mr. Lonely,* directed by Harmony Korine, Love Stream Productions, 2008.

13. Erving Goffman observed that one way to recognize an "oncoming psychosis" is through a person's disregard of his or her appearance and hygiene and disregard of societal norms about respectable "personal front"—the conscious management of one's appearance. *Behavior in Public Places,* 25–27.

14. Galembo, *Dressed for Thrills,* 12.

15. Eicher, "Clothing, Costume, and Dress," 151–52.

16. For more on the Irish traditions that influence Halloween, as well as the English celebration of Guy Fawkes Day, see Jack Santino's introduction to *Halloween and Other Festivals of Death and Life,* especially xv–xvii, and also Santino, *Hallowed Eve,* especially 14–15. For more on Irish mumming traditions, see Glassie, *All Silver and No Brass,* and the edited volume by Buckley, Ó Catháin, Mac Cárthaigh, and Mac Mathúna, *Border-Crossing.*

17. All of these statistics are from "Halloween in Indiana by the Numbers," which appeared on October 25, 2010, on the IU News Room homepage of Indiana University (http://newsinfo .iu.edu/news-archive/16065.html); the statistics are from the Indiana Business Research Center.

18. For more on the commercialization of Halloween and dressing up among corporate employees, see Belk, "Carnival, Control, and Corporate," especially 115–20.

19. For more on Halloween in shopping malls, see ibid., 120.

20. See Michael Chabon's essay in Andrew Bolton's *Superheroes* volume for a catalog of fashion inspired by the superhero costume and for essays by Chabon and Bolton discussing the power of the superhero costume to help the wearer fantasize and escape the quotidian (9) and transform himself (14).

21. Durant, "Glowing Turnips," 26.

22. Kugelmass's *Masked Culture* contains interviews with participants of the Greenwich Village parade, revealing that political costumes are a point of contention. Many feel that the parade should be about Halloween—scary, spooky, supernatural—and not about current events, even though people in the parade seize the opportunity to take a public political stand.

23. Jessica Chisum wrote "Make Your Own Sarah Palin Costume for Halloween" on the blog "Creepy LA" on September 10, 2008, in which she details the necessary items to impersonate Palin: the "Palin 'do" hairstyle, sexy librarian glasses, bronzer, mauve lipstick and gloss, and props, including a baby doll to simulate the infant Trig. Creepy Los Angeles, http://creepyla .com/2008/09/10/make-your-own-sarah-palin-costume-for-halloween, accessed on October 29, 2008.

24. The tape-recorded interview with Joseph Burnette took place on November 13, 2007.

25. McDowell, "Halloween Costuming."

26. Nina, the subject of that book's chapter 10, wants to be indistinguishable from the "crowd," while Neelam and Mukta, featured in chapters 11 and 12 respectively, prefer to stand out for their good taste in dress and adornment, and for their beauty. Shukla, *Grace of Four Moons,* 221–301.

27. Cooper, *Magnificent Entertainments.*

28. Goffman, *Presentation of Self.*

29. Severa, *Dressed for the Photographer,* and Colburn, "Well, I Wondered."

30. The reenactors in Horwitz's *Confederates in the Attic,* for example, mimic the poses captured by Brady (4). There is much written about Mathew Brady; one good book is Panzer's *Mathew Brady and the Image of History.*

1. FESTIVE SPIRIT

1. The number of Africans who were brought to Brazil exceeds the total number of European immigrants. Crowley, *African Myth and Black Reality,* 12. See Kraay, introduction to *Afro-Brazilian Culture and Politics,* for a full description of race, demography, and ethnicity in Bahia.

2. Amado, *Bahia de Todos of Santos,* 104. See Gomes, *Pelo Pelô,* for articles on the history, culture, politics, and architecture of Pelourinho.

3. This tape-recorded interview took place on May 12, 2009, at the Filhos de Gandhy headquarters, Rua Gregório de Matos, Pelourinho.

4. "Presidente Da Índia Visita O Filhos De Gandhy," BahiaNoticias website, http://www.bahia noticias.com.br/noticia/71408-presidente-da-india-visita-o-filhos-de-gandhy.html.

5. Filhos de Gandhy's association with Bahia is so strong that the government of Salvador adheres to the *bloco*'s demands, appeasing them to guarantee their presence during the carnival parade; Morales, "Afoxé Filhos de Gandhi," 272.

6. See M. Smith, *Mardi Gras Indians,* for wonderful photos and writings about the Black Indians, and also Tallant, *Gumbo Ya-Ya,* 20–23. To read a first-person account, see A. Kennedy, *Big Chief Harrison.*

7. Félix, *Filhos de Gandhi,* 25. See also Morales, "Afoxé Filhos de Gandhi," 269, and Selka, *Religion and the Politics,* 90.

8. Drewal, "Art History, Agency, and Identity," 152, and Risério, *Carnaval Ijexá,* 12.

9. Lody, *O Povo do Santo,* 143–46. See Braga, "Candomblé in Bahia," for a brief yet informative history of persecution and resistance.

10. For a discussion of the symbolism, meaning, and the varieties of *paxoró,* see Lody, *O Povo do Santo,* 214–18.

11. Félix, *Filhos de Gandhi,* 30.

12. For a discussion about polymorphous deities and their representation in religious art, see Glassie, *Prince Twins Seven-Seven,* chapter 17, "Yoruba Art," particularly 273–82.

13. Other carnival groups also have "*filhos*" or "*filhas*" in their name—for example, Filhos de Nanã, Filhos de Jhá, Filhos do Korin Efan, Filhos de Ogun de Ronda, and Filhas de Olorum.

14. Ilê Aiyê, *Organizações de Resistência Negra,* 6–8. For more on confraternities, see Selka, *Religion and the Politics,* 17–18; Kraay, *Afro-Brazilian Culture and Politics,* 12, and Omari-Tunkara, *Manipulating the Sacred,* 12.

15. These lyrics are from the song "Negros e Brancos" from the Banda Filhos de Gandhy album *Coração de Oxalá,* 1996.

16. A member of Filhos de Gandhy says this in De Almeida's documentary *A Bahia do Afoxé Filhos de Gandhy.*

17. Félix, *Filhos de Gandhi,* 19.

18. Ibid., 65 and 76.

19. For other accounts of the Festa de Yemanjá, see Amado's "Festa de Iemanjá," in *Bahia de Todos of Santos*, 137; Omari-Tunkara's chapter 4 on Yemanjá, in *Manipulating the Sacred*, especially 81–87; Drewal, "Celebrating Salt and Sweet Waters: Yemanja and Oxum in Bahia, Brazil," in *Mami Wata*, 166–75; Sterling, *African Roots, Brazilian Rites*, 71–79; and Ickes, *African-Brazilian Culture.*

20. Some Candomblé practitioners do not approve of this public display of ritual practice. Historian Paul Johnson found that priests and priestesses did not attend the Festa de Yemanjá, "either considering the heat and crowd as beneath their dignity or regarding such things as *orixá* possession in the street, without house or priest to contain and control it, a promiscuous form of spiritual prostitution." Johnson, *Secrets, Gossip, and Gods*, 146.

21. Festival T-shirts are an explicit way to communicate group membership, and they can also be used for advertising a corporate brand, a local bar, or even a favorite political leader. See Lauren Adrover, "Branding Festive Bodies," for an example of festival T-shirts in Africa, a case both similar and very different from the example of Brazil in this chapter.

22. The ritual washing of the Igreja do Nosso Senhor do Bonfim, a practice documented as early as the late eighteenth century, included washing the inside of the church. But several bans on the washing, from the 1890s, 1920s, 1930s, and as late as the 1950s, either stopped the event or confined the participants to the outside. See Ickes, *African-Brazilian Culture,* especially 60–66, 195.

23. For more on the Lavagem do Bonfim, see Sterling, *African Roots, Brazilian Rites*, 79–83.

24. Amado, "Lavagem da Igreja do Bonfim," in *Bahia de Todos of Santos*, 129–36.

25. Magalhães, *Fazendo Carnaval*, 138.

26. Each year a booklet describes the criteria of judgment and provides a map of the locations, the general schedule, and the lyrics to each school's theme song, the *samba-enredo*. I used the *Ensaio Geral* booklet from 1998 for some of the details in this chapter.

27. Magalhães, *Fazendo Carnaval*; see especially 28–57. See also Guillermoprieto, *Samba,* for a description of the entire process of carnival, including descriptions of the making of the costumes.

28. Bacelar, "Blacks in Salvador," 99.

29. Bahia Folia website, section titled "Customize Your Abadá," www.foliabahia.com.br/hp/customize.aspx, accessed on February 17, 2010.

30. Ilê Aiyê, *25 Anos de Resistência*, 28, and *A Forca das Raízes*, 43.

31. Ilê Aiyê, *América Negra,* 4. See also Drewal, "Art History, Agency, Identity," 165; Butler, "Afterword: *Ginga Baiana*," 167–68; and Sterling, *African Roots, Brazilian Rites*, 91–94, 96–100, especially 97–99, in which she describes the *Noite da Beleza Negra.*

32. Ilê Aiyê, *A Forca das Raízes*, 46.

33. Real says that the carnival parades of Pernambuco also resemble secularized Catholic processions. "Evoé!," 220. DaMatta writes that during the procession, everyone is tied together in a fraternal bond; this can apply to both religious procession and to carnival parade. *Carnivals, Rogues, and Heroes,* 76.

34. Johnson, *Secrets, Gossip, and Gods*, 94–95; Selka, *Religion and the Politics,* 35; and Sansi, *Fetishes and Monuments*, 72.

35. Crowley, *African Myth and Black Reality,* 40.

36. Omari-Tunkara describes the Baiana ensemble in detail; see *Manipulating the Sacred,* 46–48.

37. For much detail on the clothing and jewelry of the Baiana, see Lody's many publications, especially *O Traje da Baiana, Pencas de Balangandãs da Bahia,* and *Jóias de Axé.*

38. See, for example, Carybé, *As Sete Portas da Bahia,* 177, 179, 183.

39. I attended this festival in 2006. To read more about the Osun Festival in Osogbo, see Glassie, *Prince Twins Seven-Seven,* 227–33.

40. Filhos de Gandhy participate officially in many of Salvador's festivals besides Bonfim and Yemanjá. For example, they are present in the festivals for Saint Lazarus, Saints Cosmos and Damian, Santa Luzia, and Santa Barbara.

41. See Shukla, "Mahatma's Samba," for a description and analysis of the fun, frivolous, and violent behavior of some members of Filhos de Gandhy.

42. This interview took place on January 17, 1998, at Pita's house in Salvador.

43. De Almeida, *A Bahia do Afoxé Filhos de Gandhy.*

44. This conversation took place on May 13, 2009, at the store A Conta.

45. Félix, *Filhos de Gandhi,* 21.

46. Ibid., 40.

47. Real, "Evoé!," 207; Crowley, *African Myth and Black Reality,* 17; and Ickes, *African-Brazilian Culture,* 146–47.

48. His given name was Ápio da Conceição, and he was the president of Filhos de Gandhy from 1977 to 1982. See Félix, *Filhos de Gandhi,* 21, 31, 60.

49. This tape-recorded interview took place on May 15, 2009, in Santos's atelier on Rua Carlos Rabelo, in Pelourinho.

50. His representation of each orixá is illustrated in the book *Os Deuses do Panteon Africano,* by Francisco Santos. As Sansi argues, representing the *orixás* in their regalia, in dance and possession, is part of the public view of Candomblé; secret aspects of the religion such as the *assentos* and the altars are not for general consumption, and these are not imaged in paintings, postcards, etc. *Fetishes and Monuments,* 154.

51. For testimonials about the visit to Mãe Menininha's terreiro, see Félix, *Filhos de Gandhi,* 31, 56, and 76. Artists, singers, and politicians also sought Mãe Menininha's blessing; she was a hugely influential force in disseminating respect and knowledge about Afro-Brazilian culture and religion. See Sansi, *Fetishes and Monuments,* 72 and 94.

52. Most of the individual accounts in Félix's *Filhos de Gandhi* say that the original *bloco* would go to seek blessings from the Church of Bonfim and Church of Santa Luzia.

53. Johnson, *Secrets, Gossip, and Gods,* 33–34.

54. See Bascom, *Sixteen Cowries,* for more details on cowry shell divination.

55. Seu Raimundo says this in an interview in De Almeida, *A Bahia do Afoxé Filhos de Gandhy.* For a photograph of Seu Raimundo as the Mahatma Gandhi and posing with a painting of the Indian leader, see Edinger, *Carnaval,* 82–83.

56. Browning, *Samba,* 157.

57. Ibid., 65 and 130.

58. De Almeida's documentary *A Bahia do Afoxé Filhos de Gandhy* contains an extra feature that has these explanations of the symbols. While Professor Agnaldo did not make this link, the white elephant is also a symbol of the king, the *oba,* in Nigeria, a powerful Yoruba metaphor. See Ross, *Elephant,* for more on the importance of the elephant in art, metaphor, and life on the continent.

59. Amado, *War of the Saints,* 310–36. Amado's *Jubiabá* and *Tent of Miracles* also recount *orixá* appearances at Candomblé festivals.

60. Sansi, *Fetishes and Monuments,* 171.

61. The song "Filhos de Gandhy," written by Gilberto Gil, appears on the album *Gil & Jorge*, Polygram do Brasil Ltda., 1975.

62. Gil is credited with reviving the group in the 1970s in a lean moment; see Risério, *Carnaval Ijexá*, 53, for an interview with Gil about this. De Almeida, *A Bahia do Afoxé Filhos de Gandhy*, contains both footage and interviews with Gilberto Gil.

63. The 2009 costume was not designed by Francisco Santos, but rather the garment is stamped and attributed to others, "Criação e Arte Final: Murilo Ferraz e Gilsoney."

64. To read more about the church and the confraternity associated with it, see Selka, *Religion and the Politics*, 50–55.

65. This tape-recorded interview with Ildo Sousa took place on May 14, 2009, at the Filhos de Gandhy headquarters at Rua Gregório de Matos, Pelourinho.

66. Selka, *Religion and the Politics*, 35. See also Kraay, Introduction, 17–22.

67. Bacelar, "Blacks in Salvador," 97. For Candomblé practiced in secret, see Johnson's excellent book *Secrets, Gossip, and Gods;* for Candomblé as resistance, see Omari-Tunkara, *Manipulating the Sacred*, 11, and Sansi, *Fetishes and Monuments*, 75.

68. Kraay, Introduction, 22.

69. Johnson, *Secrets, Gossip, and Gods*, 98–100.

70. Sansi, *Fetishes and Monuments*, 52, 131. For more on the cultural elite and their acceptance of Afro-Brazilian culture, see Ickes, *African-Brazilian Culture*.

71. Quoted in Félix, *Filhos de Gandhi*, 92.

72. Rodrigues, "Olodum and the Black Struggle," 43.

73. For more on the *padê* of Exú in Candomblé, see Omari-Tunkara, *Manipulating the Sacred*, 102; Johnson, *Secrets, Gossip, and Gods*, 39; Selka, *Religion and the Politics*, 37. For more on the *padê* of Exú before *afoxé* events, see Lody, *O Povo do Santo*, 147–48.

74. See Félix, *Filhos de Gandhi*, 60–61. Domiense Perira Amorim, criticizing the new ritual in Pelourinho Square, calls the display a "*palhaçada*"—literally a "clownery," a disgrace.

75. Morales, "Afoxé Filhos de Gandhi," 269.

76. Kraay, Introduction, 22.

77. Ickes, *African-Brazilian Culture*, 180.

78. See Rodrigues, "Olodum and the Black Struggle," for more details on the group and its founding.

79. The band calls the marks "tribal" motifs, yet Alberto Pita, who worked closely with Timbalada's founder, Carlinhos Brown, told me they are a visual reference to Candomblé initiation body marks. See Carybé, *Iconografia dos Deuses Africanos,* for beautiful, detailed drawings of the marks for each *orixá*. See Browning, *Samba,* 143, for her opinion about the connection between Candomblé body paint and Timbalada.

80. Each year Ilê Aiyê publishes an educational booklet on that year's theme. In 2007 the book that accompanied their theme "Abidjan, Abuja, Harare e Dakar" contained information about each of the four featured African nations, plus a resource guide and instructional curriculum for teachers. *Abidjan, Abuja, Harare e Dakar: Caderno de Educação,* Vol. 15. Olodum, whose red, green, gold, and black drums instantly signal solidarity with the *Movimento Negro* (Black Movement) and with African and African-diaspora struggles for freedom, carries explicit political messages through its carnival songs and themes.

81. Crook and Johnson, "Voices from the Black Movement," 15. See also Selka, *Religion and the Politics,* 133.

82. Risério, *Carnaval Ijexá,* 254.

83. Selka, *Religion and the Politics,* 1, 12, 13, 98; see p. 30 for more on the Black Movement.

84. Pitanga, "Where Are the Blacks?," 39–40.

85. Amado, *Jubiabá,* 33, 248.

86. See Bacelar's chart of occupations, which is for 1936 but still relevant today. "Blacks in Salvador," 92.

87. In the 1930s, according to Fernando Pamplona, carnival blocos gathered on Praça XI, where there were large concentrations of recently arrived people from Bahia, and also, a concentration of Candomblé terreiros (Preface to Magalhães, *Fazendo Carnaval,* 7). According to costume designer Magalhães, each samba school has about one hundred Baianas who wear full skirts with armature, underskirts, smocks, turbans, necklaces and bracelets, and who rotate continuously, visually emphasizing the roundness of their skirts (113). See also Crowley, *African Myth and Black Reality,* 40, and especially Guillermoprieto, *Samba,* 36, 52, 61, 62–63.

88. Guillermoprieto, in describing a little boy being fitted in his Rio de Janeiro Mangueira carnival costume, notes how the costume has the power to transport him into a dream world, away from the open sewers, trash, and general misery of his surroundings. *Samba,* 201.

89. For more on Olodum's 1987 Egyptian carnival theme, see Sterling, *African Roots, Brazilian Rites,* 94–95.

90. Both of these quotes, by Jorge and Brown, are in De Almeida, *A Bahia do Afoxé Filhos de Gandhy.*

2. HERITAGE

1. Besides the general revival of folk culture—dress, dance, and music—of the 1970s, there is a current trend of folk costume as high-end fashion. For example, fashion designers in Munich, such as the Alpenmädel company, offer exquisite dirndls made of silk, satin, rhinestone, lace, and fur. These reinterpreted versions of Bavarian folk dress are worn as a form of heritage and national pride to events such as Oktoberfest. See Eddy, "Dirndl, Dress of Past."

2. In Sweden all the areas that resisted the system of land reform have strong surviving traditions of folk costume: the Lake Siljan areas of Dalarna, Vingåker in Södermanland, certain parishes in Hälsingland, and parts of Skåne. Berg and Berg, *Folk Costumes of Sweden,* 12–15. This is also true of some areas in Norway, such as Setesdal and Telemark, where the villagers were able to retain their land and their customs, including costumes. For the Setesdal example, see the articles by Sandsdalen, "Identity and Local Society," and Bø, "Role Played by Tradition."

3. See Rådström, *Wooden Horses of Sweden,* and Rosander, "'Nationalisation' of Dalecarlia."

4. Scheffy, "Sámi Religion," 233.

5. To read about Hazelius's collecting and the establishing of his museums, see Hellspong and Klein, "Folk Art and Folklife Studies." For the costumes, see Berg and Berg, *Folk Costumes of Sweden,* 15, 42, and Nylén, *Swedish Peasant Costume,* 7. For the buildings, see the *Skansen Official Guide,* 5. For more on his collecting folk costumes, see Gradén, "Folk Costume Fashion in Swedish America," especially 168–72.

6. Hellspong and Klein, "Folk Art and Folklife Studies," 21.

7. Klein, "Cultural Heritage," 60.

8. O. Löfgren, "Nationalization of Culture," 10.

9. Rosander, "'Nationalisation' of Dalecarlia," 136.

10. Edenheim, *Red Houses,* 164.

11. Buildings all over Sweden, from the seventeenth century to the present, have been painted rust or brick red. The practice of painting farmhouses and its related structures red dates to the late nineteenth century. Edenheim, *Red Houses,* 9.

12. See Edenheim, *Red Houses,* 164, for a brief description of the building, built by Gunnar Matsson, the winner of an architectural design competition.

13. Rosander, "'Nationalisation' of Dalecarlia," 123, 126, and 127. Corner timbering is the notching of logs at the corner joints.

14. Berg and Berg, *Folk Costumes of Sweden,* 140.

15. Bergman, *Folk Costumes in Sweden,* 3.

16. The interviews with Kersti, many of them tape-recorded, took place between June 17 and June 30, 2007. My email correspondence with her took place from June 2006 to November 2013.

17. Berg and Berg, *Folk Costumes of Sweden,* 11.

18. See Snowden, *Folk Dress of Europe,* for examples. The generalized components of the Swedish costume I describe here are found in northern Europe, not as much in the south.

19. Nylén, *Swedish Peasant Costume,* 26.

20. Alm, *Dräktalmanacka för Leksands socken.*

21. Kersti Jobs-Björklöf quotes Ingrid Bergman, who was in charge of the costume collection at the Nordiska Museet.

22. Karin Jobs and Kersti Jobs-Björklöf, *Almanacka för Leksandsdräkten* (Stockholm: AB Sigma-tryckeriet for Leksands Hemslöjdsförening, 1978).

23. Kersti, along with three others, has coedited a brand-new book, a third version of the almanac, complete with color photos, proper names for each garment and accessory, the appropriate contexts of use, and a short bibliography of relevant books on the topic Kersti Jobs-Björklöf, et al., *Leksandsklädd.*

24. During the period of research for this book, the website contained all of this information; at the time of this writing, however, the website no longer exists.

25. See Gradén, *On Parade,* 179 and 192, for examples of Americans consulting the Berg and Berg book to choose Swedish costume to commission and wear.

26. See Nylén, *Swedish Handcraft,* for illustrations and descriptions of these pieces.

27. Glassie, "Tradition," 176.

28. Jacobsson, "Arts of the Swedish Peasant," 81.

29. Lagerlöf, *Memories of Mårbacka,* 161–69; Lagerlöf, *Gösta Berling's Saga,* 168.

30. Eklund and Thunell, *Gustaf Ankarcrona,* 94.

31. This practice is similar to an Indian custom in Rajasthan where married women wear green scarves for a requisite time period, adhering to their proper mourning traditions by wearing green instead of the celebratory red, pink, orange, or yellow. Shukla, *Grace of Four Moons,* 325.

32. To see a photograph of Knis Karl Aronsson's funeral ceremony, see Jacobsson, "Arts of the Swedish Peasant," 81.

33. Rosander writes that the Leksand maypole might be the most famous one in all of Sweden and that in the 1950s an estimated fifty thousand people would have watched the Midsummer events in Leksand. "'Nationalisation' of Dalecarlia," 128.

34. Bergman, *Folk Costumes in Sweden,* 4.

35. This tape-recorded interview took place June 27, 2007, at the home of Karin Gärdsback.

36. The tape-recorded interview with Sven Roos took place on June 24, 2007, at his house in Tibble.

37. Metal buttons were recycled and reused among Norwegian immigrants as well. The Vesterheim Museum in Iowa has many buttons saved by immigrants for reuse at a later date. See Colburn, "Well, I Wondered When I Saw You."

38. This is Sune Björklöf's translation of Ankarcrona's slogan. "Handcraft in Sweden: Background and Development during 100 Years" delivered at the first Hungarian Handcraft Conference, Budapest, 2006. Björklöf, "Från bevararmöda till lustfylld upplevelse," in *Leksands Hemslöjd.* See Nylén, *Swedish Handcraft,* and Klein, "Moral Content of Tradition," for excellent overviews of the home craft movement and useful information about Lilli Zickerman, credited with spearheading the movement in Sweden. From this national movement arose local organizations aiming to preserve local crafts while resisting the national and, some thought, universalizing tendencies of the craft manuals and pattern books.

39. According to Kersti, members of the community raised money in 1980 to keep the collection intact. This museum within a shop features the labeled objects nestled in a series of drawers, each topped with Plexiglas.

40. Instruction at the handcraft store was always part of Lilli Zickerman's original program of the home craft movement. Klein, "Moral Content of Tradition," 177.

41. The main tape-recorded interview with Ingrid Samuelsson took place in the backroom of the Leksand Handcraft store on June 25, 2007.

42. Klein, "Cultural Heritage," 57.

43. Klein, "Folklore, Heritage Politics," 25.

44. This is a reference to the subtitle of Gradén's book *On Parade,* in which she analyzes the conscious efforts at the public display of Swedish heritage in Lindsborg, Kansas. See also Gradén, "Folk Costume Fashion."

45. The English translation of *Folkdräkter och bygdedräkter från hela Sverige, Folk Costumes of Sweden,* by Inga Arno Berg and Gunnel Hazelius Berg, has been referenced several times in this chapter. Benny Norgren, Birger Persson, and Rune Östrelund, *Sockendräkter i Dalarna.*

46. Berg and Berg, *Folk Costumes of Sweden,* 151.

47. Several recent books have been devoted entirely to specific costume traditions in Sweden, producing, for example, beautiful, in-depth studies of Svärdsjö and Enviken in Dalarna, and of Österlen in Skåne: Dandanell, *Påsöm: Folkligt Broderi från Floda i Dalarna;* Nicklasson, Danielsson, and Matsols, *Dräktbruk och linnetradition i dalasocknarna Svärjdsjö och Enviken;* and Nilsson, *Österlens Folkdräkter.*

48. The traditions and history of folk costumes in Norway have been well served by the many studies of dress by Aagot Noss and by a new, impressive three-volume compilation edited by Bjørn Sverre Hol Haugen, the *Norsk Bunadleksikon.* See Noss, *Frå tradisjonell klesskikk til bunad i Vest-Telemark,* for an example of her books on Norwegian folk dress.

49. The women's costumes, with their layered knee-length skirts, have stabilized into this form since the middle of the eighteenth century, while the men's costume has remained unchanged since the middle of the nineteenth century. Both costumes contain medieval, Renaissance, and even Viking elements, in the color scheme and geometric embroidery. See Nelson, *Norwegian Folk Art,* 144; Traetteberg, "Folk Costumes," 140–41; and Sandsdalen, "Identity and Local Society," 168.

50. Bø, "Role Played by Tradition," 154. Folk dancers at Bygdöy, the Norwegian equivalent of the outdoor museum Skansen, wear the Setesdal costume, as do the crown prince's children and the SAS flight attendants (154). Sandsdalen says the Setesdal costume has become "a symbol of everything Norwegian." "Identity and Local Society," 167. That the Setesdal costume is now regarded as a de facto national costume contradicts Colburn's claims that the regional costume of Hardanger is the model for the national costume; see her "Norwegian Folk Dress."

51. Scheffy, "Sámi Religion," 233.

52. O. Löfgren, *On Vacation*, 79; see p. 84 for a photograph of a model in Leksand folk costume. To read his argument in full, see the chapter "Telling Stories," 72–106.

53. Snowden argues in his introduction to *Folk Dress of Europe* that artists and writers throughout Europe paid particular attention to dress and other aspects of peasant life in this Romantic age, which in turn helped maintain the existing tradition of folk dress (7–8).

54. For an illustration of this painting by Stikå Erik Hansson of a wedding scene in Mora parish, see Jacobsson, "Arts of the Swedish Peasant World," 69.

55. For more on artists in Dalarna, see Klein, "Introduction to Part 4," and Rosander, "'Nationalisation' of Dalecarlia," especially 115, 124, 125.

56. See Waldén, "Women's Creativity."

57. See Klein and Widbom's exhibit catalog *Swedish Folk Art: All Tradition Is Change.*

58. Klein, "Moral Content of Tradition," 171.

59. *Skansen Official Guidebook*, 6.

60. Berg and Berg, *Folk Costumes of Sweden*, 160. In Stockholm, Urban Gunnarsson, a carver of wooden figures, told us that a female figure wearing the Sundborn costume is the second most common commission by his Swedish American customers (a figure wearing the Vingåker southern costume is the most popular). For Swedes displaced in the diaspora, the costume most associated with Carl Larsson becomes, like the Dala Horse, a symbol of the country.

61. For a discussion of the national costume and its creation, see Hellspong and Klein, "Folk Art and Folklife Studies," 26–27, and Berg and Berg, 44. Ingrid Bergman, the former curator of textiles at the Nordiska Museet, gives due credit to the costume's originator, Märta Jörgensen, in her 2005 article "När den första sverigedräkten."

62. The official ceremony takes place at Skansen and includes a segment where "children in traditional peasant costume present the royal couple with bouquets of summer flowers." Lilja and Tidholm, *Celebrating the Swedish Way*, 18. The spectacle of people, especially children, dressed in peasant costumes and honoring the monarchy is a powerful visual symbol in the rhetoric of a united nation. Bendix, in writing about nineteenth-century Bavaria, describes a comparable historical parallel; see Bendix, "Moral Integrity in Costumed Identity."

63. In 2008 Miss Norway also wore a traditional folk dress, *bunad,* during the national costume competition.

64. See Saliklis, "Dynamic Relationship," for another European example of folk dress becoming official national costume.

65. Nylén, *Swedish Peasant Costumes*, 10.

66. A picture on display at the Leksands Kulturhus, dated 1811, shows the green pleated skirt. Another example is found in Hjelt Per Persson's 1846 painting of a wedding procession outside of the Leksands Kyrka, which shows the bridesmaids in green pleated skirts worn under blue aprons with ribbon appliqué on the bottom hem. For a picture of his painting, see Svärdström's *Dalmålningar i urval*, plate 14.

67. Gradén, *On Parade,* 192. On p. 103 she describes the spectacle of people parading together, looking like members of a sports team or an army, in matching uniforms. Some refer to their costumes as a "monkey suit" or as "circus outfits" (210).

68. Both Kersti and her uncle Knis Karl welcomed new users to the costume, not wanting to be "tradition police." In the words of her friend Kerstin Sinha, Kersti believes that if outsiders show interest in her folk costume, "the Leksand people should show them how to wear the costume happily but with broad and serious appreciation of all its aspects." Sinha, email received on November 5, 2013.

69. Glassie, "Epilogue," 252. In the Swedish version of the catalog, Beate Sydhoff, director of Kulturhuset, acknowledges Glassie's book *The Spirit of Folk Art* for inspiring the subtitle of the exhibit, "All Tradition Is Change." Sydhoff, *Folkkonsten,* 187–88.

70. Glassie, "Epilogue," 254.

71. Honko, "Studies on Tradition," 10; Ben-Amos, "Seven Strands of Tradition," 122. See also Glassie, "Tradition," and Hofer, "Perception of Tradition."

72. Berg and Berg, *Folk Costumes of Sweden,* 20.

73. Ibid., 20–23.

74. See Glassie, *Stars of Ballymenone,* chapter 8, for another example of a jeremiad: Hugh Nolan's hyperbolic prediction of the future for the sake of the conservation of tradition.

75. See Hellspong and Klein, "Folk Art and Folklife Studies in Sweden." See also S. Thompson, "Folklore Trends in Scandinavia."

76. Frykman and Löfgren, *Culture Builders,* 265.

77. From J. Lofgren, preface to *Carl Larsson,* viii.

78. To read about the role of the church in controlling folk costumes use, see Berg and Berg, *Folk Costumes of Sweden,* 29–32.

79. Klein, "Swedish Folklife Research"; Noyes and Bendix, "Introduction: In Modern Dress"; Dubois, "Costuming the European Social Body."

80. Rosander, in "'Nationalisation' of Dalecarlia," argues that while outsiders, artists and scholars, have helped create the cultural identity of Dalarna, "pioneers from among the province's own inhabitants" are also to be acknowledged for their efforts (135). Knis Karl Aronsson, Kersti's uncle, is singled out as one of these "pioneers."

3. PLAY

1. Paxson, "Last Tournament," 24, in Stewart, *Known World Handbook.*

2. Ibid., 25.

3. For a slightly different version of the origin of the society and its name, see Anderson, *Time Machines,* 168.

4. From the official description of the SCA, facing the title page of Stewart, *Known World Handbook.*

5. O'Donnell, *Knights Next Door,* 201.

6. Eleanor Ide, writing as Lady Alura the Twinn, 34, in Stewart, *Known World Handbook.*

7. Elizabeth Tarnove, writing as Lady Elizabeth Tremayne, "Costuming from Mundane Patterns," 43, in Stewart, *Known World Handbook.*

8. Catherine Strand Kinsey and Robin Gandy-Harsh, writing as Baroness Liriel Correll and Lady Ragan de Wolf, "Costumes from Constructed Patterns," 53, in Stewart, *Known World Handbook.*

9. Ibid.

10. I interviewed Sarah Lash several times in her home when she lived in Bloomington, Indiana. The tape-recorded interviews I quote here took place on May 15, 2008, and April 19, 2009.

11. This tape-recorded interview took place at the Constellation Academy of Defense of the Shire of Mynydd of the Midrealm, a daylong rapier collegium at the Upper Cascades Park in Bloomington, Indiana, on June 6, 2009.

12. This tape-recorded conversation with P. J. Schultz took place in his house in Bloomington, Indiana, on April 19, 2009. Schultz is also featured in Lash's dissertation, "Singing the Dream," especially 191–206.

13. I conducted two tape-recorded interviews with Carolyn Jenkinson, both in Bloomington, Indiana: July 23, 2009, at her house, and September 29, 2009, in my office at Indiana University.

14. For more on the ballads of the SCA, see Lash, "Singing the Dream."

15. Lady Arastorm the Golden, "Basic Costuming," 39, in Stewart, *Known World Handbook.*

16. I interviewed Aimee in her home at the time, in Bloomington, Indiana, on June 4, 2008.

17. Eleanor Ide, writing as Lady Alura the Twinn, "How to Get What You Want Out of the S.C.A.," 35, in Stewart, *Known World Handbook.*

18. For Spain, see Pablo Martin Dominguez's MA thesis, "The Past Is Alive," about the Grupo Attio, an experimental archeology and performance group that used excavation and serious research to reenact and demonstrate pottery construction, iron forgery, food preservation, and even funeral rites. For the United Kingdom, see O'Donnell, *Knights Next Door,* especially 256–62. For Sweden, see Gustafsson, "Medieval Selves and Current Communities," about the Medieval Week celebration in Gotland, where the specific events in Gotland of 1961 became over time a generalized "long time ago."

19. Eleanor Ide, writing as Lady Alura the Twinn, "The Last Word: To Play at Who We Really Are.," 245, in Stewart, *Known World Handbook.*

20. Lash, "Singing the Dream," 32. In Barber's MA thesis, "The Transformation of the Shire," an informant, Conrad, explains that in reenactment, the end result is known and scripted, but in recreation, there is more possibility and flexibility in recreating a general lifestyle, instead of a bounded event (49).

4. REENACTMENT

1. This tape-recorded interview with Wayne Brunson took place at Hewell's Pottery, in Gillsville, Georgia, on October 4, 2008.

2. Some reenactors become ardent preservationists. Robert Lee Hodge, who is on the cover and in the pages of Horwitz's *Confederates in the Attic,* sits on the board of the Central Virginia Battlefields Trust and has helped save acres of land around both Fredericksburg and Chancellorsville. Purdom, "Preservation Battle Cry," 11.

3. These are the regulations on the registration forms for two living history museums in Indiana: Billie Creek Village and Conner Prairie Museum, respectively.

4. These rules are from appendix E, "American Civil War Commemorative Committee and Napoleonic Tactics, Incorporated Gettysburg Reenactment Regulations, 1988," reprinted in Hadden, *Reliving the Civil War,* 169–75.

5. Appendix C in Hadden, *Reliving the Civil War,* 164.

6. *150th Civil War Commemorative Program,* 67.

7. Hadden, *Reliving the Civil War,*14.

8. There are, of course, varying degrees of achieved authenticity in terms of dress, accoutrements, weapons, and behaviors and attitudes. Most internal and external judgments about an authentic impression, however, center on the dress of the reenactor; see Strauss, "Framework for Assessing Military Dress Authenticity."

9. See Hadden, *Reliving the Civil War,* endnote 6, 211–12n6, and glossary, 219–20.

10. Horwitz, *Confederates in the Attic,* 10–11.

11. For more on "hard-core" reenactors, see ibid., 7, and Hadden, *Reliving the Civil War,* 138–40.

12. Jim Kincade, a reenactor with the Seventh Arkansas Infantry, calls these men "Ramada Inn soldiers." Kincade is interviewed and quoted in Clements, "Randolph County Rebel," 17.

13. This tape-recorded interview with Mark LaPointe took place in my office at Indiana University on April 19, 2010.

14. In Horwitz's *Confederates in the Attic* reenactors compliment one another on having lost weight and exchange low-calorie recipes to "achieve the gaunt, hollow-eyed look of underfed Confederates" (12). In Leslie Wheeler's novel *Murder at Gettysburg,* the protagonist starves himself into anorexia trying to achieve the proper physique of a Confederate soldier. Looking through the photographs in Stephen Sylvia's *North South Trader's Manassas Reenactment Commemorative 125th Civil War Anniversary,* it is strikingly apparent how much thinner (and younger) the reenactors were in 1986.

15. Jake Jennette, the CSA general at the first Manassas reenactment on July 23 and 24, 2011, estimates the cost of uniforms and equipment at $1,500 to $2,500. *150th Civil War Commemorative Program,* 73. Likewise, Schroeder, in *Man of War,* estimates the cost of basic equipment and uniform for Nazi World War II reenactors at $2,500 (18).

16. This tape-recorded interview with Dwight Hensley took place at the event commemorating the 150th anniversary of start of the Civil War, in Manassas, Virginia, on July 21, 2011.

17. This tape-recorded interview with Niles Clark also took place in Manassas, Virginia, on July 21, 2011.

18. The Confederate Army Uniform Regulations, General Orders No. 9, adopted in June 1861 in Richmond, Virginia, specifies this regulation for the brigadier general's coat. The text of the regulation addresses the kinds of details that a reenactor has at his disposal: "Two rows of buttons on the breast, eight in each row, placed in pairs; the distance between the rows four inches at top and three inches at bottom; stand up collar, to rise no higher than to permit the chin to turn freely over it; to hook in front at the bottom, and slope thence up and backward, at an angle of thirty degrees, on each side; cuffs two and a half inches deep on the under side, there to be buttoned with three small buttons, and sloped upwards to a point, at a distance of four inches from the end of the sleeve; pockets in the folds of the skirt, with one button at the hip and one at the end of each pocket, making four buttons on the back and skirt of the tunic, the hip buttons to range with the lowest breast buttons." Confederate Uniforms and Equipage, http://confederateuniforms.org/conun/confederateuniforms-ca01.php, accessed June 2, 2014.

19. I met, interviewed, and tape-recorded Jay Vogel at the reenactment of the Battle of Gettysburg in Pennsylvania on July 3, 2010, and we talked again at the reenactment of the Battle of Bull Run in Virginia on July 21 and 22, 2011.

20. See, for example, Shaara, *Killer Angels,* xvi.

21. This tape-recorded interview with Frank Orlando took place on March 24, 2010, at the Gettysburg National Military Park Visitor's Center.

22. The film *Gettysburg* is an adaptation of Michael Shaara's novel *The Killer Angels.* The film was released in 1993 and features thousands of reenactors as extras. The movie is a source of history for many people. Jay Vogel, as General Longstreet, spends much time correcting the historical inaccuracies of the film in his explanation of what actually happened on the battlefield in 1863.

23. I met, interviewed, and tape-recorded Mike Sipes at the reenactment of the Battle of Gettysburg, in Pennsylvania on July 3, 2010, and interviewed him again at the reenactment of the Battle of Bull Run, in Virginia, on July 21 and 22, 2011.

24. Courtney, *Returning to the Civil War,* 19–20.

25. Kimberley Miller-Spillman finds that a large number, 85 percent, of reenactors say they have experienced a magic moment while reenacting. "Male Civil War Reenactors' Dress," 464. She also shows that for the majority of her respondents, accurate clothing is very important for the achievement of the magic moment (466).

26. Courtney, in *Returning to the Civil War,* describes reenacting as a spiritual, almost religious experience (7, 8, 14, 20).

27. This tape-recorded interview with Jim Opdenaker took place in Manassas, Virginia, on July 21, 2011, at the event commemorating the 150th anniversary of the start of the Civil War.

28. Jenny Thompson found that among twentieth-century war reenactors (reenactors of World War I, World War II, Korean War, and Vietnam War), many men moved away from reenacting the Civil War because of the involvement of wives and children. They found this focus on family a distraction from the hard-core experience of reenacting war. *War Games,* 61–62.

29. Rory Turner, in his article "Bloodless Battles," notes that although reenacting allows individuals to find self-expression and experience camaraderie, the hobby can also perpetuate the identities and ideologies of the past instead of questioning them. Mark LaPointe exemplifies the reenactor who thinks through the values of the Civil War and aligns his present views with those of the men he is portraying.

30. See Strauss, "Identity Construction," for more on people who reenact as Confederate soldiers as a way of expressing their ideology and as an act of criticism of the contemporary political situation. These reenactors project personal meanings onto the uniforms and the flags of the Confederacy.

31. I met Mark Sloane during the military parade at the reenactment of the Battle of Bull Run in Virginia on July 22, 2011.

32. I received this email from Mark Sloane on August 7, 2011.

33. At the sesquicentennial of the Civil War, where I met Mark Sloane, there were many Northerners portraying Southerners. According to Jake Jennette, the CSA general at the first Manassas reenactment, Confederate units were present from Canada, Massachusetts, Vermont, New York, Pennsylvania, Ohio, Michigan, Indiana, and Arizona.

34. I bought Wexler's *The Authentic South of* Gone with the Wind at the Atlanta Cyclorama museum. On pages 126–29, in recounting Sherman's March to the Sea, the author's description conflates historical facts with the fictional actions of Rhett, Scarlett, and Melanie, and with Margaret Mitchell's personal opinion about the "looting and burning" in the hands of the Yankees.

35. This tape-recorded interaction took place in Manassas, Virginia, on July 21, 2011.

1. This estimate of visitation is often given, including in Baumgarten, *What Clothes Reveal*, vi. This number varies. In the 2010 Annual President's Report, a public document found on the foundation's website, President Colin Campbell says that "1.7 million people walked our streets." Colin G. Campbell, "Stewards of the Future," President's Report, Colonial Williamsburg Foundation, http://www.history.org/Foundation/Annualrpt10/index.cfm?showSite=mobile, accessed June 2, 2014. This could mean those who paid admission to the museum or just visitors to the former state capital, for it is possible to walk the public streets of Williamsburg without purchasing an admission ticket that allows visitors access inside the buildings.

2. Preface to the *Colonial Williamsburg Official Guidebook and Map*, 1976 edition.

3. *Official Guide to Colonial Williamsburg*, 2007 edition, 24.

4. Theobald, *Colonial Williamsburg*, 29. For more on Rockefeller and his desire for authenticity, see Magelssen, *Living History Museums*, 29–30, Handler and Gable, *New History in an Old Museum*, 31–36, and Greenspan, *Creating Colonial Williamsburg*, 16–39.

5. Colonial Williamsburg, mission statement, http://www.history.org/foundation/mission .cfm, accessed June 2, 2014.

6. Ibid.

7. *Official Guide to Colonial Williamsburg*, 2007 edition, 7 and 25 respectively.

8. Theobald, *Colonial Williamsburg*, 30.

9. This tape-recorded interview with Karen Schlict took place on March 19, 2010.

10. This tape-recorded interview took place on March 19, 2010 at the Costume Design Center. I also use information shared by Brenda on a series of follow-up email messages.

11. Baumgarten, *Eighteenth-Century Clothing*, 7.

12. Ibid. For more on the "hostesses, selected for their charm and southern hospitality," see Theobald, *Colonial Williamsburg*, 29; Greenspan, *Creating Colonial Williamsburg*, 46, and Handler and Gable, *New History in an Old Museum*, 177–86.

13. The seminar, symposium, and exhibition all date to March 2011.

14. This tape-recorded interview with Linda Baumgarten took place on March 18, 2010 in her office.

15. Baumgarten, *Eighteenth-Century Clothing*, 7.

16. In the book *Diary of a Williamsburg Hostess*, written in the 1940s, Helen Campbell recounts early instances where the "Costume Head" makes sure the hostesses were not wearing red nail polish, contemporary hairdos, or colored hose; see pages 28 and 125.

17. *Colonial Williamsburg Costume Handbook*, Costume Design Center, Colonial Williamsburg Foundation, 2005, 23.

18. Ibid.

19. Ibid.

20. Ibid., 3.

21. This information was shared by Christopher Daley, Historical Clothing Services supervisor at the Jamestown-Yorktown Foundation, during the presentation of his paper titled "'Counterfeited According to Truth': The Challenges of Accurately Clothing Powhatan Indians at Jamestown Settlement" at the seminar I attended, "A Reconstructed Visitable Past," at Colonial Williamsburg, on March 17, 2011. See http://fashionablefrolick.blogspot.com/2011/03/reconstructed-visitable-past-day-one.html, accessed June 2, 2014. Magelssen, referencing Maxine Feifer and

John Urry, describes "post-tourists," who, unlike tourists seeking the authentic, thrill in the inauthenticity of tourist experience (*Living History Museums*, 133).

22. See the 2009 publication *Revolutionary City* by editors Kopper and Weldon for scripts of each episode of the play. To read more about "Revolutionary City" and its precursor, "Days of History," see Magelssen, *Living History Museums*, 31–23, Greenspan, *Creating Colonial Williamsburg*, 177–80, and Carson, "End of History Museums" 19–22. Many people believe most living history museums in the United States center on great men, in keeping with a general historical trend. Horwitz notes in his book *A Voyage Long and Strange*—about current celebrations of the founding of America—that the past is used to explain "extraordinary individuals: men make the times, not the other way around" (51).

23. Native Americans also use costumed reenactments to further their own educational agendas and messages in historic sites other than Colonial Williamsburg; see Peers, *Playing Ourselves*, especially 64–68.

24. I met and interviewed Mark Schneider on March 18, 2010.

25. Rowe, "Biographical Sketch of Gowan Pamphlet," Colonial Williamsburg Research Division, http://research.history.org/Historical_Research/Research_Themes/Theme Religion/Gowan.cfm, accessed April 28, 2012. See also Kopper and Weldon, *Revolutionary City*, 72–75.

26. Carson, "Lost in the Fun House," 143–46.

27. In 1994 Colonial Williamsburg staged a slave auction as part of their interpretative program on African American history. The event received much attention and stirred a minor controversy. To read about this, see Magelssen, *Living History Museums*, 119–22, 136–38, 147–49; and Greenspan, *Creating Colonial Williamsburg*, 163–64. To read about the interpretation of difficult topics, see Roth, *Past into Present* chapter 15, in which she talks about history museums, including Colonial Williamsburg. For more on the politics and practices of exhibitions of slavery beyond the United States, see Walvin, "What Should We Know about Slavery?" For memorializing African American history in the United States, see Doss, *Memorial Mania*, particularly chapter 5, "Shame."

28. Two of the episodes of "Revolutionary City"—"Running to Freedom" and "The Promised Land" with Gowan Pamphlet—feature slaves and a discussion of their future options and paths; see Kopper and Weldon, *Revolutionary City*, 68–75. See also Greenspan, *Creating Colonial Williamsburg*, 180.

29. Likewise, many Native Americans who work at history museums find it important to portray and interpret Native American traditions and peoples for museum visitors, to control their own agenda and message within the framework of the museum, and to represent not just the character they are portraying but their communities and their shared past and present as well. See Peer, *Playing Ourselves*, particularly 64–68.

30. *Colonial Williamsburg Official Guidebook*, 1976 edition, vi.

31. Carson, "Lost in the Fun House," 146, and Theobald, *Colonial Williamsburg*, 41–47.

32. Carson, "Living Museums," 26–27.

33. Ibid. To read more about the new social history at Colonial Williamsburg and the 1977 Curriculum Committee, see Magelssen, *Living History Museums*, 43–44, 76–78; Handler and Gable, *New History in an Old Museum*, 66–70, 102–125; and Theobald, *Colonial Williamsburg*, 52–61.

34. Anderson, *Time Machines*, 12.

35. This tape-recorded interview with Terry Thon took place on March 18, 2010.

36. At Colonial Williamsburg the visitors generally prefer to relate to elite instead of "lower sort people." Magelssen, *Living History Museums,* 310. John D. Rockefeller Jr. was interested in the life and culture of the elite more than of those less prominent. Greenspan, *Creating Colonial Williamsburg,* 40–41.

37. To read more about Colonial Williamsburg's and women's history, see Theobald, *Colonial Williamsburg,* 62, and Greenspan, *Creating Colonial Williamsburg,* 158–59.

38. This tape-recorded interview with Sarah Woodyard took place on March 19, 2010, behind the Margaret Hunter Shop in Colonial Williamsburg.

39. See Baumgarten, *What Clothes Reveal,* 40, for support of Sarah's comment.

40. This is the figure for the summer months.

41. Crews, "The Millinery Shop," originally published in *Colonial Williamsburg* (Winter 1997–1998): 63–67, and also found on the foundation website, http://www.history.org/history/cloth ing/milliner/millinershop.cfm, accessed May 10, 2012.

42. Neal Hurst completed his apprenticeship with Mark Hutter in June 2011. Mark's new apprentice is Michael McCarty, who began his apprenticeship in August 2012. I learned this fact from a follow-up email from Mark Hutter on November 6, 2013.

43. See Anderson, *Time Machines,* 17–21, for more on Skansen and its influence on living history museums.

44. Anderson, "Serious Play," in *Living History Reader,* 216. See also Anderson, *Time Machines,* part 2.

45. Carson, "End of History Museums," 17.

46. Malcolm-Davies, "Borrowed Robes," see particularly 278–79 and 285.

6. ART

1. To read more about Agbo, see Glassie, *Prince Twins Seven-Seven,* 220–23, and 229–31.

2. For more on masquerades, see Cole's excellent introduction to *I Am Not Myself,* 15–27.

3. *The Last Emperor,* directed by Bernardo Bertolucci, Columbia Pictures, 1987.

4. See Glassie, *All Silver and No Brass,* 115–18. For a historical and comparative essay on the strawboys in Ireland, Norway, and Scotland, see Gunnell, "Skotrarar, Skudlers."

5. For more on English mumming, see Chambers, *English Folk-Play;* for a description of the costumes of the various characters, see 83–87. For an updated account of mumming in England today, see Cass and Roud, *Room, Room.*

6. See also Glassie, *Stars of Ballymenone,* chapter 5, especially 55–63.

7. The mumming play incorporated some stock characters akin to the Commedia dell'Arte in Italy, which consisted of characters that would be recognizable by their costume, attributes, and personalities, but could differ in the exact interpretation from place to place and throughout time. And like the Commedia dell'Arte, Irish mumming also has a Doctor and a Captain. See Duchartre's reissued and well-illustrated *Italian Comedy,* in which he describes the general costume and variations of each character.

8. As Glassie explains, the play had served an important function in maintaining harmony among the divided community of Catholic and Protestant farmers while granting everyone the pleasure of drama and live performance. The play was for them, as it is now for us, a welcome suspension of the mundane aspects of daily life, inspiring and entertaining the audience with poetry

and grand action, human emotions and values recast as mannerist and stylized art. Glassie, *All Silver and No Brass*, 60.

9. Ibid., 28.

10. Ibid., 122–42.

11. For more on contemporary mumming in England, see Cass and Roud, *Room, Room*, 21–23. For Ireland, see Cashman, "Christmas Mumming Today," "Mumming on the Irish Border," and "Mumming with the Neighbors." For mumming in other parts of Europe, see Buckley et al., *Border-Crossing*. As Mac Cárthaigh documents, in Northern Ireland the play now involves more elaborate choreography, costumes, and makeup. Mac Cárthaigh claims that as the drama transforms from a house visitation to a paying spectacle, the audience expectations have risen and there is now demand for a more sophisticated and polished performance. As the costumes become more professional, they also become more realistic. Mac Cárthaigh, "Room to Rhyme," 169.

12. While I have spoken with Vincent Woods on many occasions since meeting him in 2003, this tape-recorded interview took place on November 9, 2010.

13. Clurman, *Lies Like Truth*, 271–72.

14. Artaud, *Theater and Its Double*.

15. This tape-recorded interview with Charles Morey took place on January 23, 2009, at the Pioneer Theatre in Salt Lake City, Utah.

16. This play ran from May 4 to June 2, 2007.

17. Shaw, *Arms and the Man*, 28.

18. This interview with Molly Trainer took place on May 19, 2007, at the Lyric Stage Company theater in Boston.

19. Ebrahimian, *Sculpting Space*, 61 and 68.

20. Ibid, 61.

21. Cunningham, *Magic Garment*, 1.

22. Two excellent books that outline the process of costume design are Cunningham, *Magic Garment*, and Ingham and Covey, *Costume Designer's Handbook*.

23. Haire, in *The Folk Costume Book*, explains that her book is useful for theater directors if they focus only on the "general effect and richness of color" of the ethnic costumes she describes, resisting the urge to reproduce the costume in material or in workmanship (v–vi). Russell, in *Adaptable Stage Costume for Women*, shows how two basic gowns can be converted into fourteen period garments with the addition of trim, lace, sleeves, skirts, and so on. All they have to do onstage is to give the *effect* of historic dresses from the fifteenth to the nineteenth centuries.

24. Cunningham, in *Magic Garment*, has a list and job description of these and other costume personnel; see box 8A, 216–17.

25. See Cunningham, *Magic Garment*, 14. The collective known as Motley says, in *Designing and Making Stage Costumes*, that the success of a costume designer depends on her collaboration with the director (11). Ingham and Covey, in *Costume Designer's Manual*, teach the aspiring designer that "theatre is a collaboration and not a place where individual artists make individual statements" (165). However, they do warn the reader that actors might have strong opinions about the clothes they are asked to wear, especially if it is contemporary dress, and that the designer should keep the focus on the characters and on the script, not on "the actors' own likes and dislikes" (170). Russell, in *Adaptable Stage Costume for Women*, however, does suggest that good costume design must be comfortable for the actor who will wear the clothes (1).

26. This conversation took place on January 23, 2009, in Salt Lake City, Utah, where Lena played Claire Clairmont in Charles Morey's *The Yellow Leaf* at the Pioneer Theatre. Lena is now known as Lena Hart, and she has relocated to San Francisco.

27. The tape-recorded interview with Rafael Jaen took place on May 18, 2007, in his office at Emerson College in Boston. We also exchanged several email messages, including two particularly informative ones on May 29, 2007 and July 10, 2007.

28. *Project Runway* is a reality television show on the Bravo network that features a competition for the best fashion design within the restrictions of time, theme, and materials.

29. For the creation of the "New Look," see Dior, *Dior by Dior.* For an analysis of Dior's style, see Wilcox, *Golden Age of Couture,* and Palmer, *Dior.*

30. This production was at the Lyric Stage Company theater in Boston, in the winter of 2007.

31. Kennedy, "Scary Truths."

32. This production was staged at Boston's Publick Theatre in 2005 and was directed by the artistic director Diego Arciniegas.

33. These references to Luce (or Nell, played as either one or two separate characters in different productions) appear in Shakespeare, *Comedy of Errors,* act 3, scene 2, line 88; act 3, scene 2, line 114; act 5, scene 1, line 114; act 4, scene 4, line 153.

34. This interview took place in Boston on March 3, 2007.

35. This production was staged at Boston's Publick Theatre, in the summer of 2006 and was directed by the artistic director Diego Arciniegas.

36. This email message was received on June 2, 2007.

37. This production was staged at Boston's Publick Theatre in the summer of 2005.

38. The Norton Awards are given in different categories, since the size of the theater greatly affects its budget and its resources. *Arcadia* won in 2006 in the category "Outstanding Production by a Small Resident Company." That same year the play's director, Diego Arciniegas, won the "Outstanding Director, Small/Midsize Company" for *Arcadia.*

39. All of these are in the "Small Company" category.

40. This email message was received on June 2, 2007.

41. Costume designer Pamela Keech says a costume is good when it is "made from the inside out," with the proper techniques and materials: "To me the greatest accomplishment is when the costumes on stage look like real *clothing.* Nine-tenths of that is being able to construct the silhouette of the period." Keech, "Powerful Secrets," 39.

42. This tape-recorded interview with Lewis Wheeler took place in Boston on May 19, 2007.

43. Gielgud, *Acting Shakespeare,* 97.

44. Witcover, *Living on Stage,* xiii.

45. This play was directed by Rick Lombardo, at the New Repertory Theatre in Boston in January 2007.

46. Lewis and Lewis, *Costume: The Performing Partner.*

47. This play was part of the American Shakespeare Center's "Piercing Eloquence" tour of 2007–2008.

48. Ellen Adair kept a blog, "Bardolatry: True Confessions of a Shakespeare Nerd," about her American Shakespeare Center experience. See http://bardolatry.wordpress.com, accessed June 2, 2014.

49. *More Than What* was directed by Joe Antoun for the BCA Plaza Black Box Theatre in Boston. I saw the play on March 3, 2007.

50. *Marie Antoinette: The Color of Flesh* was written by Joel Gross and was directed by Daniel Burson for the Portland Stage. I saw the play on May 18, 2012.

51. This email message was received on July 27, 2007.

52. This is the title of Clurman's book on theater review and essays.

53. Lahr, "He That Plays the King," *New Yorker,* August 27, 2007, 56.

54. This play was directed by David Wheeler at the American Repertory Theatre from May 12 through June 10, 2007.

55. This poem is from Ellen Adair's upcoming volume, *Curtain Speech,* a collection of poems about acting.

CONCLUSION

1. For more on these master contexts—creation, consumption, and communication—see Glassie, *Material Culture,* chapter 2, 41–86.

2. Ibid., 41.

3. My approach has been shaped in line with the folkloristic paradigm of performance, articulated in Hymes, *Foundations in Sociolinguists,* and Bauman, *Verbal Art as Performance,* and exemplified in Glassie, *Passing the Time in Ballymenone* and *Turkish Traditional Art Today.*

4. Schroder, in *Man of War,* says there are fifty thousand Civil War reenactors today (46), as does Saguto in "Reflections on Reenacting," 77.

5. Mistress Siobhan Medhbh O'Roarke, in the article "What Is the SCA," found on the SCA website (http://socsen.sca.org/what-is-the-sca, accessed June 2, 2014). In the article "Serious Play," in his *Living History Reader,* Anderson says that "living history synthesizes the mental challenges of the work place with the physically and emotionally satisfying benefits of recreation" (217).

6. Thomas lives in St. Louis, Missouri, but I met him at the Constellation Academy of Defense of the Shire of Mynydd of the Midrealm, a daylong rapier collegium, at the Upper Cascades Park in Bloomington, Indiana, on June 6, 2009.

7. Thomas sent me this email on June 30, 2009.

8. I attended the premier of *A Cry from Heaven* at the Abbey Theatre in Dublin on June 9, 2005.

9. This quote is from Ellen Adair's poem "Stratford," from her volume, *Curtain Speech.*

10. Adair, "Song of the Young Poet," in *Curtain Speech.*

11. Adair, "Stratford."

12. See Kennedy, *Big Chief Harrison.* To read about his social activism through his role as a leader of the Mardi Gras Indians, see chapter 2, "The Resistance of the Elders"; chapter 8, "Shoot My Pistol on Mardi Gras Day"; and chapter 10, "Walking across New Orleans."

13. Magelssen, *Living History Museums,* 25; Snow, *Performing the Pilgrims,* 33–40, 195; Anderson, "Living History" in *Living History Reader,* 6–9.

14. Deetz, "The Link from Object to Person to Concept," in Anderson, *Living History Reader.* For interpretation of the past at Plimoth Plantation, see also Deetz, *In Small Things Forgotten* and Deetz and Deetz, *Times of Their Lives.*

15. I met and interviewed Jim Gossert at the Monroe County History Center's Civil War event on June 9, 2007.

16. I met and interviewed Susan Claassen at the Costume Society of America annual symposium in Phoenix, Arizona, on May 30, 2009. She performed *A Conversation with Edith Head* that evening for the conference participants.

17. The tape-recorded interview with Mickey Woods took place on November 13, 2007.

18. Kugelmass, in his book about the Greenwich Village Halloween parade, observes that many gay people like Halloween because they are "accustomed to hiding identity and masquerading the inner self in the trappings of someone else's codes of conduct." *Masked Culture,* 96.

19. Clark, *Shakespeare and Costume,* 38.

20. Kimberly Miller's study of gender and costumes of reenactors shows that for men, wearing a historical or military uniform as a costume was a legitimate, socially acceptable, masculine choice for a costume; her respondents also said that as men they felt they had fewer opportunities to express themselves through dress, and therefore, the enjoyed donning the military uniform for reenactment. "Gender Comparisons within Reenactment Costume," 53 and 54.

21. Lahr, "He That Plays the King," 52.

22. Joanne Eicher asserts that there is a public self, a private self, and a secret self that are expressed through wearing certain clothes in specific contexts; see her "Influences of Changing Resources." See also Davis, "Clothing, Fashion," and Kimberly Miller, "Dress."

23. See Shukla, *Grace of Four Moons,* 211–18, section "Choice and Collaboration," and for a broader summary, chapter 16, "The Study of Body Art."

24. Ben-Amos, "Toward a Definition of Folklore in Context," 14.

25. Ibid.

26. Glassie, *Stars of Ballymenone,* chapter 8.

BIBLIOGRAPHY

150th Civil War Commemorative Program: The Moment That Changed America. Prince William and Manassas Conventions and Visitors Bureau, 2011.

Abraham, Donna J. *The Way They Were: Dressed in 1860–1865: A Photographic Reference.* Gettysburg, PA: Abraham's Lady, LLC, 2008.

Adair, Ellen. *Curtain Speech.* Boston: Pen and Anvil Press, 2013.

Adrover, Lauren. "Branding Festive Bodies: Corporate Logos and Chiefly Image T-Shirts in Ghana." In *African Dress: Fashion, Agency, Performance,* edited by Karen Tranberg Hansen and D. Soyini Madison, 45–59. London: Bloomsbury, 2013.

Ågren, Per-Uno. "Country Photographers." In *Swedish Folk Art: All Tradition Is Change,* edited by Barbro Klein and Mats Widbom, 113–27. New York: Harry N. Abrams, 1994.

Alm, Albert. *Dräktalmanacka för Leksands socken.* Oskarhamn, Leksand, Sweden:1923.

Allen, Stacy D. *Corinth: Crossroads of the Western Confederacy.* Columbus, OH: Blue & Gray Magazine, 2007.

Alver, Bente Gullveig, Tove Ingebjørg Fjell, and Ørjar Øyen, eds. *Research Ethics in Studies of Culture and Social Life.* Helsinki: Academia Scientiarum Fennica, 2007.

Amado, Jorge. *Bahia de Todos of Santos.* São Paulo: Livraria Martins Editôra, 1945.

———. *Jubiabá.* New York: Avon Books, 1984 [1935].

———. *O País do Carnaval.* Rio de Janeiro: Editora Record, 1978 [1931].

———. *Tent of Miracles.* Madison: University of Wisconsin Press, 1971 [1969].

———. *The War of the Saints.* New York: Dial Press, 2005 [1988].

Amado, Jorge, Flávio Damm, and Carybé. *Bahia Boa Terra Bahia.* Rio de Janeiro: Agência Jornalística Image, n.d.

Anderson, Jay, ed. *A Living History Reader.* Vol. 1, *Museums.* Nashville: American Association for State and Local History, 1991.

———. *The Living History Sourcebook.* Nashville: American Association for State and Local History, 1985.

———. *Time Machines: The World of Living History.* Nashville: American Association for State and Local History, 1984.

Anttonen, Pertti, ed. *Folklore, Heritage Politics, and Ethnic Diversity: A Festschrift for Barbro Klein.* Botkyrka, Sweden: Multicultural Centre, 2000.

Araujo, Emanoel. *Carybé.* São Paulo: Ipsis Gráfica e Editora, n.d.

Armstrong, Jennifer. *Photo by Brady: A Picture of the Civil War.* New York: Athenaeum Books for Young Readers, 2005.

Artaud, Antonin. *The Theater and Its Double.* New York: Grove Press, 1994 [1938].

Bacelar, Jeferson. "Blacks in Salvador: Racial Paths." In Crook and Johnson, *Black Brazil,* 85–101.

Balfour, Emma Harrison. *Mrs. Balfour's Civil War Diary: A Personal Account for the Siege of Vicksburg.* Gordon Cotton, ed., n.p., 2006.

Barber, Suzanne. "The Transformation of a Shire: Local Negotiation in the Society for Creative Anachronism." MA thesis. Western Kentucky University, 2011.

Barber, Suzanne, and Matt Hale. "Enacting the Never-Was: Upcycling the Part, Present, and Future in Steampunk." In *Steaming into a Victorian Future: A Steampunk Anthology,* edited by Julie Anne Taddeo and Cynthia J. Miller, 165–84. Lanham, MD: Scarecrow Press, 2013.

Bascom, William. *Sixteen Cowries: Yoruba Divination from Africa to the New World.* Bloomington: Indiana University Press, 1980.

Bauman, Richard. *Story, Performance, and Event: Contextual Studies of Oral Narrative.* Cambridge, UK: Cambridge University Press, 1986.

———. *Verbal Art as Performance.* Rowley, MA: Newbury House, 1977.

———. *A World of Others' Words: Cross-Cultural Perspectives on Intertextuality.* Malden, MA: Blackwell, 2004.

Baumgarten, Linda. *Eighteenth-Century Clothing at Williamsburg.* Williamsburg, VA: Colonial Williamsburg Foundation, 1986.

———. *What Clothes Reveal: The Language of Clothing in Colonial and Federal America.* New Haven, CT: Yale University Press, 2002.

Belk, Russell. "Carnival, Control, and Corporate Culture in Contemporary Halloween Celebrations." In Santino, *Halloween and Other Festivals,* 105–132.

Ben-Amos, Dan. "The Seven Strands of Tradition: Varieties in Its Meaning in American Folklore Studies." *Journal of Folklore Research* 21, no. 2/3 (1984): 97–131.

————. "Toward a Definition of Folklore in Context." In *Toward New Perspectives in Folklore,* edited by Américo Paredes and Richard Bauman, 4–19. Bloomington, IN: Trickster Press, 2000 [1972].

Bendix, Regina. "Moral Integrity in Costumed Identity: Negotiating 'National Costume' in 19th-Century Bavaria." In Bendix and Noyes, "In Modern Dress," 133–45.

Bendix, Regina, and Dorothy Noyes, eds. "In Modern Dress: Costuming the European Social Body, 17th-20th Centuries." Special issue, *Journal of American Folklore* 111, no. 440 (1998).

Berg, Inga Arnö, and Gunnel Hazelius Berg. *Folk Costumes of Sweden: A Living Tradition.* Translated by W. E. Ottercrans. Västerås, Sweden: ICA Bokförlag, 1975.

Bergman, Ingrid. *Folk Costumes in Sweden.* Stockholm: Swedish Institute, 2001.

————. "När den första sverigedräkten lanserades i Falun." In *Dalarna 2005: Utgiven av Dalarnas Fornminnes och Hembygdsförbund,* 195–204.

Björklöf, Sune, ed. *Leksands Hemslöjd: 100 år Av Skaparglädje och Gott Hantverk.* Laholm, Sweden: Trydells Tryckeri AB, 2004.

Bø, Olav. "The Role Played by Tradition in a Local Community Today and Earlier." *Arv* 42 (1986): 143–57.

Boman, Eric. *Rare Bird of Fashion: The Irreverent Iris Apfel.* New York: Thames and Hudson, 2007.

Braga, Júlio. "Candomblé in Bahia: Repression and Resistance." In Crook and Johnson, *Black Brazil,* 201–212.

————. *Na Gamela do Feitiço: Represssão e Resistência nos Candomblés da Bahia.* Salvador: Editora Universidade Federal da Bahia, 1995.

Bridal, Tessa. *Exploring Museum Theatre.* Lanham, MD: Altamira Press, 2004.

Bronner, Simon J. *The Carver's Art: Crafting Meaning from Wood.* Lexington: University Press of Kentucky, 1985.

Browning, Barbara. *Samba: Resistance in Motion.* Bloomington: Indiana University Press, 1995.

Bruzzi, Stella. *Undressing Cinema: Clothing and Identity in the Movies.* London: Routledge, 1997.

Buckley, Anthony, Séamas Ó Catháin, Críostóir Mac Cárthaigh, and Séamus Mac Mathúna, eds. *Border-Crossing: Mumming in Cross-Border and Cross-Community Contexts.* Dundalk, Sweden: Dundalgan Press, 2007.

Burrison, John A. *Brothers in Clay: The Story of Georgia Folk Pottery.* Athens: University of Georgia Press, 1983.

————. *From Mud to Jug: The Folk Potters and Pottery of Northeast Georgia.* Athens: University of Georgia Press, 2010.

Butler, Kim. D. "Afterword: *Ginga Baiana*—The Politics of Race, Class, Culture, and Power in Salvador, Bahia." In Kraay, *Afro-Brazilian Culture and Politics,* 134–57.

Campbell, Helen Jones. *Diary of a Williamsburg Hostess.* New York: G. P. Putnam's Sons, 1946.

Carson, Cary. "The End of History Museums: What's Plan B?" *Public Historian* 30, no. 4 (2008): 9–27.

———. "Living Museums of Everyman's History." In Anderson, *Living History Reader,* 25–31.

———. "Lost in the Fun House: A Commentary on Anthropologists' First Contact with History Museums." *Journal of American History* 81, no. 1 (1994): 137–50.

———. "Mirror, Mirror, on the Wall, Whose History Is the Fairest of Them All?" *Public Historian* 17, no. 4 (1995): 61–67.

Carybé. *As Sete Portas da Bahia.* Rio de Janeiro: Editora Record, 1976.

———. *Iconografia dos Deuses Africanos no Candomblé da Bahia.* São Paulo: Editora Raízes Artes Gráficas, 1980.

Cashman, Ray. "Christmas Mumming Today in Northern Ireland." *Midwestern Folklore* 26, no. 1 (2000): 27–47.

———. "Mumming on the Irish Border: Social and Political Implications." In Buckley et al., *Border-Crossing,* 39–56.

———. "Mumming with the Neighbors in West Tyrone." *Journal of Folklore Research* 37, no. 1 (2000): 73–84.

Cass, Eddie, and Steve Roud. *Room, Room, Ladies and Gentlemen: An Introduction to the English Mummers' Play.* London: English Folk Dance and Song Society, 2002.

Chabon, Michael. "Secret Skin: An Essay in Unitard Theory." In *Superheroes: Fashion and Fantasy,* edited by Andrew Bolton, 12–23. New Haven, CT: Yale University Press.

Chambers, E. K. *The English Folk-Play.* New York: Russell & Russell, 1964 [1933].

Chierichetti, David. *Edith Head: The Life and Times of Hollywood's Celebrated Costume Designer.* New York: Perennial, 2003.

———. *Hollywood Costume Design.* New York: Harmony Books, 1976.

Clark, Cumberland. *Shakespeare and Costume.* London: Mitre Press, 1937.

Clark, Elizabeth Stewart. *The Dressmaker's Guide to Fit & Fashion.* Idaho Falls: Elizabeth Stewart Clark and Company, 2004.

———. *Skirting the Issue: A Workbook for Skirts and Petticoats.* Idaho Falls: Elizabeth Stewart Clark and Company, 2004.

Clements, Derek Allen. "Randolph County Rebel: Jim Kincade, the 7th Arkansas Infantry, and Reenacting the American Civil War." *Arkansas Reviewer* 38, no. 1 (2007): 13–21.

Clurman, Harold. *Lies Like Truth: Theatre Reviews and Essays.* New York: Grove Press, 1958.

Colburn, Carol Huset. "Norwegian Folk Dress in America." In Nelson, *Norwegian Folk Art,* 156–69.

———. "'Well, I Wondered When I Saw You, What All These New Clothes Meant.'" In Nelson, *Material Culture,* 118–55.

Cole, Herbert M., ed. *I Am Not Myself: The Art of African Masquerade.* Los Angeles: Museum of Cultural History, UCLA, 1985.

Colonial Williamsburg Costume Handbook. Costume Design Center, Colonial Williamsburg Foundation, 2005.

Colonial Williamsburg Official Guidebook. Williamsburg, VA: Colonial Williamsburg Foundation, 1976.

Cooper, Cynthia. *Magnificent Entertainments: Fancy Dress Balls of Canada's Governors General 1876–1898.* Quebec: Canadian Museum of Civilization, 1997.

Coski, John M. *A Century of Collecting: The History of the Museum of the Confederacy.* Richmond, VA: Museum of the Confederacy, 1996.

Courtney, Kent. *Returning to the Civil War: Grand Reenactments of an Anguished Time.* Salt Lake City: Gibbs-Smith, 1997.

Crews, Edward. "The Millinery Shop." *Colonial Williamsburg* (Winter 1997–1998): 63–67.

Crook, Larry, and Randal Johnson, eds. *Black Brazil: Culture, Identity, and Social Mobilization.* Los Angeles: UCLA Latin American Center Publications, 1999.

———. "Voices from the Black Movement." In Crook and Johnson, *Black Brazil,* 15–16.

Crowley, Daniel J. *African Myth and Black Reality in Bahian Carnaval.* Monograph Series 25. Los Angeles: Museum of Cultural History, 1984.

Cunningham, Rebecca. *The Magic Garment: Principles of Costume Design.* Long Grove, IL: Waveland Press, 1994 [1989].

Da Silva, Ornato José. *A Linguagem Correta dos Orixás.* Rio de Janeiro: Pallas, 1994.

DaMatta, Roberto. *Carnivals, Rogues, and Heroes: An Interpretation of the Brazilian Dilemma.* Notre Dame, IN: University of Notre Dame Press, 1991 [1979].

Dandanell, Birgitta. *Dalarnas Hembygdsbok 1989.* Falun, Sweden: Dala-Offset AB, 1990.

———. *Påsöm: Folklight Broderi Fran Floda i Dalarna.* Falun, Sweden: Strålins Tryckeri AB, 1992.

Davis, Fred. "Clothing, Fashion, and the Dialectic of Identity." In *Communication and Social Structure,* edited by David R. Maines and Carl J. Couch, 23–38. Springfield, IL: Charles C. Thomas, 1988.

De Almeida, Lino. *A Bahia do Afoxé Filhos de Gandhy.* Filme documentário. Salvador: 912 Produções, 2004.

Deetz, James. *In Small Things Forgotten: An Archaeology of Early American Life.* New York: Anchor Books, 1996 [1977].

———. "The Link from Object to Person to Concept." In Anderson, *Living History Reader,* 206–212.

Deetz, James, and Patricia Scott Deetz. *The Times of Their Lives: Life, Love, and Death in Plymouth Colony.* New York: W. H. Freeman, 2000.

Dior, Christian. *Dior by Dior: The Autobiography of Christian Dior.* Translated by Antonia Fraser. London: Victoria and Albert Publications, 2007 [1957].

Dominguez, Pablo Martin. "The Past Is Alive: Celtiberian Re-enactment in Central Spain." MA thesis. Indiana University, 2012.

Doss, Erika. *Memorial Mania: Public Feeling in America.* Chicago: University of Chicago Press, 2010.

Drewal, Henry John. "Art History, Agency, and Identity: Yorùbá Transcultural Currents in the Making of Black Brazil." In Crook and Johnson, *Black Brazil,* 143–74.

———. *Mami Wata: Arts for Water Spirits in Africa and Its Diaspora.* Los Angeles: UCLA Fowler Museum of Cultural History, 2008.

Drewal, Henry John, and John Mason, eds. *Beads, Body, and Soul: Art and Light in the Yoruba Universe.* Los Angeles: UCLA Fowler Museum of Cultural History, 1998.

Dubois, Thomas A. "Costuming the European Social Body: A Response." In Bendix and Noyes, "In Modern Dress," 218–24.

Duchartre, Pierre Louis. *The Italian Comedy.* New York: Dover Publications, 1966 [1929].

Durant, Mark Alice. "Glowing Turnips, Pointy Black Hats, and Insomniac Aliens: The Hybrid History of Halloween." In Galembo, *Dressed for Thrills,* 15–27.

Ebrahimian, Babak. *Sculpting Space in the Theater: Conversations with the Top Set, Light, and Costume Designers.* Burlington, MA: Focal Press, 2006

Edenheim, Ralph. *The Red Houses.* Malmö, Sweden: Byggförlaget, 2005.

Edinger, Claudio. *Carnaval.* São Paulo: Dórea Books and Art, 1996.

Eddy, Melissa. "Dirndl, Dress of Past, Makes a Comeback in Bavaria." *New York Times,* September 29, 2013, 6.

Eff, Elaine. *The Painted Screens of Baltimore: An Urban Folk Art Revealed.* Jackson: University Press of Mississippi, 2013.

Eicher, Joanne B. *Berg Encyclopedia of World Dress and Fashion,* 10 vols. New York: Berg, 2010.

———. "Clothing, Costume, and Dress." In Steele, *Berg Companion to Fashion,* 151–52.

———. "Influences of Changing Resources on Clothing, Textiles, and the Quality of Life: Dressing for Reality, Fun, and Fantasy." In *Combined Proceedings, Eastern, Central, and Western Regional Meetings of Association of College Professor of Textiles and Clothing,* 36–41. Denver: ACPTC, 1981.

Eklund, Gun-Britt, and Inger Thunell. *Gustaf Ankarcrona, 1869–1933.* Leksand, Sweden: Leksands Kommun, 2001.

Ensaio Geral. Informative da Liesa. Ano III, No. 3, Fevereiro 1998. Rio de Janeiro.

Evans, Timothy H. *King of the Western Saddle: The Sheridan Saddle and the Art of Don King.* Jackson: University Press of Mississippi, 1998.

Félix, Anísio. *Filhos de Gandhi: A História de Um Afoxé.* Salvador: Gráfica Central Ltda., 1987.

Ferris, William. *Local Color: A Sense of Place in Folk Art.* New York: McGraw-Hill, 1982.

Forrsell Gafstrom, Christian Didrik, and Anders Abraham. *Ett år I Sverge.* Stockholm: Johan Horberg, 1827.

Fry, Gladys-Marie. *Stitched from the Soul: Slave Quilts from the Ante-Bellum South.* New York: Dutton Studio Books, 1990.

Frykman, Jonas, and Orvar Löfgren. *Culture Builders: A Historical Anthropology of Middle-Class Life.* Translated by Alan Crozier. New Brunswick, NJ: Rutgers University Press, 1987.

Gailey, Alan. *Irish Folk Drama.* Cork: Mercier Press, 1969.

Galembo, Phyllis. *Dressed for Thrills: 100 Years of Halloween Costumes and Masquerades.* New York: Harry N. Abrams, 2002.

Garduño, Blanca, and José Antonio Rodríguez, eds. *Pasion for Frida.* Museo Estudio Diego Rivera. Mexico City: De Grazia Art and Cultural Foundation, 1991.

Gates, Henry Louis, Jr. "Celebrating Candomblé in Bahia." *The Root* (daily online magazine), http://www.theroot.com/articles/history/2010/02/henry_louis_gates_the_african_roots_of_brazils_carnival.html, February 16, 2010.

Gielgud, John. *Acting Shakespeare.* New York: Charles Scribner's Sons, 1991.

Gil, Gilberto. *Gil & Jorge.* Polygram do Brasil Ltda., 1975.

Glassie, Henry. *All Silver and No Brass: An Irish Christmas Mumming.* Philadelphia: University of Pennsylvania Press, 1983 [1975].

———. *Art and Life in Bangladesh.* Bloomington: Indiana University Press, 1997.

———. "Epilogue: The Spirit of Swedish Folk Art." In Klein and Widbom, *Swedish Folk Art,* 247–55.

———. *Folk Housing in Middle Virginia: A Structural Analysis of Historic Artifacts.* Knoxville: University of Tennessee Press, 1976.

———. "The Idea of Folk Art." In *Folkkonsten: All Tradition Är Förändring,* edited by Beate Sydhoff. 189–92. Stockholm: Carlsson Bokförlag, 1992.

———. *Material Culture.* Bloomington: Indiana University Press, 1999.

———. *Passing the Time in Ballymenone: Culture and History of an Ulster Community.* Philadelphia: University of Pennsylvania Press, 1982.

———. *The Potter's Art.* Bloomington: Indiana University Press, 1999.

———. *Prince Twins Seven-Seven: His Art, His Life in Nigeria, His Exile in America.* Bloomington: Indiana University Press, 2010.

———. *The Spirit of Folk Art.* New York: Harry N. Abrams, 1989.

———. *The Stars of Ballymenone.* Bloomington: Indiana University Press, 2006.

———. "Tradition." In *Eight Words for the Study of Expressive Culture,* edited by Burt Feintuch, 176–97. Urbana: University of Illinois Press, 2003.

———. *Turkish Traditional Art Today.* Bloomington: Indiana University Press, 1993.

Goffman, Erving. *Behavior in Public Places: Notes on the Social Organization of Gatherings.* New York: Free Press, 1963.

———. *The Presentation of Self in Everyday Life.* New York: Double Day/Anchor Books, 1959.

Gomes, Marco Aurélio A. de Filgueiras, ed. *Pelo Pelô: História, Cultura e Cidade.* Salvador: Editora da Universidade Federal da Bahia, 1995.

Gradén, Lizette. "Christmas in Lindsborg." In *Creating Diversities: Folklore, Religion, and the Politics of Heritage,* edited by Anna-Leena Siikala, Barbro Klein, and Stein R. Mathisen, 276–91. Helsinki: Finnish Literature Society, 2004.

———. "Folk Costume Fashion in Swedish America: Crafting Cultural Heritage and Diversity through Dress." *Swedish-American Historical Quarterly* 62, no. 3 (2011): 166–203.

———. *On Parade: Making Heritage in Lindsborg, Kansas.* Uppsala: Uppsala University Library, 2003.

Green, Martin, and John Swan. *The Triumph of Pierrot: The Commedia dell'Arte and the Modern Imagination.* University Park: Pennsylvania State University, 1986.

Greenspan, Anders. *Creating Colonial Williamsburg: The Restoration of Virginia's Eighteenth-Century Capital.* Chapel Hill: University of North Carolina Press, 2002.

Guillermoprieto, Alma. *Samba.* New York: Vintage Departures, 1990.

Gunnell, Terry. "Skotrarar, Skudlers, Colloughs and Strawboys: Wedding Guising Traditions in Norway, Shetland and Ireland, Past and Present." In *Atlantic Currents: Essays on Lore, Literature and Language,* edited by Bo Almqvist, Críostóir Mac Cárthaigh, Liam Mac Mathúna, Seamus Mac Mathúna, and Seosamh Watson, 241–68. Dublin: University College Dublin Press, 2012.

Gustafsson, Lotten. "Medieval Selves and Current Communities: Playing with Identity at an Intersection of Rootedness and Mobility." In Anttonen, ed. *Folklore, Heritage Politics,* 158–76.

Gustafsson, Lotten. "The Play about the Plot: History on Stage and at Stake during the Medieval Week in Visby." *Ethnologia Europaea* 28, no. 1 (1998): 17–26.

Hadden, R. Lee. *Reliving the Civil War: A Reenactor's Handbook,* 2nd ed. Mechanicsburg, PA: Stackpole Books, 1999.

Hahn, Daniel, and Rosemary Linnell. *Shakespeare's Globe Exhibition.* London: International Shakespeare Globe Centre, 2001.

Haire, Frances H. *The Folk Costume Book.* New York: A. S. Barnes, 1927.

Hammar-Moeschlin, Elsa. *Blom-Kari.* Translated by Alan Crozier. Grycksbo, Sweden: Strålins AB for Leksands Kommun, 1998 [1911].

Handler, Richard, and Eric Gable. *The New History in an Old Museum: Creating the Past at Colonial Williamsburg.* Durham, NC: Duke University Press, 1997.

Haring, Lee. *Verbal Arts in Madagascar: Performance in Historical Perspective.* Philadelphia: University of Pennsylvania Press, 1992.

Haugen, Bjørn Sverre Hol, ed. *Norsk Bunadleksikon,* 3 vols. N. W. Damm and Son, 2006.

Head, Edith, and Jane Kesner Ardmore. *The Dress Doctor.* Boston: Little, Brown, 1959.

Head, Edith, and Paddy Calistro. *Edith Head's Hollywood.* Santa Monica: Angel City Press, 2008 [1983].

Hedin, Svante. *Kunglig Bildskatt, 1850–1950.* Stockholm: Royal Books, 1994.

Hellspong, Mats, and Barbro Klein. "Folk Art and Folklife Studies in Sweden." In Klein and Widbom, *Swedish Folk Art,* 17–39.

Hofer, Tamas. "The Perception of Tradition in European Ethnology." *Journal of Folklore Research* 21, no. 2/3 (1984): 133–47.

Hofrén, Erik, and Birgitta Dandanell, eds. *Textil Tradition: Speglad i Dalarnas Museums Samlingar.* Falun, Sweden: Dala-Offset AB for Dalarnas Hembygdsbok, 1982.

Holtzberg, Maggie. *Keepers of Tradition: Art and Folk Heritage of Massachusetts.* Lexington: Massachusetts Cultural Council, 2008.

Honko, Lauri. "Studies on Tradition and Cultural Identity: An Introduction." *Arv* 42 (1986): 7–26.

Horwitz, Tony. *Confederates in the Attic: Dispatches from the Unfinished Civil War.* New York: Vintage Books, 1999.

———. *A Voyage Long and Strange: Rediscovering the New World.* New York: Henry Holt, 2008.

Hymes, Dell. *Foundations in Sociolinguistics: An Ethnographic Approach.* Philadelphia: University of Pennsylvania Press, 1974.

Ickes, Scott. *African-Brazilian Culture and Regional Identity in Bahia, Brazil.* Gainesville: University Press of Florida, 2013.

Ilê Aiyê. *25 Anos de Resistência.* Salvador: Associação Cultural Bloco Carnavalesco Ilê Aiyê, 1999.

———. *Abidjan, Abuja, Harare e Dakar: Caderno de Educação,* Vol. 15. Salvador: Associação Cultural Bloco Carnavalesco Ilê Aiyê, 2007.

———. *América Negra: "O Sonho Africano."* Salvador: Associação Cultural Bloco Carnavalesco Ilê Aiyê, 1993.

———. *A Forca das Raízes: Caderno de Educação, Vol.IV.* Salvador: Associação Cultural Bloco Carnavalesco Ilê Aiyê, 1996.

———. *Organizações de Resistência Negra: Caderno de Educação, Vol. I.* Salvador: Associação Cultural Bloco Carnavalesco Ilê Aiyê, 1995.

Ingham, Rosemary, and Liz Covey. *The Costume Designer's Handbook.* Portsmouth, NH: Heinemann, 1992 [1983].

Jacobsson, Bengt. "The Arts of the Swedish Peasant World." In Klein and Widbom, *Swedish Folk Art,* 55–81.

Jensen, Les. *A Catalogue of Uniforms in the Collection of the Museum of the Confederacy.* Richmond, VA: Museum of the Confederacy, 2000.

Jobs, Karin, and Kersti Jobs-Björklöf. *Almanacka för Leksandsdräkten.* Stockholm: AB Sigma-tryckeriet for Leksands Hemslöjdsförening, 1978.

Jobs-Björklöf, Kersti, Elisabeth Näs, Kristina Kvarnbäck, and Charlotte Lautmann. *Leksandsklädd: i Leksand, Djura och Siljansäs, med almanacka för Leksandsdräkten och kyrkoåret.* Gävle, Sweden: Leksands Hemslöjdsvänner, 2013.

Johnson, Paul Christopher. *Secrets, Gossip, and Gods: The Transformation of Bra-zilian Candomblé.* New York: Oxford University Press, 2002.

Jones, Ann Rosalind, and Peter Stallybrass. *Renaissance Clothing and the Materi-als of Memory.* Cambridge, UK: Cambridge University Press, 2000.

Jones, Michael Owen. *Craftsman of the Cumberlands: Tradition and Creativity.* Lexington: University Press of Kentucky, 1989.

Joseph-Witham, Heather. *Star Trek Fans and Costume Art.* Jackson: University of Mississippi Press, 1996.

Kaivola-Bregenhøj, Annikki, Barbro Klein, and Ulf Palmenfelt, eds. *Narrating, Doing, Experiencing: Nordic Folkloristic Perspectives.* Helsinki: Hakapaino Oy, 2006.

Keech, Pamela. "Powerful Secrets: An Interview with Pamela Keech." *Parabola* 19, no. 3 (1992): 34–42.

Kennedy, Al. *Big Chief Harrison and the Mardi Gras Indians.* Gretna, LA: Pelican, 2010.

Kennedy, Louise. "Scary Truths Resonate in Dark Musical." *Boston Globe,* Janu-ary 9, 2007.

Klein, Barbro. "Cultural Heritage, the Swedish Folklife Sphere, and the Others." *Cultural Analysis* 5 (2006): 57–80.

———. "Folklore, Heritage Politics and Ethnic Diversity: Thinking about the Past and the Future." In Anttonen, *Folklore, Heritage Politics,* 23–36.

———. "Introduction to Part 4." In Klein and Widbom, *Swedish Folk Art,* 191–93.

———. "The Moral Content of Tradition: Homecraft, Ethnology, and Swedish Life in the Twentieth Century." *Western Folklore* 59, no. 2 (2000): 171–95.

———. "Swedish Folklife Research in the 1980s." *Journal of American Folklore* 99, no. 394 (1986): 461–69.

Klein, Barbro, and Mats Widbom, eds. *Swedish Folk Art: All Tradition Is Change.* New York: Harry N. Abrams, 1994.

Kopper, Philip, and Bill Weldon, eds. *Revolutionary City.* Williamsburg, VA: Co-lonial Williamsburg Foundation, 2009.

Kraay, Hendrik. *Afro-Brazilian Culture and Politics: Bahia, 1790s to 1990s.* Ar-monk, NY: M. E. Sharpe, 1998.

———. Introduction to *Afro-Brazilian Culture and Politics,* 3–29.

Kugelmass, Jack. "Designing the Greenwich Village Halloween Parade." *Journal of American Folklore* 104, no. 414 (1991): 443–65.

———. *Masked Culture: The Greenwich Village Halloween Parade.* New York: Co-lumbia University Press, 1994.

La Motte, Richard. *Costume Design 101: The Art and Business of Costume Design for Film and Television.* Studio City, CA: Michael Wiese Productions, 2001.

Lagerlöf, Selma. *Gösta Berling's Saga.* Translated by Lillie Tudeer. New York: Dover Publications, 2004 [1918].

———. *Memories of Mårbacka.* Edited by Greta Anderson. Iowa City: Penfield Press, 1996.

Lahr, John. "He That Plays the King." *New Yorker,* August 27, 2007, 48–59.

Landis, Deborah Nadoolman. *Screencraft: Costume Design.* Burlington, MA: Focal Press, 2003.

Lash, Sarah K. "Singing the Dream: The Bardic Arts of the Society for Creative Anachronism." PhD dissertation. Indiana University, 2009.

Leese, Elizabeth. *Costume Design in the Movies.* New York: Dover Publications, 1991.

Lewis, Jac, and Miriam Striezheff Lewis. *Costume: The Performing Partner.* Colorado Springs: Meriwether, 1990.

Ligiéro, Zeca. *Iniciação ao Candomblé.* Rio de Janeiro: Editora Record, 1993.

Lilja, Agneta, and Po Tidholm. *Celebrating the Swedish Way.* Stockholm: Swedish Institute, 2004.

Linthicum, M. Channing. *Costume in the Drama of Shakespeare and His Contemporaries.* New York: Russell and Russell, 1963.

Lody, Raul. *Afoxé.* Cadernos de Folclore, 7. Rio de Janeiro: Ministério da Educação e Cultura, Departmamento de Assuntos Culturais, Fundação Nacional de Arte, 1976.

———. *Jóias de Axé.* Rio de Janeiro: Bertrand Brasil, 2001.

———. *O Negro No Museu Brasileiro: Construindo Identidades.* Bertrand Brasil, 2005.

———. *Pencas de Balangandãs da Bahia: Um Estudo Etnográfico das Jóias-Amuletos.* Rio de Janeiro: Instituto Nacional do Folclore, 1988.

———. *O Povo do Santo: Religião, História e Cultura dos Orixás, Voduns, Inquices e Caboclos.* Rio de Janeiro: Pallas, 1995.

———. *A Roupa de Baiana.* Salvador: Associação das Baianas de Acarajé e Mingau do Estado da Bahia, 2003.

———. *O Traje da Baiana.* Salvador: Museu do Traje, n.d. [c. 1990].

Lofgren, John Z., ed. *Carl Larsson: The Autobiography of Sweden's Most Beloved Artist.* Iowa City: Penfield Press, 1992.

Löfgren, Orvar. "The Disappearance and Return of the National: The Swedish Experience 1950–2000." In *Folklore, Heritage Politics, and Ethnic Diversity: A Festschrift for Barbro Klein,* edited by Pertti Anttonen, 230–52. Botkyrka, Sweden: Multicultural Centre, 2000.

———. "Historical Perspectives on Scandinavian Peasantries." *Annual Review of Anthropology* 9 (1980): 187–215.

————. "The Nationalization of Culture." *Ethnologia Europaea* 19, no. 1 (1989): 5–24.

————. *On Vacation: A History of Vacationing.* Berkeley: University of California Press, 1999.

Mac Cárthaigh, Críostóir. "Room to Rhyme: Irish Christmas Mumming in Transition." In Buckley et al., *Border-Crossing,* 146–70.

Magalhães, Rosa. *Fazendo Carnaval: The Making of Carnival.* Rio de Janeiro: Editora Nova Aguilar, 1997.

Magelseen, Scott. *Living History Museums: Undoing History through Performance.* Lanham, MD: Scarecrow Press, 2007.

Malcolm-Davies, Jane. "Borrowed Robes: The Educational Value of Costumed Interpretation at Historic Sites." *International Journal of Heritage Studies* 10, no. 3 (2004): 277–93.

Manifold, Marjorie Cohee. "Life as Theater and Theater as Life: Art Expressions of Information-Age Youth." *Journal of Cultural Research in Art Education* 23 (2005): 1–16.

Mann, Kathleen. *Peasant Costume in Europe.* London: Adam and Charles Black, 1961 [1931, 1936].

McDowell, John H. "Halloween Costuming among Young Adults in Bloomington, Indiana: A Local Exotic." *Indiana Folklore and Oral History* 14 (1985): 1–18.

Mikhaila, Ninya, and Jane Malcolm-Davies. *The Tudor Tailor: Reconstructing 16th-Century Dress.* London: Batsford, 2006.

Miller, Kimberly A. "Dress: Private and Secret Self-Expression." *Clothing and Textiles Research Journal* 15, no. 4 (1997): 223–34.

————. "Gender Comparisons within Reenactment Costume: Theoretical Interpretations." *Family and Consumer Sciences Research Journal* 27, no. 1 (1998): 35–61.

Miller-Spillman, Kimberley A. "Male Civil War Reenactors' Dress and Magic Moments." In *Men's Fashion Reader,* edited by Andrew Reilly and Sarah Cosbey, 455–74. New York: Fairchild, 2008.

Morales, Anamaria. "Afoxé Filhos de Gandhi Pede Paz." In *Escravidão & Invenção da Liberdade: Estudos Sobre O Negro No Brasil,* edited by João José Reis, 264–74. São Paulo: Editora Brasiliense, 1988.

Motley. *Designing and Making Stage Costumes.* New York: Watson-Guptill Publications, 1964.

Nagler, A. M. *Shakespeare's Stage.* New Haven, CT: Yale University Press, 1981 [1958].

Nelson, Marion, ed. *Material Culture and People's Art among the Norwegians in America.* Northfield, MN: Norwegian-American Historical Association, 1994.

———. *Norwegian Folk Art: The Migration of a Tradition.* New York: Abbeville Press, 1995.

A New Members' Guide to the Society for Creative Anachronism (pamphlet). Society for Creative Anachronism, 2000.

Nicklasson, Hasnis Eva, Hams Ulla Danielsson, and Hans Matsols. *Dräktbruk och Linnetradition: i Dalasocknarna Svärsjö och Enviken.* Falun, Sweden: Strålins Tryckeri AB, 1997.

Nilsson, Hakan. *Österlens Folkdräkter.* Ystad, Sweden: AB Ystads Centraltryckeri, 2000.

Norgren, Benny, Birger Persson, and Rune Österlund. *Sockendräkter i Dalarna.* Falun, Sweden: Esselte-Herzogs AB, 1973.

Noss, Aagot. *Frå tradisjonell klesskikk til bunad i Vest-Telemark.* Oslo, Norway: Novus forlag, 2003.

———. "Rural Norwegian Dress and Its Symbolic Functions." In *Norwegian Folk Art: The Migration of a Tradition,* edited by Marion Nelson, 149–55. New York: Abbeville Press, 1995.

Noyes, Dorothy, and Regina Bendix. Introduction to "In Modern Dress," by Bendix and Noyes, 107–114.

Nylén, Anna-Maja. *Swedish Handcraft.* Translated by Anne-Charlotte Hanes Harvey. Lund: Berlingska Boktryckeriet, 1976 [1968].

———. *Swedish Peasant Costumes.* Stockholm: Nordiska Museet, 1949.

O'Donnell, Patrick. *The Knights Next Door: Everyday People Living Middle Ages Dreams.* New York: iUniverse, 2004.

Official Guide to Colonial Williamsburg. Williamsburg, VA: Colonial Williamsburg Foundation, 2007.

Omari-Tunkara, Mikelle Smith. *Manipulating the Sacred: Yoruba Art, Ritual and Resistance in Brazilian Candomblé.* Detroit: Wayne State University Press, 2005.

Palmer, Alexandra. *Dior: A New Look, A New Enterprise (1947–1957).* London: Victoria and Albert Museum, 2009.

Panzer, Mary. *Mathew Brady and the Image of History.* Washington, DC: Smithsonian Institution Press, 1997.

Patterson, Daniel W. *The True Image: Gravestone Art and Culture of Scotch Irish Settlers in the Pennsylvania and Carolina Backcountry.* Chapel Hill: University of North Carolina Press, 2012.

Peers, Laura. *Playing Ourselves: Interpreting Native Histories at Historic Recon-structions.* Lanham, MD: Altamira Press, 2007.

Phillips, Ruth B. *Representing Women: Sande Masquerades of the Mende of Sierra Leone.* Los Angeles: UCLA Fowler Museum of Cultural History, 1995.

Piddick, Julianne. *Contemporary Costume Film.* London: British Film Institute, 2004.

Pitanga, Antônio. "Where Are the Blacks?" In Crook and Johnson, *Black Brazil,* 31–42.

The Pleasure Book. New Mexico: Raymond's Quiet Press, 1987.

Pocius, Gerald L. *A Place to Belong: Community Order and Everyday Space in Cal-vert, Newfoundland.* Athens: University of Georgia Press, 1991.

Purdom, Gwendolyn. "A Preservation Battle Cry." *Preservation.* National Trust for Historic Preservation (Fall 2012): 11.

Rådström, Anne Marie. *Wooden Horses of Sweden: From Folk Art to National Symbol.* Translated by Skans Victoria Airey. Värnamo, Sweden: Fälths Tryckeri, 1992.

Real, Katarina. "Evoé!: The Carnaval of Recife and Olinda in Pernambuco, Bra-zil." In *¡Carnaval!,* edited by Barbara Maudin, 203–237. Seattle: University of Washington Press, 2004.

Reis, João José, ed., *Escravidão & Invenção da Liberdade: Estudos Sobre O Negro No Brasil.* São Paulo: Editora Brasiliense, 1988.

Riley, Mara. *Whatever Shall I Wear? A Guide to Assembling a Women's Basic 18th-Century Wardrobe.* Excelsior Springs, MO: Graphics/Fine Arts Press, 2002.

Rinzler, Ralph, and Robert Sayers. *The Meaders Family: North Georgia Potters.* Washington, DC: Smithsonian Institution Press, 1980.

Risério, Antônio. *Carnaval Ijexá.* Salvador: Corrupio, 1981.

———. "Carnival: The Colors of Change." In *Black Brazil: Culture, Identity, and Social Mobilization,* edited by Larry Crook and Randal Johnson, 249–60. Los Angeles: UCLA Latin American Center Publications, 1999.

Roach-Higgins, Mary Ellen, and Joanne B. Eicher. "Dress and Identity." In *Dress and Identity,* edited by Mary Ellen Roach-Higgins, Joanne B. Eicher, and Kim K. P. Johnson, 7–18. New York: Fairchild Publications, 1995.

Rodrigues, João Jorge Santos. "Olodum and the Black Struggle in Brazil." In Crook and Johnson, *Black Brazil,* 43–51.

Rodrigues, Nina. *Os Africanos no Brasil.* Brasília: Editora Universidade de Brasí-lia, 1988 [1932].

Rosander, Göran. "The 'Nationalisation' of Dalecarlia: How a Special Province Becomes a National Symbol for Sweden." *Arv* 42 (1986): 93–142.

Rosenzweig, Denise, and Magdalena Rosenzweig, eds. *Self-Portrait in a Velvet Dress: Frida's Wardrobe.* San Francisco: Chronicle Books, 2007.

Ross, Doran, ed. *Elephant: The Animal and Its Ivory in African Culture.* Los Angeles: UCLA Fowler Museum of Cultural History, 1992.

Roth, Stacy F. *Past into Present: Effective Techniques for First-Person Historical Interpretation.* Chapel Hill: University of North Carolina, 1998.

Rowe, Linda. "A Biographical Sketch of Gowan Pamphlet." Colonial Williamsburg Research Division, http://research.history.org/Historical_Research/Research_Themes/ThemeReligion/Gowan.cfm, accessed April 28, 2012.

Russell, Elizabeth. *Adaptable Stage Costume for Women.* London: J. Garnet Miller, 1979 [1974].

Saguto, D. A. "Reflections on Reenacting: Seeking an Authentic Past in a Specious Present." *Colonial Williamsburg Journal* (Winter 2011).

Saliklis, Ruta. "The Dynamic Relationship between Lithuanian National Costumes and Folk Dress." In *Folk Dress in Europe and Anatolia: Beliefs about Protection and Fertility,* edited by Linda Welters, 211–34. New York: Berg, 1999.

Sandsdalen, Unni. "Identity and Local Society: Setesdal Today." *Arv* 42 (1986): 159–73.

Sansi, Roger. *Fetishes and Monuments: Afro-Brazilian Art and Culture in the 20th Century.* New York: Berghahn Books, 2010 [2007].

Santino, Jack, ed., *Halloween and Other Festivals of Death and Life.* Knoxville: University of Tennessee Press, 1994.

———. *The Hallowed Eve: Dimensions of Culture in a Calendar Festival in Northern Ireland.* Lexington: University of Kentucky Press, 1998.

Santos, Francisco. *Os Deuses do Panteon Africano.* Salvador: EGBA, 2003.

Scheffy, Zoë-Hateehc Durrah. "Sámi Religion in Museums and Artistry." In Siikala et al., *Creating Diversities,* 225–59.

Schouvaloff, Alexander. *Set and Costume Designs for Ballet and Theatre: The Thyseen-Bornemisza Collection.* New York: Vendome Press, 1987.

Schroeder, Charlie. *Man of War: My Adventures in the World of Historical Reenactment.* New York: Hudson Street Press, 2012.

Selka, Stephen. *Religion and the Politics of Ethnic Identity in Bahia, Brazil.* Gainesville: University Press of Florida, 2007.

Severa, Joan L. *Dressed for the Photographer: Ordinary Americans and Fashion, 1840–1900.* Kent, OH: Kent State University Press, 1995.

———. *My Likeness Taken: Daguerreian Portraits in America.* Kent, OH: Kent State University Press, 2005.

Shaara, Michael. *The Killer Angels.* New York: Ballantine Books, 2003 [1975].

Shakespeare, William. *The Comedy of Errors.* Hertfordshire: Wordsworth Classics, 1995.

———. *The Merchant of Venice.* London: Arden Shakespeare, 2005.

Shaw, Bernard. *Arms and the Man.* New York: Penguin Books, 2006 [1926].

Shukla, Pravina. "Afro-Brazilian Avatars: Gandhi's Sons Samba in South America." *Indian Folklore Research Journal* 1, no. 1 (2001): 35–45.

———. "Beads of Identity in Salvador da Bahia." In *Beads, Body, and Soul: Art and Light in the Yoruba Universe,* edited by Henry John Drewal and John Mason, 187–97. Los Angeles: UCLA Fowler Museum of Cultural History, 1998.

———. "Carnival Costume in Brazil." *Berg Encyclopedia of World Dress and Fashion,* Vol. 2. *Latin America and the Caribbean,* publishing on the Berg Fashion Library online, August 2013. http://www.bergfashionlibrary.com/view/bewdf/BEWDF-v2/EDch2612.xml.

———. "Fashion in the East: Dress in Modern India." In *Fusion Fashion: Culture Beyond Orientalism and Occidentalism,* edited by Gertrud Lehnert and Gabriele Mentges, 89–104. Frankfurt am Main: Peter Lang, 2013.

———. "Filhos de Gandhy (Afro-Brazilian carnival group)." In *Encyclopedia of African American Folklore,* edited by Anand Prahlad. Vol. 1, 435–37. Westport, CT: Greenwood, 2006.

———. *The Grace of Four Moons: Dress, Adornment, and the Art of the Body in Modern India.* Bloomington: Indiana University Press, 2008.

———. "The Mahatma's Samba." In John H. McDowell and Pravina Shukla, *Dancing the Ancestors in South America.* Bloomington, IN: Mathers Museum of World Cultures, 2001: 13–23.

———. "The Maintenance of Heritage: Kersti Jobs-Björklöf and Swedish Folk Costume." In *The Individual and Tradition: Folkloristic Perspectives,* edited by Ray Cashman, Tom Mould, and Pravina Shukla, 144–69. Bloomington: Indiana University Press, 2011.

Siikala, Anna-Leena, Barbro Klein, and Stein R. Mathisen, eds. *Creating Diversities: Folklore, Religion, and the Politics of Heritage.* Helsinki: Finnish Literature Society, 2004.

Skansen Official Guide. Uppsala, Sweden: Sandvikens Tryckeri AB, 2005.

Smith, Michael P. *Mardi Gras Indians.* Gretna, LA: Pelican, 2007.

Smith, Robin, and Ron Field. *Uniforms of the Civil War: An Illustrated Guide for Historians, Collectors, and Reenactors.* Guilford, CT: Lyons Press, 2001.

Snow, Stephen Eddy. *Performing the Pilgrims: A Study of Ethnohistorical Role-Playing at Plimoth Plantation.* Jackson: University Press of Mississippi, 1993.

Snowden, James. *The Folk Dress of Europe.* New York: Mayflower Books, 1979.

Steele, Valerie. *The Berg Companion to Fashion.* New York: Berg, 2010.

———. *Daphne Guinness.* New Haven, CT: Yale University Press, 2011.

———, ed. *Encyclopedia of Clothing and Fashion,* 3 vols. New York: Charles Scribners and Sons, 2004.

———. Foreword to Phyllis Galembo, *100 Years of Halloween Costumes and Masquerades.* New York: Harry N. Abrams, 2002, 12.

Stewart, Baron Alwyn, ed. *The Known World Handbook.* Milpitas, CA: Society for Creative Anachronism, 1995.

Sterling, Cheryl. *African Roots, Brazilian Rites: Cultural and National Identity in Brazil.* New York: Palgrave Macmillan, 2012.

Stoppard, Tom. *Arcadia.* London: Faber and Faber, 1993.

Strauss, Mitchell D. "A Framework for Assessing Military Dress Authenticity in Civil War Reenacting." *Clothing and Textiles Research Journal* 19 (2001): 145–57.

———. "Identity Construction among Confederate Civil War Reenactors: A Study of Dress, Stage Props, and Discourse." *Clothing and Textiles Research Journal* 21 (2003): 149–61.

Svärdström, Svante. *Dalmålningar i Urval.* Stockholm: Albert Bonniers Förlag, 1975 [1957].

Sydhoff, Beate. *Folkkonsten: All Tradition Är Förändring.* Stockholm: Carlsson Bokförlag, 1992.

Sylvia, Stephen W. *North South Trader's Manassas Reenactment Commemorative 125th Civil War Anniversary.* Fredericksburg, VA: North South Press, 1986.

Tallant, Robert. *Gumbo Ya-Ya: A Collection of Louisiana Folk Tales.* Boston: Houghton Mifflin, 1945.

Theobald, Mary Miley. *Colonial Williamsburg: The First 75 Years.* Williamsburg, VA: Colonial Williamsburg Foundation, 2001.

Thompson, Jenny. *War Games: Inside the World of 20th-Century War Reenactors.* Washington, DC: Smithsonian Books, 2004.

Thompson, Stith. "Folklore Trends in Scandinavia." *Journal of American Folklore* 74, no. 294 (1961): 313–20.

Tilden, Freeman. *Interpreting Our Heritage.* Chapel Hill: University of North Carolina Press, 2007 [1957].

Traetteberg, Gunvor. "Folk Costumes." In *The Native Arts of Norway,* edited by Roar Hauglid, 137–74. Oslo: Mittet and Co., 1953.

Troiani, Don. *Don Troiani's Civil War: Infantry.* Mechanicsburg: Stackpole Books, 2002.

Trotzig, Liv, Hams Ulla Danielsson, Sven-Olof Gudmunds, Gösta Andersson, and Erik Hofrén. *Sockendräkter Dalarna.* Falun, Sweden: Stftelsen Dalarnas Museum, 1976.

Turner, Rory. "Bloodless Battles: The Civil War Reenacted." *Drama Review* 34, no. 4 (1990): 123–36.

———. "The Play of History: Civil War Reenactments and Their Use of the Past." *Folklore Forum* 22, no. 1/2 (1989): 54–61.

Vlach, John Michael. *Charleston Blacksmith: The Work of Philip Simmons.* Columbia: University of South Carolina Press, 1992.

Wafer, Jim. *The Taste of Blood: Spirit Possession in Brazilian Candomblé.* Philadelphia: University of Pennsylvania Press, 1991.

Waldén, Louise. *Genom Symaskinens Nålsöga* [Through the Eye of the Sewing Machine Needle]. Stockholm: Carlsson Bokfördag, 1990.

———. "Women's Creativity and the Swedish Study Circle." In Klein and Widbom, *Swedish Folk Art,* 181–88.

Walvin, James. "What Should We Know about Slavery? Slavery, Abolition, and Public History." In *Historical Reenactment: From Realism to the Affective Turn,* edited by Ian McCalman and Paul A. Pickering, 63–78. New York: Palgrave Macmillan, 2010.

Wexler, Bruce. *The Authentic South of* Gone with the Wind: *The Illustrated Guide to the Grandeur of a Lost Era.* Philadelphia: Courage Books, 2007.

Wheeler, Leslie. *Murder at Gettysburg.* Toronto: Five Star Publishing, 2007.

Wilcox, Claire. *The Golden Age of Couture: Paris and London 1947–57.* London: Victoria and Albert Publications, 2007.

Witcover, Walt. *Living on Stage: Acting from the Inside Out, a Practical Process.* New York: Back Stage Books, 2004.

Woods, Vincent. "At the Black Pig's Dyke." In *Far from the Land: Contemporary Irish Plays,* edited by John Fairleigh. London: Methuen Drama, 1998.

———. *A Cry from Heaven.* York, UK: Methuen Drama, 2005.

Zug, Charles G. *Turners and Burners: The Folk Potters of North Carolina.* Chapel Hill: University of North Carolina Press, 1986.

INDEX

Pravina Shukla

IS ASSOCIATE PROFESSOR IN THE DEPARTMENT OF FOLKLORE AND Ethnomusicology at Indiana University. She is the author of *The Grace of Four Moons: Dress, Adornment, and the Art of the Body in Modern India* (Indiana University Press, 2008), winner of both the Millia Davenport Award of the Costume Society of America and the A. K. Coomaraswamy Book Prize by the South Asia Council of the Association for Asian Studies. She is also co-editor of *The Individual and Tradition: Folklorist Perspectives* (Indiana University Press, 2011). Three-time winner of the Indiana University Trustees Teaching Award, Professor Shukla has lectured on material culture, dress, and adornment within the United States as well as in India, Bangladesh, Canada, Israel, and Germany.